JOHNNY

U

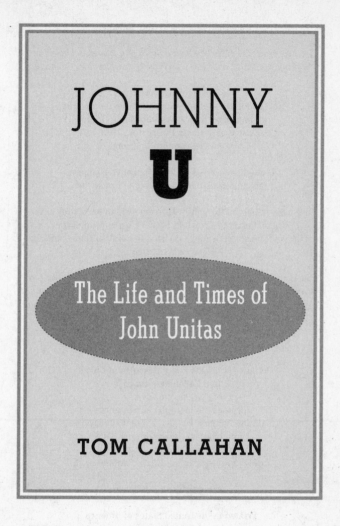

JOHNNY U

The Life and Times of
John Unitas

TOM CALLAHAN

THREE RIVERS PRESS • NEW YORK

This book contains an excerpt from the forthcoming book *The GM: The Inside Story of a Dream Job and the Nightmares That Go with It* by Tom Callahan. This excerpt has been set for this edition only and may not reflect the final content of the forthcoming edition.

Library of Congress Cataloging-in-Publication Data
Callahan, Tom.
Johnny U : the life and times of John Unitas /
Tom Callahan.—1st ed.
p. cm.
Includes bibliographical references.
1. Unitas, Johnny, 1933– 2. Football players—
United States—Biography.   I. Title.
GV939.U5U653   2006
796.332092—dc22   2006000754

ISBN 978-1-4000-8140-0

Printed in the United States of America

DESIGN BY BARBARA STURMAN

10 9 8 7 6 5 4 3

First Paperback Edition

*With thanks to Larry Harris for
gathering the photographs*

CONTENTS

JOHNNY
U

"You almost had to know all of us to know any of us."

It Was the Players' Game Then

O n black-and-white televisions, in a black or white time, men played football for something less than a living and something more than money. They didn't deny the attractiveness of money. On their own scale, they were as venal a collection of chiselers and money-grubbers as professional athletes are today. But they were football players first. If the Browns cut them in Hiram, Ohio, they hitchhiked to Westminster, Maryland, to try out for the Colts; and if Baltimore had no use for them either, they would play for the *Annapolis* Colts, or the Bloomfield Rams. If the sandlots were full, they might form their own semipro team and call themselves the Antioch Hornets. They were going to play football.

Most of them were white; a few were black. (Black-and-white is their color, all right.) On average, the white ones were just about as bigoted as the country. Yet there were surprising incidents of en-lightenment, fellowship, even brotherhood. The pro football play-ers of the 1950s were regular guys who, by and large, stayed regular guys. They were slightly less famous, somewhat less pros-perous, than the baseball players. But literally and figuratively, they were in the same ballpark. When the World Trade Center crashed down on September 11, 2001, among the small, exquisite details was the fact that Carl Furillo, retired batting champion of the Brooklyn Dodgers, had worked in the construction of the Twin Towers, installing Otis elevators. Today's pro athletes won't be installing any elevators. That's the thing that sports will never get back. Once, the players were one of us. They lived right next door. They don't anymore.

On September 11, 2002, the first anniversary of that horror, the legendary quarterback Johnny Unitas died of a heart attack. "He was a football player," said Unitas's primary receiver, Raymond Berry. Those words don't look like much on the page, but you should have heard Berry say them. "Unitas was *the* football player," said Sam Huff, an old linebacker for the New York Giants. The *best* player of Huff, Berry, and Unitas's day—and maybe of any day—was Cleveland fullback Jim Brown, who, in a conversation with the writer George Plimpton, once mentioned a Pro Bowl practice conducted by Giant coach Allie Sherman. "All right," Sherman called out across the field, "let's have the first team offense over here." But no lists of first or second strings had been posted. Every player present was a starter and a star. Nevertheless, one by one, with scarcely a word spoken, hardly a glance exchanged, eleven of them moseyed over and took their places. "Ballplayers know," Brown told Plimpton. And if one of the eleven had been too modest to step forward immediately? "The others," Jim said, "would have waited for him. The position would have stayed open until he walked in and filled it. Can you imagine any other quarterback, no matter who the guy was, shoving John Unitas aside to get into an All-Star lineup? No, man, no way."

Unless it was Sonny Jurgensen of Washington, sticking a friendly needle in Unitas. "Don't you remember," Jurgensen asked a sportswriter not long ago, "what I said to him that day we were all together in his restaurant? Remember how he howled? He howled!" Of course the sportswriter remembered. The restaurant was the Golden Arm in Baltimore. The fourth man in the booth was a round bartender named Rocky Thornton. "I'd like to thank you, John," Sonny told Unitas earnestly, "for naming the place after me." Not waiting for John to stop laughing, he added, "Back when we were playing, I don't remember you being this eloquent with the press." Unitas sipped his beer—the sportswriter had never seen him drink anything except beer—and said through that toothy, crooked smile, "I always figured being a little dull was part of being a pro. Win or lose, I never walked off a professional foot-ball field without first thinking of something boring to say to [*Baltimore Sun* beat man] Cameron Snyder."

Almost every celebrated athlete has an original story of being burned in print. John's involved a New York journalist named Leonard Schecter. "I was at a golf outing in the early years," Unitas said, "an airline junket: American Airlines. After the golf, we were all sitting around the clubhouse, just like we are now. Everybody was drinking. Nobody was taking notes. I said a few things I shouldn't have, questioning Weeb [Baltimore head coach Weeb Ewbank] in a way, contrasting our offensive philosophies. The story came out: 'What Johnny Unitas would do differently if he were the coach of the Colts.' Ain't that a kick in the head? The les-son I learned there kept me pretty quiet the rest of my career. If you don't know who you're talking to, you better be careful what you say."

Several years earlier, at his home in Oxford, Ohio, Ewbank told the same story, but better. "One of those first off-seasons," he said, "John phoned here to say, 'Weeb, there's a magazine article just out that is going to be very embarrassing to you. A fellow named Schecter wrote it, but it sounds like I wrote it myself. It lists all of the little things I'd change if I were the coach instead of you. I want you to know that everything in there is absolutely accurate. It's exactly how I feel. I honestly have no idea how the guy was able to keep it straight. He didn't take a single note. But I also want you to know that I didn't mean for it to be printed. I apologize.'" Think-ing back, Ewbank chuckled and said, "That's Unitas." Punching his visitor in the arm, he said, "Nine hundred and ninety-nine players out of a thousand would swear they were misquoted or that what they said had been taken out of context. Not him. It was exactly how he felt. I just said, 'Forget it, John. Thanks for calling.' To tell you the truth, I'm not sure if I ever even saw that article."

Through the beery mist of the Golden Arm, the conversation staggered in many different directions until, as usual, it had reeled its way back around to Berry, Gino Marchetti, Jim Mutscheller, Lenny Moore, Jim Parker, Alan "the Horse" Ameche, Artie Donovan, Bert Rechichar, Bill Pellington, Jimmy Orr, Gene "Big Daddy" Lipscomb, Alex "Captain Who?" Hawkins, L. G. "Long Gone" Dupre, and an era of life and football that was also long gone. "If you knew any of us," Jurgensen said for the entire National Football League in the 1950s and 1960s, "you knew all of us." Not to contradict Sonny, speaking only for the old Colts, Unitas reworked the sentence slightly. "I think you almost had to know all of us to know any of us," he said.

This is a book about all of them, in the pursuit of trying to know one of them, Johnny U. It begins and ends with him. But it is as much about a certain time as a single player. It is less about a specific place in the country than a place where the whole country used to be. Of course, it flies in the face of Plimpton's literary maxim that the smaller the ball, the richer the subject. Pro football isn't usually thought of as a romance, but that's the way it is offered here, in black-and-white.

"Ours was the great era of professional football," Jurgensen said, "because it was the players' game then. It's the coaches' game now. In those days quarterbacks looked their own guys right in the eye, and then stared across the line at the other guys. Who's ready to do it? Who's starting to quit? We controlled the game. We applied the psychology in the huddle. You know, if in the first or second quarter we found a defensive player we could take advantage of, we didn't always show him up right away."

"We might save him for later," Unitas agreed.

"We're in scoring territory now, the game's on the line." Sonny set up the play.

"All right, let's abuse him," John said, and they laughed.

After Jurgensen and Thornton departed, and the notebook was put away, Unitas posed a question of his own. "Doesn't it make you sick today," he said, "seeing so many jigs in the end zone?" Though the word was "jigs," the sportswriter heard "jigaboos," and answered too quickly, "I'm not going to listen to that, John."

"To what?" Unitas asked.

"Jigs."

"Dances," he said.

The sportswriter apologized twice. "Don't be sorry," Unitas said softly, "but shouldn't you know me better than that by now?"

"John, I don't know you at all."

"Don't worry about it," he said. "Nobody does."

ONE

"Well, I'm going to play professional football."

Francis Unitas and Helen Superfisky

"**M**y father's name was Leonard Unitas," states the autobiography of Johnny Unitas, *Pro Quarterback,* published in 1965 by Grosset and Dunlap. The funny thing is, his father's name was not Leonard. His brother's name was. Reading the book in 1965, Cameron Snyder of the *Baltimore Sun* noticed how reminiscent many of the passages were of newspaper stories Snyder had written or read. Whole columns by John Steadman of the *News-Post and Sunday American* appeared to have been redrawn in the first person and incorporated into the narrative. *"I always remember how surprised John Steadman, the sportswriter, was the morning of the championship game. . . ."*

When next he saw Unitas, Snyder said dryly, "I got your book and I have only one question. Did you write it?"

"Hell," Unitas said, "I didn't even read it."

◆

His father's name was Francis Joseph Unitas. Always Francis, never Frank (just as John was never Jack or even, as a boy,

Johnny). When his mother died and his father could not cope, Francis was dispatched with two brothers, twins, to a Pittsburgh orphanage called the Toner Institute and Seraphic Home for Boys. (Two sisters and another brother were scattered elsewhere.) Both twins died in the orphanage, leaving Francis alone. The name of the one who died of influenza has been forgotten in time. The little boy who was run over by a train while trying to escape was named Adam.

At sixteen, the maximum age, Francis was sprung from the Toner Institute. Wrapping two shirts around an old baseball glove and waving good-bye to the Sisters of Divine Providence and the Capuchin Franciscan Fathers, he made for the coal country of West Virginia, hoping to pick up the trail of his lost siblings in a large Lithuanian community of miners. No relatives turned up then (one would, years later), but in an Old World enclave known as Century, Francis did make a significant find. She was a Lithuanian immigrant who worked in the company store and therefore, by necessity, could speak not only Lithuanian and English but also Russian and Polish. A self-taught piano player—a self-taught everything—she was the organist for Sunday Mass at the Catholic church. It seemed to Francis that there was nothing Helen Superfisky couldn't do.

To Helen, Francis was equally remarkable. He was tall—right around six feet—gangly, but amazingly powerful, almost in the manner of a circus strongman. He had huge hands, bigger than Lennie's in *Of Mice and Men,* busier than Wing Biddlebaum's in *Winesburg, Ohio.* Francis liked to lift things just to prove he could do it, roadside boulders and even the back wheels of coal trucks. Despite a comically improper technique, he out-tossed all of the local shot-putters (a regional specialty) and could fling a rock practically out of sight. Combing his brown hair in a confident wave, he was a showy character in every way, an all-around performer who boxed like a lighter man and could be plugged into any position on the town baseball team. They married.

Not quickly but by hard increments, over ten sweaty years, Francis and Helen Unitas worked their way up to owning a small coal truck and establishing their own delivery business back in the Brookline section of Pittsburgh. Though coal furnaces abounded, it was the 1930s; profits were meager. But the entire country was toiling for the minimum. To be working at all was the main thing. They lived more than modestly in a one-bathroom house that was rather like a hive, buzzing as it did with a swarm of Superfiskys that included Helen's parents, several layers of cousins and in-laws, and a great-uncle, Tony, who was stricken with silicosis ("miner's asthma"). Hanging bedsheets for privacy, Francis, Helen, and all four of their children—Leonard, Millicent, John, and Shirley—slept together in the dining room.

Stood up by his helpers in the bitter September of 1938, Francis put in a long day doing his own job, dropping the black piles here and there all over town, and then a longer night doing theirs, assembling the chutes and shoveling the coal into basement bins. Working at breakneck speed, he took on the task as another exhibition of superhuman strength—an impossible race against daybreak—and won. But he caught pneumonia and died, technically of uremia, kidney failure. Francis Joseph Unitas wasn't quite thirty-eight years old. John Constantine Unitas, born on the seventh of May 1933, was five.

"John was the apple of his dad's eye," said big brother Leonard without resentment. The unread autobiography wasn't so wrong at that. In a way, Leonard *was* John's father. Eleven years old when Francis died, Leonard was already as averse to melodrama and immune to sentimentality as John would grow up to be. For instance, Leonard could believe that one of his orphaned uncles was killed hopping a freight train, but he always wondered if the "escape" part of Adam's story wasn't embroidery. "There weren't any railroad tracks," Leonard said with twinkling eyes, "anywhere near the Toner Institute." Sister Millie, three years younger than Leonard, three years older than John, didn't care one way or the other. But the "children," John and Shirley, never questioned the family's heroic tragedy. It thrilled them and broke their hearts.

"I have pictures of us with Dad and the truck," Shirley said, "but no recollections of him at all. I don't even remember the sound of his voice. The only memories I have are little ones that John shared with me: like Dad flying up the stairs three steps at a time to make sure Mom wasn't hurting John in the bath. I think there was a lot of my dad in John that we didn't know or recognize, but Mom did." He had those same big dukes. (Anyone who ever shook the hand of Johnny Unitas never forgot it.)

One year apart, John and Shirley were Jem and Scout. He called her Tootsie. The others laughed at how quiet he was. "He very seldom spoke," according to Leonard. "Once in a while he'd come out with something." But Shirley understood his silences. "John was always thinking," she said. And blinking. Many who later huddled with him swore they could hear his eyeballs clicking as he double-checked his calculations. At ages ten and nine, John and Shirley were fused together permanently by forty-two plunges of a syringe. Shirley said, "John loved animals more than anything, you know. We always had a dog." Tippy was killed in traffic. Skippy wasn't nearly as adventurous. Weegee was another story entirely. The sweetest in the long line of mysteriously bred mutts that Leonard kept rescuing from the pound, Weegee was the only dog they ever had who could give the okay signal with his tail. Missing for three days, he came home wet, bedraggled, and rabid. As John and Shirley were washing him in a tin tub, Weegee changed personalities. Both kids were nipped on the face and nose.

Panting turned to growling turned to screaming. Summoned from work, Leonard was able to trap Weegee in the cellar. While nobody slept, the poor dog moaned all night and made toothpicks out of his side of the door. When Leonard opened it a crack in the morning, Weegee lay there exhausted, his face bathed in a white froth and his jaws dripping foam. The police strapped him into an ugly leather harness and took him out in a bag. Two days later, John and Shirley were called to Southside Hospital for rabies shots. The hardest part was sitting through a torturous school day before climbing onto the streetcar alone. All the way there and back, they held hands.

In the same room, each received twenty-one injections, first in the stomach, then in one buttock, then in the other, then in one arm, then in the other, then back in the stomach, and around again, and again and again. Did John cry? "Oh, God, no," Shirley said. "I couldn't either, in front of him." On the return trip, as the streetcar approached their stop, John whispered the first full sentence of the day: "It's only a needle, Toots." He was Johnny Unitas at ten.

◆

With Francis gone, Helen streamlined the family and dropped down a social notch to a two-bedroom house on unpaved William Street in Mount Washington. "The highlight of the year," said a neighbor, Joe Chilleo, "was when the scrapers came up to scrape the street just before the election. We'd go out there and watch them. We thought it was wonderful." Helen, Millie, and Shirley shared one of the bedrooms; Leonard, John, and Great-Uncle Tony the other. Although he could cough with Doc Holliday, Tony was good company. There still was only one bath. To Millie, it was "like living on the tip of a mountaintop." From the porch of their yellow house, which looked orange at sunset, you could see the city, a few tall buildings at least, the Monongahela River, and the bridge where the streetcars crossed over. "The automobiles were just specks," she said.

Until Leonard was old enough to drive the coal truck, men were hired to work under Helen's supervision. They set no records for sobriety. The sisters at Saint Justin's School, including a six-foot-three nun whom everybody called Big Red, pretended not to notice Leonard's grogginess in the morning (he had been up since four-thirty shoveling coal), and they sighed sympathetically every afternoon to see him hustling back to the job. Eventually, John would pull his share of after-school turns with the shovel. "If you put in three tons," he said with a grin, "you got a dollar fifty. It wasn't bad." Helen fielded the coal orders and worked for a bakery in the morning, sold insurance in the afternoon, and cleaned office buildings at night. Though lacking a high school diploma, she studied bookkeeping, passed the civil service exam with the highest possible mark, and ended up in the employ of the city of Pittsburgh.

"Just watching my mother, how hard she had to work for everything we had," John said, "was the greatest thing I ever saw. Sometimes I'd come home from a ball game all beat up and she'd say, 'You know Mrs. Wrigley up the street?' and I'd say, 'Yeah, I know Mrs. Wrigley up the street,' and she'd say, 'Well, she has three tons of coal sitting out in front of her house. See that it gets put in.' I could hardly move, and I'd say, 'Ma, it's raining.' And she'd say, 'Yeah, it's raining. Go do it.' And I did."

It was Millie's job to wake the kids and get them off to school. Rousing John was a particular challenge. "You know how much the man liked to play football?" Leonard said. "That's how much the boy loved to sleep." The children stumbled downstairs every morning to what Shirley called "Mom's infamous notes" on the kitchen table. "She'd leave, like, mother's oats and stuff on top of the double boiler, so that they would still be warm, along with the day's instructions." Under no circumstances was anyone to leave the house that afternoon until the following things were taken care of. "And you knew, boy, you didn't dare. 'Start the dinner, peel the potatoes . . .' John's job was to keep the furnace banked. If Mom came home to a cold house, there'd be hell to pay."

Helen was a fervent Catholic. The family marched in a loose formation to Sunday Mass in the basement of Saint Justin's High School. Sometimes, after everyone else was gone, the Unitas family lingered to walk the Stations of the Cross. "She was never flowery,"

Shirley said. "You didn't get kisses and hugs from my mom. You knew she loved you because she was taking care of you. If you complained about something, she'd say, 'You ate, didn't you?'" All of Helen's harsh sayings have been stitched into samplers in her children's memories. "If you have to clean toilets for a living, make them shine." "Show me where it's written that *you're* supposed to be happy." "If you have a 'need,' we'll talk about it. But if it's only a 'want,' don't bring it up."

Though her large extended family had split off and spread out, Helen remained the matriarch in an Old World sense. With hats in hand, uncles came to the house on William Street to fidget and squirm on the edge of their chairs while requesting her permission to marry. "I was very young then," Shirley said. "I couldn't imagine these big boobs asking my mother this." At Christmas, the whole family came back together. Shirley remembered a few bleak Christmases. "Sometimes we'd go down to the tree and there'd be nothing under there. Or you'd get a little doll or a tiny purse. I remember one year my sister got a brush and a comb." But many of the Christmases were brilliant. Helen's brother the priest, Father Constantine Superfisky (Father Connie to the children, and the contributor of John's middle name), would arrive from Tiltonsville, Ohio, in an automobile loaded like a sleigh with presents.

In Lithuanian homes, Christmas Eve was the day of Kucios, a special seven- or even ten-fish supper. Ordinarily Helen was the plainest of cooks. Though no one ever had the nerve to say so, her spaghetti sauce and her chili tasted exactly the same; one had beans. Once a week, she served liver and onions. But for Kucios each branch of the family brought a dish. Not so much for the smelt or the herring, but for the ritual (and the potato pancakes), John and Shirley loved Christmas Eve most of all. There was one catch. In order to receive their gifts, the children were required to perform. One year John sang "I'm Popeye the Sailor Man."

He had a worse than average singing voice. At the peak of Unitas's fame, a Baltimore confectioner, Mary Sue Candies, hired him to warble its Easter jingle on television. *(Mary Sue Easter Eggs / they're the best Easter Eggs / honey, your money can buy / So rich and nutritious / and mmm-mmm delicious / so Mary Sue Easter Eggs, try.)* Anyone who ever heard that commercial can still call back the sensation in the metal filling of a tooth. But Unitas had a meter if not a melody. The silent boy who you never knew was even in the house turned into a constant whistler. "Not that you could recognize what he was whistling," Shirley said. "But you always knew where he was."

He may have been moved to song by the Notre Dame football coach Knute Rockne.

●

A baseball mitt or, later, football shoes clearly fell into the category of "want," not "need." "My brother Leonard thought of those things," Shirley said. "He was our dad that way. Once, John and I were throwing a ball around the house and we broke the globe on a lamp. In a panic we called Leonard. Somehow—I have no idea how—he came up with an exact replacement before Mom got home. Leonard was incredible. When the games started to take over John's life, Leonard always saw to it that John had whatever he needed to play."

Until the games started, Shirley was one of the gang on William Street. She hung out with John and the boys who sat on a corner curb in front of McGuinness's drugstore nursing a pint of ice cream. When the beat cop came along to rap his billy club against the fence, she scattered with the others. Even after John discovered the games, he didn't coldly jettison Tootsie. She went on swinging the backyard tire through which he spun his football, and they continued to make most of their regular rounds, like following up a stiff Sunday Mass by sitting back in the grass beside the Baptist church enjoying the amazing music and watching the building shake.

"John loved all of the games, and he was good at all of them," said Joe Chilleo, a classmate and teammate from third grade through the end of high school. "I don't call him a natural athlete; he just had more push. We played baseball at a place called Cargo, where there was no left field. For that matter, right field was in a gully. The right fielder was actually out of sight. You had to yell at him, 'Look out, the ball is coming!' I can remember that." The Mount Washington Owls, as they named themselves, scheduled a few formal baseball games with other nonuniformed teams, but mostly they competed against one another, playing a version of baseball called roundies. Three men batted, everyone else took a position in the field, and whoever made the putout changed places with the hitter. If the three batters ever filled the bases, the lead runner was automatically out. So there were numerous plays at home plate. "And Cargo was one of those fields you had to oil," Chilleo said, "to keep the dust down." Because there was no left field, anyone who hit the ball to the left side of second base was also out.

"One day," Chilleo said, "John turned around and started batting left-handed. He didn't say anything about it; he just did it. That's how he was. Pretty soon, we were all hitting left-handed. We were an entire team of left-hand hitters. It just made sense, with no left field. There was a recreation center nearby where we could swim in the summer—in the nude, as a matter of fact—and play softball or paddleball. John seemed to think paddleball was unmanly. So none of us played paddleball. In basketball, he was probably our second-tallest [and their thinnest] guy; he could have been our center. But John was the playmaker. He just was. Of course, in football, he was always the quarterback."

"In school," John told Steve Sabol of NFL Films, "I think it was the eighth grade or seventh, we had a substitute teacher by the name of Mrs. O'Connor. Beautiful girl. Boy, I had a bad crush on her. She went around the room asking everybody what they wanted to do with their life. And when she got to me, for some reason—don't ask me why, I don't know—I said, 'Well, I'm going to play professional football.'"

Chilleo's father was a railroader, an engineer. He was a silent, undemonstrative man, a stickler for schedules and rules, as someone who operates a locomotive might naturally be. He enjoyed cowboy books, Zane Grey. "In those days," Joe said, "you didn't ask questions about who died or what. But I knew John didn't have a father. Because he was always asking me about mine. I didn't know what to say. I remember John's surprise when I told him that my dad had never let me ride up front with him in the engine. I said, 'John, he could be fired for that.' John said, 'Well, my father used to let me ride on the running board of our truck.' He claimed to remember—come on, a four- or five-year-old's memory—that the door flew open once and knocked him right under the wheels. He said he would have been run over and killed if his dad hadn't slammed on the breaks just in the nick of time. The back wheel supposedly stopped an inch from his head. But John said, 'He still let me ride on the running board.' I gave him that one. I always felt sorry that John didn't have a dad."

In school, John paid relatively close attention and always did his homework. But he was an undistinguished student. Surprisingly, he preferred oral tests to written ones, and he could navigate multiple-choice and true-false questions far better than essays. On report card day, the old, gray pastor of Saint Justin's, Father Barry, handed out the cards personally. To be more precise, he flipped them out, along with sarcastic, not to say sadistic, commentary. "Look at this one," he'd tell the class, skimming it over their heads like a pebble across the water. "You'll make a good truck driver someday. Oh, here's another one. You'll be digging ditches." The prospect of being mentioned by Father Barry chilled John more than any of the prophecies.

Except for comic books, he wasn't an avid reader. "We always had comic books," Shirley said. "John would stretch out on the floor and read them for hours and hours." But in the first big upset of his career, he did happen upon a library once where he discovered the adolescent sports literature of John R. Tunis and reveled in the escapades of a young protagonist named Roy Tucker. Partly because Unitas was Catholic, mostly because quarterback Johnny Lujack was from western Pennsylvania (Connellsville), John also fell in love with the University of Notre Dame. Just as the single-wing offense was giving way to a modified T-formation, Lujack became the Irish quarterback in 1943, when Angelo Bertelli ("the Springfield Rifle") was called into the marines. After his own time-out for war, Lujack returned in 1946 to tackle Doc Blanchard in the open field and save a scoreless tie against Army. That allowed the Irish to replace the Cadets as college football's national champions. Unitas was conversant in every detail and statistic. By comparison, of course, the NFL was a minor league.

John checked out the book *Knute Rockne* so many times that the librarian ran out of space for stamping a return date and, in an impromptu ceremony—exactly like retiring a trophy—presented it to him. According to *Knute Rockne,* Coach Rockne hit on the idea for Notre Dame's shifting backfield while watching a line of chorus girls dancing on a stage. John would sooner play paddleball than dance, but he started to see football as more than a display of toughness—as a game of precision and timing with its own rhythm and even choreography.

Unitas never discussed his theories of music with the sportswriters, only with receiver Raymond Berry and dancer Gene Kelly. In December of 1958, during a rehearsal for the live television special *Dancing: A Man's Game* for *Omnibus,* John demonstrated for Mickey Mantle, Bob Cousy, Sugar Ray Robinson, and Kelly the precise steps involved in dropping back to pass, and the intricate spins required in completing a full battery of fakes after the ball has been handed off. To Milton Richman of United Press International, the Pittsburgher Kelly (South Hills High, class of '29, about two hundred yards from Saint Justin's) quoted Unitas as saying,

"Fred Astaire's a dancer, Gene. You're an athlete." Kelly told Richman, "That's the greatest compliment I ever received."

Like the Baptist church, football had a beat. John could whistle it. Not that anyone could recognize what he was whistling.

●

He came home from his first day of high school to let Shirley in on exactly what he had learned: they were poor. "Before that, we thought everybody was just like us," Shirley said. "John didn't spell it out and I didn't really understand. But when I followed him there the next year, I got it. The kids from Mount Lebanon or Brookline had to pay to go to Saint Justin's High School. In Mount Washington, we didn't pay. On our street, the children all wore the same clothes. [Joe Chilleo's mother made his shirts.] These kids, gosh, had a different outfit every day, and more than one pair of shoes. Before we could go to the movies, we had to find bottles and collect the deposits. They had allowances. It didn't devastate us or anything like that, but high school was the first time John and I realized we were poor."

Big Red was a hell of a lot of Mercy nun. "If she turned suddenly," Shirley said, "it knocked her habit just a bit off kilter and you might get a glimpse of her bright red hair." If Big Red was barreling somewhere and you were in her path, she would just pick you up by the elbows and move you over. "If you misbehaved in or out of class," Shirley said, "she would take her pointer and put it across the back of your legs. You were marked for the rest of the day. Of course, Mom would look at the stripe and say, 'You must have deserved it.' The nuns were the law."

A less flamboyant member of the order, Sister Theresa Marie, was the first person to read inspiration into John's last name. "'Unite us,'" she said when they met. "You must be the leader." From the second day of football practice on, he was. Leonard said, "He came home from the first day of practice all bent out of shape, muttering, 'They say I'm too light to play football. They're afraid I'll get hurt.' This was a couple of years before Max Carey became the coach. Two other guys shared the job. 'You go back tomorrow,' I told John. 'I'll be over there. I'll talk to them.' But by the time I arrived, he was already in the huddle. I saw him jump up and rifle a pass over the middle for a completion. His whole face, his whole body, was a smile. I turned around and went back to work."

Speaking of rifles and firearms in general, the first time John was shot, Leonard shot him. The second time, John shot himself. "That first time was the year Dad died," Leonard said. "I was eleven, John five. This wasn't the smartest thing I ever did, by the way. A buddy of mine—his father was a detective for the city of Pittsburgh—gave me a thirty-eight caliber bullet. In our backyard, there was a wall Dad had built out of curbstones. He carried each one of them back there by himself. Incredible. Wedging the shell into a piece of a split telephone pole, I crouched down behind the wall and shot at it with my BB gun. Awfully small target. I kept telling John to stay down, but after a while I must have convinced him I couldn't hit it, because he hopped up on the wall just a split second before the explosion."

Not the bullet, but the casing, tore into John's right leg. Leonard lifted him up and carried him off in his arms. In the retelling, Leonard added drolly, "He ain't heavy; he's my brother." Some of the metal was tweezed out, some was left. ("That's why I can't run any faster than this," Unitas joked forever.) "When Mom got home," Leonard said, "she took that BB gun and broke the stock right off over her knee. Better the knee than me. Pretty soon, her knee blew up as big as a balloon. I went into hiding for a few days."

No more shots rang out in Mount Washington until John was a junior at Saint Justin's High and well established as the Saint J's quarterback, whose specialty was the jump pass over the middle. His uniform number was 18. Reacting to reports of a prowler in the area, a friend named Howard Gibbs lent Helen a Colt 380 automatic pistol, which she kept fully loaded on the living room mantel.

(It still works today.) Taking it down for cleaning, John removed the clip and, needless to say, forgot about the bullet in the chamber. He shot himself straight through the middle finger of his some-day-to-be-world-famous right hand. "I wrapped the hand in a towel," Shirley said, "and we ran up the side of the hill to the doctor's office. Do you know, because it was a gunshot wound, that man wouldn't touch him? I was scared John was going to bleed to death right there in the office. We raced back down the hill to Joe Chilleo's house. The Chilleos were the only family on our street that had a car."

As Joe picked up the narrative, "Here came Shirley on the dead run, screaming, 'John shot himself!' And here's John, lack-adaisically strolling along behind her, holding up his hand in a bloody towel, saying, 'I don't know what she's so excited about. It's only a hole in my finger.' Thank God, my dad was home. We drove them to the hospital." That evening, two policemen came to Helen's house to investigate the shooting. "This one cop," Leonard said, "started bad-mouthing John for being so stupid. My mother did everything but throw that man down them steps."

Ralph Green, Saint Justin's right halfback, said, "All of this took place just before our first dress game of the season. We went down to play Moon—a school from Moon Township—and for the whole game nobody could take their eyes off John's right hand. He had this big splint on the center finger sticking straight up above the football. It looked like a yardstick. On the first play—I suppose it could have been the second play, but I honestly think it was the first one—John threw that goddamned ball fifty-some yards for a touchdown. He had massive hands, you know. It would have blown my finger clean off."

Before the Moon game, before every game, John went to church. In or out of the state of grace, he would do this throughout his career. "The church was underneath the school at that time," Green said. "After we'd suit up, if we were going on the bus, he'd lead a bunch of us down to the altar to pray." In their regular crowd, the B League—Saint Mary's, Saint Michael's, Saint Vincent's, Saint Wendelin's—they more than held their own. When they ventured out into the larger world—Bradford, Ambridge—prayer was less effective. The big Catholic high schools in Pittsburgh, the football powers, were North Catholic and Central Catholic. Speaking for North Catholic, former quarterback Daniel Rooney said, "We had about a thousand boys. Central Catholic had at least twelve hundred, maybe thirteen hundred boys. Saint Justin's couldn't have had two hundred and fifty boys and girls. My senior year, John's junior year, we won the Catholic championship. When the All-Catholic team came out, I couldn't believe my eyes. Many of my teammates were on it, but I was only second-team. *He* was first-team. My friends razzed me, 'How in the world did this B League kid from this jerkwater school beat you out?' But John was good. I knew he was good. We had played them his sophomore year, my junior year, and well, they upset us. But you know, it was a fluke. It was a total fluke."

Rooney and Unitas would cross paths again. Dan's father owned the Pittsburgh Steelers.

◆

In John's junior season, James "Max" Carey became Saint Justin's coach. His influence on Unitas would be immense. All head football coaches of the day paced the sidelines like gents in creased fedoras and long overcoats. But Carey truly was a gentleman. If Ohio legend Paul Brown brought to mind a homicide inspector viewing the body, Carey resembled a stockbroker who had just missed his train. Even at practice, Max was unanimated and businesslike. Skipping the customary locker room slogans ("When the going gets tough . . ."), he never exhorted the players at the top of his lungs. "Before Carey," Joe Chilleo said, "Saint Justin's coaches were all screamers. 'Cheese and rice!' they'd yell. (Within earshot of Big Red, they better not yell, 'Jesus Christ!') 'Cheese and rice! Can't anybody make a tackle?' Whether they were players or coaches, John hated screamers. He'd chew on you himself in the huddle, but he never screamed at you, even when he was saying, 'Shut up.'"

Having schooled Unitas on the offense, Carey informed him, "It's your job to call the plays, but when you come over to me afterward, you damn sure better have a good reason for everything you did." John later said, "Max Carey was the person who taught me that a quarterback can't just be one of the boys. You really have to be a little aloof from everyone else even though you want to be friends with them and join in all of the different things they want to do. You just can't do it. You can sit with them. You can have a joke. You can have a drink. But you always have to keep a certain distance."

In the classroom, John continued to meet the minimum requirements. "Why do we have to take Latin?" he grumbled to Shirley. "Are we all going to be speaking Latin someday? Are there verbs out there in the real world that are going to need conjugating?"

On a crowded bus bound for a basketball game, John rose to offer his seat to a brassy cheerleader named Dorothy Jean Hoelle. It was a classic attraction of opposites. "Polar opposites," Shirley said tersely, as if more than two words might be dangerous. While Dorothy sought center stage, John hid in the third row of the team photograph. She loved to dance, especially the exuberant bop and jive of the day. True to his principles, John escorted her to the school hops, waited outside while she lassoed partners (including an annoyingly avid one John dubbed Twinkletoes), and then saw her home. His schoolwork fell to third place on the depth chart.

Thanks to Carey's contacts, to John's brief notices in the newspapers, to a letter from a Saint Justin's priest, and—probably most critically—to a telephone call from a Saint J's alumnus who was one of the biggest beer distributors in Pittsburgh, Unitas won the lottery: an actual tryout at Notre Dame. On a cloud and a train, he arrived in South Bend, Indiana, to find that the golden dome was even shinier in fact than it was in fantasy. All of the famous ghosts, from George Gipp to the Four Horsemen, were on parade.

Of course, John knew everything there was to know about Knute
Rockne, about half of which was true. The real Gipp was a gam-
bling and pool-shooting reprobate whose favorite things next to
blondes were skipping whole semesters of classes and blowing
smoke rings into Rockne's putty face. As the Gipper lay dying of a
rampaging infection, he *could* have asked Rock to win one for him
someday. It's possible. But it would have been much more in character for Gipp to want to get a little something down on the strep-
tococci. Never mind. Unitas bought the legend in its entirety.

John was anxious to meet coach Frank Leahy, who never
emerged from the cathedral. Following Hunk Anderson and Elmer
Layden to Rockne's throne, Leahy had been deemphasizing oratory while re-establishing invincibility. An assistant coach, the
former All-America halfback Bernie Crimmins, presided at a week-
long tryout for two dozen extras. In the end, Crimmins told John
he was terrific. But because he weighed only 137 pounds, he was
just too slight for Notre Dame. More to the point, he was too frail
for the company Notre Dame kept. ("Bernie Crimmins said, 'Geez,
I like what you do, but God, you're so small. You're five eleven, a
hundred thirty-some pounds. We're liable to be sued for manslaughter up here.' So, that was it.") Never having seen John's
report cards, Crimmins recommended the Ivy League. As a matter
of fact, on his own nickel, he placed several telephone calls. A couple of the Ivies actually made inquiries. Nothing came of them.

At Carey's urging, Indiana University glanced at John but
never called back. John and one of Dan Rooney's former North
Catholic teammates, Richie McCabe, auditioned together for Pitt.
Both were offered scholarships, but only McCabe passed the entrance exam. For college football's bluest chippers (even then),
being able to read wasn't absolutely mandatory. But John wasn't a
star; he was just a bit player. When he flunked the test, Pitt turned
away. Unitas felt a tug of shame for the rest of his life and, at the
first crossroads in his pro career, seriously wondered if the
coaches somehow knew of this failure and marked it against him.

Much later, the quarterback celebrated for never trading in alibis told Doug Brown of the *Baltimore Evening Sun,* "Maybe if I had had a dad, he'd have made me study."

Enter Frank Gitschier of Sharon, Pennsylvania, just one year out of the University of Louisville. Though Louisville was far from a football power, Gitschier had quarterbacked the Cardinals to a commendable 8–3 record in 1949 against the likes of Catawba, Bradley, and Murray State (all victories). However, the following season, Gitschier's first as an assistant coach, the team slipped to 3–6–1 versus such schools as Mississippi Southern, Duquesne, and Washington and Lee (all losses). Straining just to pay the assistants' salaries, $3,300 a year in Gitschier's case, Louisville had no budget for recruiting, not even for telephone calls. Out-of-town prospects had to be courted by mail. Quizzing his players for leads, Gitschier heard from two of them about a gritty kid in Pittsburgh's B League who could really throw the football.

Like Unitas, Gitschier came from coal. When Frank was eight or nine, back in Sharon, his father would give him fifty cents to go to the lumber yard and collect pieces of coal that had dropped off the trucks—what they called slack—in a burlap bag. "By the time the bag was full, I'd be dragging it," Gitschier said, "and pretty soon there'd be a hole in the bottom. I'd be trailing a black line of coal dust all the way home. Then I'd rush back with a paper sack and retrieve what little bits I could."

In December of 1950, Louisville head coach Frank Camp made the casual suggestion to Gitschier, "If you're planning to go home for Christmas anyway, why don't you stop off and see this Unitas kid?" (In other words, don't even think of expensing it.) Gitschier recalled, "I went to a gym where John was supposed to be playing basketball, but I just missed him. So I drove up to the Unitas house on the top of William Street. I remember, it was a freezing cold night and dark as pitch when I got there. Snow was on the ground. The lights were on inside. I climbed up the steps to the porch, and do you know what I saw there? A burlap bag with a black hole in the bottom. I knew this kid."

Without ever seeing John play, without ever seeing him throw so much as one ball on a practice field, Gitschier offered him room, board, books, and tuition to come to the University of Louisville. Fifteen dollars a month spending money was also a possibility, but not guaranteed. To Helen, sitting next to John on the living room sofa, Gitschier made two firm pledges. "'Mrs. Unitas,' I said, 'I promise you that he'll go to Mass every Sunday, and I promise you that he'll graduate.' I'll never forget the way she smiled." Helen answered in a letter that said simply, "John wants to come," and after another woeful exam, saved by a personal appearance before the university board, he was ultimately admitted on academic probation.

There are several other versions of how Unitas was discovered by Louisville. But none of the heroes of those stories would be chosen by John to introduce him at his induction into the Pro Football Hall of Fame. Gitschier would be.

(By the way, Helen would marry Howard Gibbs, the friend who lent her the pistol, and be widowed a second time. Shirley Unitas and Ralph Green, the Saint Justin's halfback whose normal-sized finger would have been "blown clear off," also wed. On the night their son Scott died of lymphoma at twenty-eight, Shirley opened the front door and there stood John. "That was the first time I ever saw him cry," she said. "The second time was the next year, when Mom passed away." To John, Helen had seemed indestructible. At seventy, a decade before she died, Helen was hit by a car in Pittsburgh, broke both legs and her right arm, and didn't think a thing of it. "She was in a nursing home with Alzheimer's at the end," Shirley said. "You know how they put those bands on their arms? She'd look at hers and say to me, 'Who is this? Why is this name on here? I'm Helen Superfisky.'" Helen had gone home in her mind to Century, West Virginia, where Shirley was her sister

Mary and John was an attractive strongman with big hands. He'd kiss her on the forehead and call her Mom, but in the next instant she'd whisper to Shirley, "Boy, he's tall. Who is he, Mary?")

In 1951, eighteen-year-old John Unitas headed off to college. Most of the Mount Washington Owls, an entire team of left-hand hitters, did not. Though accepted at Duquesne, Joe Chilleo went into the navy. "When I was coming home from the service," he said, "the train was stopped in Johnstown and there was a knock at the window. I looked out and it was my dad. His train was pulled up right next to mine. He grabbed my bag, and when I started for the coal tender, getting ready to duck down in a little house behind the engine, he pulled me right up into the cab. He could have been fired, but I was riding with him. 'My kid!' he kept shouting, blowing the whistle. 'It's my kid!' I was full of soot by the time we got home, but it was wonderful. I thought of John. I wished he could have seen me."

TWO

1951

"You run the ball; I'll call the plays."

Losing in Louisville

Louisville in the postwar years was a streetcar school, "the oldest municipal university west of the Allegheny Mountains," situated right at the horseshoe where the streetcars turned around. The football players were the rare students who lived on campus—in White Hall, a stark wooden navy barrack left over from the V-12 program. John didn't object to spartan quarters and enjoyed the camaraderie. He eventually joined the Air Force ROTC, not minding the blue uniform, liking the extra few dollars. After a summer of lifting weights and jumping rope, Unitas was up to 145 pounds. Still, on the first day of practice, Coach Camp mistook him for the water boy.

Big hands and feet. Long arms and legs. As bowlegged as a ranch hand. Somewhat sunken chest. Slightly rounded shoulders. ("He ran a little like a camel," Baltimore teammate Alex Hawkins would later say, "like a really pissed-off camel.") Only when Unitas cracked his knees to spread his hands under center Otto Knop's considerable rump did John's football pants nearly fit. Otherwise, the knee pads drooped down around his shins like George Bailey's coming home from the dance. (Colts receiver

Jimmy Orr said, "John threw a sharp pass that came on you quick but, for some reason, was easy to catch. Some balls are softer than others, you know. John had a ball that was so soft you could catch it and keep on going. You didn't have to concentrate on it. It was a great thing to have, that soft-feeling fastball.") Easy for Orr to say. Jimmy was equipped with talons. Louisville receivers Dave Rivenbark, Kenny Anderson, and Babe Ray had ordinary human hands that, following a pass-and-catch session with Unitas, glowed like crepes suzette.

Another freshman, Bill Campbell, was named the starting quarterback for the Cardinals' opener at Wayne State, but a crumpled knee the week before put Campbell out for the season. Junior Jack Browning was the most experienced quarterback on the team; however, an emergency tonsillectomy scratched him, too. So, in Detroit, sophomore Jim Olmstead did the playing, and freshman John Unitas the standing by. John's new number was 16. Wayne was the only game on the schedule that the Cardinals were favored to win, and they did, 28–12. Then, with Browning doing most of the signal calling, they were thumped in quick succession by Boston University (39–7), Cincinnati (38–0), and Xavier (47–6).

Like Max Carey of Saint Justin's, Frank Camp was diminutive and quiet. In fact, Camp had the edge on Carey in both departments. His interchangeable nicknames were the Little Man and the Silent Man, though the people who knew him best emphasized the second. "He was a man's man and a lady's man," said his wife, Nancy. "He liked to go to the racetrack, and when I wasn't with him, I know, the women would flock to him at Churchill Downs. But Frank was a man you could trust. He was just the straightest person I think you could ever meet." Equal parts offensive theorist and unbending taskmaster, Camp might also be described (in the shorthand of Kentucky pedigrees) as being by Bill Walsh out of Vince Lombardi. Camp's teams scrimmaged full-speed every day and the survivors played on Saturdays. "He never shouted, he never cursed," said assistant coach Clark Wood, who oversaw the defense. "But he was a very strict person, and he would delegate a lot of that to me. He'd say, 'Clark, after practice I want you to take those two out and run them until they go home.'"

Joe Trabue, Frank Gitschier's former backfield mate and fellow fledgling assistant, knew Camp the longest. Trabue played for the Silent Man not only at Louisville but also in high school, and even before that, in something called "animal leagues" in the southern Kentucky town of Glasgow. Trabue said, "Coach Camp rounded up all of us grade-schoolers into little teams—the Tigers, the Bears, and what have you—to learn the fundamentals of football. Whatever the level, once you had the basics down, he encouraged every player—not just the quarterback—to be innovative, to try things. He was a 'Try anything if it's the right thing to try' kind of coach. Spread the line a little, if it feels right. Don't do everything exactly the same way every time. Do some little thing spasmodically that won't have any effect on the immediate play but will make a difference later on and by then won't be noticed. He'd drill you, drill you, drill you, on the meat and potatoes you had to have, and then he'd teach you how to be creative, the dessert. It was very unusual."

Better-known football coaches in the area, men like Blanton Collier of the University of Kentucky, came to Camp for ideas. "Camp ran the Chicago Cardinals' offense," Collier said when he was the head coach of the Cleveland Browns, "before the Chicago Cardinals." (In the late 1940s, a regular Louisville opponent was Washington University in Saint Louis. Camp's football was a particular fascination to the Washington coach, Weeb Ewbank.) When he could find a durable enough fullback and a resourceful enough quarterback, Camp was inclined to feature a one-back offense. In 1951, he was ready to rotate a couple of tough ball carriers, both juniors: Jim Williams and Bill Pence, whom the newspapermen dubbed Battering Bill. But where was the thoughtful quarterback? Well, he was off to one side of the practice field rehearsing by himself. Out of a corner of an eye, Camp began to notice him. Because of their size and activity, John's hands drew attention as they flashed in and out of the sunlight. Extending his open left hand like a white-gloved cop directing traffic, Unitas double-cocked his right arm so far back that the knuckles seemed to touch the ground. Only his ring and little fingers were as far forward on the ball as the laces. ("He followed through like he was cutting it," Orr said, using a golf term.) The right hand turned completely over, like Tom Seaver's. The old quarterback, Gitschier, tried to coach some of the rolling wrist out of John's delivery. But Gitschier knew enough not to change too much. "How's your boy doing?" Camp asked after work. (He *was* Gitschier's boy. When Camp sentenced Unitas to run five laps for taking a sip of water, Gitschier ran the laps alongside John.) One day, Camp said, "How's *our* boy doing?" and Gitschier knew John's moment had come.

Louisville's fifth game was against Saint Bonaventure in Olean, New York, four days before Halloween, and Unitas was starting. In a chilly, dreary rain, John took almost an entire half to get comfortable, by which time the Bonnies led, 19–0. Their quarterback was a sprint-out runner and passer from Franklin, Pennsylvania (south of Erie, north of Pittsburgh), Ted Marchibroda. "I can't honestly say I knew then who it was over there on the other side," Marchibroda said, "but somebody was bringing them back." In the second half, John completed eleven consecutive passes— three for touchdowns—to open a 21–19 Louisville lead. When time had seemed to expire, the Cardinals stormed the field in premature triumph. But a few more seconds were found, enough for Saint Bonaventure to attempt a field goal. After the kick was missed, the visitors celebrated again. But this time, a penalty flag was thrown. "We eventually kicked a field goal on the so-called last play of the game," Marchibroda said, "to win, I think, twenty-two to twenty-one, something like that. Not until about ten years later did I hear a story about a student manager who ran the clock that day. Maybe it's only a story, but it did take an awfully long time for those last few seconds to run off."

With a defensive player named Jack Butler at the wheel, Marchibroda and Unitas would one day ride together from Pittsburgh back to that exact field in Olean, where the Steelers trained.

●

Beating North Carolina State (26–2), Houston (35–28), Washington and Lee (14–7), and Mississippi Southern (14–13), the Cardinals finished the season with four straight victories, a 5–4 record, and a permanent quarterback. The Houston game, played before just three thousand people in Louisville's duPont Stadium, was John's Rubicon. Twice against the Cougars, who were nineteen-point favorites, he faced make-or-break decisions. After the second one, the team was his. "Now it can be told," staff writer Baxter Melton wrote a number of weeks later in the *Louisville Times*. "The teams were tied at 21–21 and U. of L. had fourth down on the Cougar 35, with two yards needed for the first down. 'Unitas called for a pass,' said Battering Bill Pence, 'and I checked signals. I told him I could make two yards anytime. If not, there was no use for me to be out there.'" Coldly, the freshman quarterback informed the junior fullback, "You run the ball when I call your signal, and I'll call the plays." Faking to Pence, John threw a pass to end Dave Rivenbark, standing alone in the center of the field. Rivenbark loped into the end zone.

Later, third-and-three at his own seven-yard line, Unitas ordered up another unexpected play, to Babe Ray this time. Pence just smiled and blocked. That ninety-three-yard touchdown pass, John's fourth of the day, was a Louisville record. "In the dressing room after the Houston game," Camp told Melton, "I asked of no one in particular, 'What made the difference in this ball club?'" Of course, the coach knew the answer—everyone knew the answer—but he wanted to hear someone say it. "Bill Pence, one of our fullbacks, spoke up. 'That Unitas.' 'You mean to tell me, Pence, that one man, a freshman, did it? How?'" This question went unanswered in the room, but it was sort of answered in the last line of Melton's piece: "The publicity resulting from his performance isn't all deserved, John believes. He said, 'I just felt sure of myself when I took over and that's all there was to it.'" Accompanying the story was a photograph of Unitas, whose shock of hair (a particular shock on him) brought to mind James Dean. Under the picture, the cutline read, "U.L. Boss Man."

The season finale against Mississippi Southern was also played at duPont, in a whistling squall before only a dedicated twelve hundred spectators. Primarily a high school field, its grass was already worn out from the big Male-Manual game two days earlier. By an account in the *Courier-Journal,* "Both the U.L. and the Mississippi Southern players were instantly caked with mud, and the ball was nothing more than a soggy clod of dirt. The conditions deprived Louisville of its most potent weapon, Johnny Unitas' passing [no longer John but Johnny], although his one completion [a fourteen-yard touchdown pass to Kenny Anderson] won the game." In their locker room, where nobody's number could be read for the mud, the Cardinals rolled around on the floor like happy children. It was as if they had won the national championship.

That spring, roommates Pence and Jack Browning (the quarterback John replaced) were drinking beer too long at White Hall. Browning, who was from Hamilton, Ohio, not far from Cincinnati, had his father's Oldsmobile. Around midnight they drove to a school hangout on Floyd Street called the Kampus Korner, where backup center Keith Myers and two young women, twenty-two-year-old Gloria Busby and eighteen-year-old Carlene Reagen, joined in the search for more beer. In what started out as a rollicking collegiate caper, a case of beer was swiped from the Cardinal Inn. Soon a police car appeared and a chase ensued. Browning thought the Cardinal Inn had called the cops. It hadn't. By cutting his lights, he shook the first pursuer. The passengers went on laughing and drinking. Helling south on Third Street with the headlights still off, they flew by a parked cruiser. Veering left onto

Southern Parkway at an estimated eighty miles an hour, Browning missed a curve and hit a tree, sheering off the right side of the car. After careering into another tree two hundred yards farther on, the Oldsmobile finally came to a stop in the middle of the parkway. Five bottles of beer were found in the car. Many bottles had been tossed out during the chase. Browning and Miss Reagen were only slightly injured. Miss Busby broke a leg and a hip. Keith Myers and Battering Bill Pence were dead.

The era was over, and it had just begun. That would be Unitas's only winning team at Louisville. As John and most of the other players sat dead-eyed in a courtroom, assistant coach Clark Wood told the judge, "I don't know of three boys who had a better record. They were three high-type, superior boys." Charged with two counts of manslaughter plus drunken and reckless driving, Browning was offered a deal that required his immediate enlistment in the army. Momentarily losing its heart for football, the university began to listen harder to the campus voices that had perennially argued for deemphasizing sports. A new president, a former football player for Ole Miss, reduced the scholarships and toughened the academic standards for athletes. As a result, Unitas came back for his sophomore year to find that fifteen returning lettermen had flunked out. For his own part, John had no trouble meeting the new mark. Surprisingly, he was thriving in the classroom. His academic probation was lifted.

●

Down to nineteen players in 1952, Louisville filled out the team with walk-on freshmen, including one, a 190-pound tackle named Larry "Bumpy" Simmons, who made history without leaving a mark. A full fourteen years before the color line was broken at the University of Kentucky, Camp sent in Simmons during the fourth quarter of the opener against Wayne State, a 19–12 Louisville victory at home. The *Times* reported, "Simmons looked okay in the

few minutes he played against Wayne. Ever since his enrollment at
U.L., where he's studying physical education, the big boy has been
a big hit with all the Cardinal gridders. Ask any of them about
Larry and they'll tell you he's all right." Obviously, he had to be left
home from Florida State, Chattanooga, Memphis State, and Mississippi Southern. Simmons didn't play enough to letter. He just kind
of faded away. When asked to name the first black athlete at the
university, most Louisville people say Lenny Lyles, who was the
first to receive a scholarship, the first to become a star. Lyles always says, "Larry Simmons."

Increasingly ambitious football schedules, necessarily drawn
up years in advance, started to kick in at the least felicitous time.
On the other hand, the simultaneous return of one-platoon football
was a blessing to Louisville, especially welcome to John. He had
liked playing safety at Saint Justin's and was glad to be going both
ways again. "Back to single-platoon," Clark Wood said; "the rules
allowed for the substitution of just one man. Naturally, most teams
pulled out the quarterback. But we kept John in. He was our
smartest *defensive* player, too, our leading interceptor, our surest
tackler."

Louisville followed up the Wayne victory with a 41–14 miracle
against Florida State in Tallahassee. John was buffeted around so
turbulently by onrushing Seminoles that at one point he found it
convenient to throw a left-handed pass between his legs—for a
fifteen-yard completion. "You should have seen him," said Lee
Corso, who didn't see him either, but who was the Florida State
quarterback a year later and saw the film. "Holy mackerel, was this
guy good. A kind of rawboned-looking, bowlegged guy. Not fast but
quick. Unbelievably quick release. Boom! Drop back in that pocket.
Boom! The Seminoles didn't have a chance. He riddled them."
Unitas completed sixteen of twenty-two passes for 198 yards and
three touchdowns. But it was a last hurrah for the Cardinals. They
beat only Eastern Kentucky the rest of the way and finished the season 3-and-5. The newspapers pretty well summarized the year in

one sentence before the Memphis State game—"Unitas was unable to hold up his right arm at practice yesterday, but he's expected to start Saturday"—and one headline after it: "Unitas' Passes Scare Foe But Cardinals Lose 29-25."

Because life is stranger than anything the mind can invent, it turned out that Bernie Crimmins, the assistant coach who had said "no" for Notre Dame, grew up in Louisville, where he was a three-sport sensation at Saint Xavier High. His brother, a local politician captivated by Unitas, kept Bernie apprised of every turn in the Louisville saga. In 1952, when Indiana University hired Crimmins to be its head coach, he quietly called John, first to recheck his weight ("Almost a hundred and seventy pounds," John exaggerated), eventually to propose a transfer. Taking a teammate into his confidence, Unitas told tackle Bob Bender, "With our ball club torn to pieces the way it is, Crimmins doesn't see any point in my staying here. If I transferred to Indiana, I'd have to sit out a whole year, but I'd still have two full seasons of eligibility left, two Western Conference [Big Ten] seasons to show the pros what I can do." Crimmins slipped into Louisville to meet with Unitas. ("He talked to me like a Dutch uncle," John said.) Without informing Coach Camp, John made a trip to Bloomington. Senior center Otto Knop gave him a lift.

"I was really mad at Otto," Bender said. "I told John, 'How can you possibly go back to a guy who didn't want you?' He said, 'You're right,' but that didn't tell me anything. I had no idea what John was going to do. Of course, I wasn't what you would call an Indiana lover, and I'm still not." A local product, Bender had originally signed with Purdue. But, missing his girlfriend, Norma, he came home from West Lafayette for a weekend visit to find Clark Wood sitting on his porch. "You know, freshmen can play at Louisville," Wood told him coyly. Bender said, "John and I fell in together at the first team meeting and were friends from that moment on. He was in Norma's and my wedding, and became our daughter Donna's godfather. You know, John loved football more

than I did, more than anybody did. Louisville had only two TV stations in those days: CBS and NBC. On Sundays, one showed the
Bears, the other the Browns. Every week, John sat and watched
both games. 'C'mon, it's a beautiful day, let's go out,' I'd say. 'No, I
have to see the games.' 'You mean to tell me that after practicing
all week, after sitting through all the meetings, after playing every
single down of every single game, you still haven't had enough
football?' 'Nope.' None of the rest of us knew exactly what we
wanted to be. He did. So, I couldn't root against him on the Indiana
thing. But I didn't want to lose him, either."

Returning from Bloomington, John finally went to see Coach
Camp. Starting with Camp, Gitschier, and Wood, he polled virtually
everyone he knew. "I don't want to do anything underhanded," he
told Bender. John called his brother, Leonard, and his girlfriend,
Dorothy. He even consulted the Louisville sportswriters. To a man,
the writers said he should go. More than one teammate expressed
the opinion that John was crazy if he *didn't* go. Of all the people
Unitas contacted, only his old high school coach, Max Carey, argued for neither side, listing the pros and cons before saying what
he had always said about big plays that came along: "It's a decision
you have to make by yourself." After hanging up with Carey, John
called Crimmins and thanked him. Then, within earshot of Bender,
he said, "These people took me when no one else wanted me. I'm
staying here." Crimmins's Indiana teams won just two games each
of the next two seasons, but keeping tabs in the newspapers as the
Hoosiers prepared to face Ohio State, Michigan, or even Notre
Dame, Unitas sometimes ached with jealousy. He wondered if he
had thrown away his only chance.

◆

In 1953, the Cardinals won just the opener, 19–14 over Murray
State, dropping the rest of their eight games by a combined score
of 262–51. Sliding up and down the line, John involuntarily be-

came an option quarterback, and with three running touchdowns—
eighteen measly points—he led the team in scoring. Returning
to Tallahassee, Louisville was buried by Florida State, 59–0. "It
was so bad," Bender said, "the cannon they fired off after touchdowns ran out of shells." "It wasn't fair," said Corso, who started
at quarterback for the Seminoles and returned a punt fifty-nine
yards for a touchdown. "Louisville had almost no players except
John. Overnight, it had turned into a high school team. We over-
ran him, crushed him, killed him. But you still couldn't take your
eyes off him. Studying the film from the year before, I couldn't
get over how good he was. Now, I couldn't get over how tough
he was."

(Later, when Unitas was with the Colts, Corso sought him out
at practice. "I needed to know him," Lee said. Beginning his college coaching career near Baltimore, with assistant's jobs at Navy
and the University of Maryland, Corso stayed close to John. When
a heart attack forced Frank Camp's retirement in 1968, Lee applied to replace him. "I was, like, four hundred and fifteenth on the
list," he said, "until John called them for me. I went straight to
number one. That's how I got the University of Louisville job. Because I knew a god.")

"The schedule kept getting tougher and tougher," Clark Wood
said, "and we kept getting worse and worse. We couldn't bring in
anyone at all. There was nothing we could do except our best. John
took it like any intelligent person would. He was realistic." *Show
me where it's written that you're supposed to be happy. If you
have to clean toilets for a living, make them shine.*

"He understood the game of football," Wood continued, "and
got pleasure in just trying to do the right things. Of course, he
didn't give a damn about statistics, especially his own. Despite
everything, somebody came in one day and said, 'Do you know,
you're the third-rated small-college passer in the nation?' John
laughed and said, 'Big deal.' Our blockers gave him so little time to
throw that he was often forced on the run to sort of drop the ball

over the defensive line to a receiver. It didn't even look like a pass. 'Looks don't count,' he said.

"Losing didn't kill his self-confidence, I can tell you that. He was the most confident person—confident in his own ability—that I ever met, that I think anyone ever met. Maybe going through all of this was what made him what he was in years to come. Did you ever think of that? Unless something really tries to destroy you, how can you know you're indestructible? John knew he was indestructible. All I can tell you is that we lost at Tennessee that year, fifty-nine to six. Yet, everyone in the stadium knew that John was the best football player on the field. When he left, it was to a standing ovation. I don't expect anyone to believe that who didn't see it."

●

An old silent film, black-and-white, is playing in a smoky light on a cinder-block wall in Knoxville. The opening shot is of a marching band spelling out a T on a lined and numbered football field. It's a day game. An American flag is shown beyond one end zone to record the wind, just a breeze, as a legion of white-helmeted Tennessee players tramps onto the field. The Louisville Cardinals, in dark jerseys, are sporting old Notre Dame–style leather helmets with padded crossbars on the dome, like the one Paul Hornung used to wear. No face masks, of course. (The Cardinals have recently switched from plastic white helmets of their own, which were cracking in two.) For the first quarter only, the old film is accidentally flopped: all of the numbers are reversed and everybody is left-handed. But the picture is clear. The Volunteers in their single-wing attack are rolling over the visitors.

Unitas, number 16, is playing a kind of center field on defense, and is in on most of the tackles. Nobody in a white helmet can be stopped at the scrimmage line. The Vols station four men in the offensive backfield. Mostly the ball is hiked to the deepest man, the tailback. There are a few tricky turns and switches, but generally the backs just go one, two, three, four, straight through the center of the Louisville line. The last man through has the ball. They almost never pass. After the touchdowns and the conversions, they kick off to Unitas, who on one return swivels his hips a little and lugs the ball more than thirty yards, all the way to midfield. Then he sets up as the quarterback in a T-formation either with a full-house backfield or a two-man set with another back split out to the right. John takes the direct snap and hands the ball off left and right, deftly, usually making at least one full revolution. He is remarkably light on his feet, a trickster carrying out many sleights of hand. He spins and backpedals and goes to pass and stops, and goes to pass again and stops again, and scrambles to the left and finally delivers his pass. Almost every throw is catchable, even when someone has a hold of the quarterback's right arm, forcing him to whip a long rope trick of a spiral underhanded with his left. That pass, which seems to come from the ground up, bounces off the receiver's chest. Many of John's passes are dropped. But it is a ballet of pitches and fake pitches and handoffs and fake handoffs. The visitors move the ball well enough in the center of the field, but every time it matters, they are stopped on downs. And the juggernaut comes back on. Just before halftime, John is staggered and number 12, sophomore quarterback Jim Houser, comes in for a few plays. But Unitas returns in the second half to field the kickoff.

With the clock winding down in the third quarter of a 39–0 game, John is running a belly series along the line, and waiting until the absolute last instant to snatch the ball back out of the runner's stomach, to pitch it or keep it. At Louisville's twenty-seven-yard line, one of his ball-carrying workhorses goes down, and Unitas lifts him up in his arms and carries him off the field. Taking the next snap, John links up with a runner and they cradle the ball together for about three strides before John yanks it away and continues around the right end alone. After *gaining about eight more yards—just a beat before he is paved over by the whole Tennessee defense—he makes a no-look pitch to an outside trailer, who speeds down the right sideline to the Volunteers' twenty-nine. Three plays later, with the ball at the twenty-two, the third quarter ends. To mark the time, the cameraman pans the stands of the crowded but not jammed stadium to an end zone scoreboard that reads "Shields-Watkins Field," and in brightening lightbulbs declares, "4th Down, 3 Yards to Go, 22-Yard Line."*

As two running backs bend over in three-point stances behind him, Unitas takes the snap and turns left, feigning a handoff to the first back and a pitchout to the second. Keeping the ball himself, he bucks straight ahead through the line, shakes off one linebacker, jukes another, and runs over a defensive back into the end zone. Then he holds for the extra point, which is missed. His next offensive series, he drives the visitors to the Tennessee sixteen-yard line, but gets up limping from another quarterback keeper. Houser returns to the game and throws an interception at the goal line that is run back one hundred yards for a touchdown. The final score is 59–6.

In the most one-sided of losses, John has carried the ball nine times, for fifty-two yards. He has completed nine of nineteen passes, for seventy-three yards. He has returned six kickoffs, for eighty-five yards. He has fielded one punt, for three yards. His offense has chalked up sixteen first downs and gained 290 yards, mostly in the middle of the field. And Unitas is credited with making 86 percent of Louisville's tackles. Unable to raise either arm in the locker room afterward, he cannot take off his jersey. Out of range of the cameraman, the number 16 shirt is cut away with shears. The next morning, in the Knoxville News-Sentinel, *Bob Wilson writes:*

> *The Volunteers dominated the game, but Johnny Unitas, Louisville's lanky quarterback, stole the show. Hailed*

mainly as a passing star, the 6-1, 185-pound Unitas was a terrific performer in all departments against the Vols. He not only directed the Cardinals' attack brilliantly, but passed expertly, punted well, ran like a halfback, and kicked off and tackled like a demon. With Tennessee leading, 39–0, at the start of the fourth quarter, Unitas still refused to surrender. On the first play of that final quarter, he broke through the Tennessee defense and went 22 yards to score the visitors' only touchdown. Battered and bruised, Unitas was helped off the field later in the final period as the spectators saluted his gifted and courageous play with an ovation that resounded across Loudon Lake.

Before the 1954 season, Unitas recruited his cousin Joe to join him for one last college try. Joe's father, Bill Unitas, the only brother who had not been sent to the Toner Institute, resurfaced too late to know Francis but in time to meet Francis's children and to introduce them to his own son before, in a puff of smoke, Bill disappeared again. ("That was when I was about eleven," Joe Unitas said. "He went out west, apparently." In San Francisco years later, lounging in a hotel room, John received a phone call from the front desk. "There's a fellow down here who says he's your uncle Bill." "Send him up." For most of the afternoon, they talked. Rather, Bill talked and John listened. Describing himself as a treasury agent, a counterfeit expert, Bill was full of dramatic stories. But as none of them involved Francis, John was disappointed.)

"I played football at South Hills High in Pittsburgh," Joe said, "and got a scholarship to Lenoir-Rhyne College in Hickory, North Carolina. But they weren't playing me there. One afternoon during the summer, I ran into John on Brookline Boulevard, and he said, 'Why don't you come back with me to Louisville? I can get you a tryout. We can use you.' So, I did. He had just bought a green 1941 Plymouth—the 'Green Hornet.'" (It burned a little oil, trailed a little smoke, and cost exactly $400.) "He'd pat it on the dashboard and say, 'Come on, baby.'" They drove back to Louisville early, to get a jump on the season. "John was so happy to be returning to football," Joe said, "he whistled almost all of the way there." Dragging their mattresses out on the lawn beside White Hall, they lifted each other instead of weights. "He'd get on my back and then I'd get on his and we'd do our deep knee bends. The day the players checked in, John was measured at six foot one, a hundred and seventy-six pounds. He was the captain, of course. John had a dignity about him that was unexplainable. I think it came from his mother, from his respect for her." John and Joe grew close that year, though it didn't keep John from telling Joe in the huddle, "If you can't block this guy, there's someone on the bench who can."

A week before the first game, against Murray State, John was hurt in a scrimmage. He threw an interception, made the tackle, and came up holding his right ankle. ("Whenever John threw an interception," said Don Shula, Unitas's future teammate and coach, "he *always* made the tackle.") John thought the ankle was sprained. In fact, it was broken, a hairline fracture. He missed the Murray State game, but swaddled in tape and bandages, he played all of the others with minimum mobility. For injured teammates who had lower thresholds of pain, John regularly prescribed the same medical treatment. "Try spitting on it," he'd say. "That seems to work." Only partly because of the weakened ankle, Unitas would someday be the last "skills" player in all of football still decked out in high-top shoes. ("They work," he said. "Why switch to low-tops? For looks?") Looks don't count.

Louisville won just three of its nine games in John's final season, but the scores were reasonable again. The heat was off the football program and scholarships were back on offer. John was still swimming in a sea of freshmen, but this new batch, led by black running back Lenny Lyles, had talent. (Three years later, they would win nine of ten games plus the Sun Bowl; and with 1,207 yards, Lyles would lead the nation in rushing.) Frank Camp's wife, Nancy, said, "My husband came from Glasgow, Kentucky. I came from Patchardsville, right next door." Where the impulse to change the world came from, she had no idea. After all, Louisville was still the South, and this was a full year before the murder of fourteen-year-old Emmett Till in Mississippi. "I don't know," she said. "I just think Frank was a coach and a man who tried to do the right things."

Lyles was the son of a hod carrier who moved his family from Tennessee to Kentucky when Lenny was three. Lenny's mother worked as a maid at the Brown Hotel. They lived on the east end of Louisville, "Smoke Town." Through his senior year at Central High, the dominant fact of Lyles's life was segregation. "And I had already left for Lincoln University, a black school in Missouri," he said. "Coach Camp had to come and get me. His main selling point was that if I went to the University of Louisville, three other blacks could go, too—George Cain, Andy Walker, and a kid from Alabama. But I was the one who was supposed to have an immediate impact, and I wasn't really ready to play that first year. I had so much to learn. But I could run. People kind of admired that." ("He could run?" exclaimed Johnny Sample, who would be Lyles's first roommate in the pros. "Is that what Leonard told you? He could run? I'll tell you something. He was the fastest man in football equipment I ever saw. And I saw Bob Hayes. From the beginning of time until today, nineteen thirty, nineteen fifty, I don't care when, nobody ever ran faster in pads than Lenny Lyles.") Lyles posted a 9.4 in the 100-yard dash when 9.3 was the world record. "That belonged to Mel Patton," Lenny said, "who wasn't a black guy, by the way. Then came Jim Golliday, Dave Sime, Bobby Morrow, and all that bunch, Ira Murchison, Hayes . . . I could run with all of them. That made up for a lot."

The bleak barrack, White Hall, "was really nice," Lyles said, "much better than what I had at home." After a tenement house, the projects had been a step up. "I thought I was in heaven when we got to the projects," he said, "and I could sleep by myself on the couch. Now, George Cain and I had our own room." They were subject to the customary slights, but encountered some generosity, too. "On their way to sorority parties, the other players would say, 'Don't worry, we'll bring you back something.' But that was okay. That was how it was. You experience all kinds of stuff, but you can't hold blame. You'll end up being something you won't like to be. 'Who's going to the drive-in?' Unitas called out one day. 'Get in the trunk, Lyles. You're going.'" John snuck Lenny into a restricted theater in the Green Hornet.

The school cafeteria was closed on weekends. "One Sunday," Lyles said, "I took John home with me, John and another player, named Jack Meade. My mother fixed a meal for us: beef, green beans, corn, some of the best corn bread you ever tasted. John always asked about my mother. Her name was Alice. It was nice just sitting there, talking about nothing." (Of course, there was no problem with white folks coming into black neighborhoods. The problem was with black folks coming into white neighborhoods.) "John and I never talked about anything so serious. Several times we'd almost start to talk about it and here'd come somebody else and we'd stop. He wasn't a guy who let you inside, anyway. I don't even think he let himself inside."

No matter what Jimmy Orr says, Lyles found John's ball all but impossible to catch. "John could knock you down, you know," Lenny said. "Even in practice, he could just throw it through my hands." Before long, a phobia took hold. "It wasn't so much that I couldn't catch the ball. It was—how do I say this?—I couldn't get away from the fear of maybe missing it. I'd go out for a pass and John would throw it and I'd say to myself, Oh Lord, let me catch this ball. Don't let me drop it in front of everybody. I wanted to talk it over with John, but what could I say to him? 'When you throw the ball to me, could you throw it a little softer?' I guess I hoped he'd pull me aside and show me, 'Lenny, here's the way you catch a pass.' But as a freshman I was too immature to go up to him. I couldn't even get to where I could say to John, 'Let's go throw some balls.' If I'd have asked him, I'm sure he'd have done it. But you had to ask him and I didn't know how. I just stood back and watched."

Coach Camp employed a head-on hitting drill, one ball carrier against one tackler, that the players called "the hamburger drill." "The king of the hamburger drill," Lyles said, "was a guy named John Sowa—the meanest Polish bastard I ever saw in my life." Not only did Unitas take his turn with everybody else in the hamburger drill, he moved up or dropped back so he could get Sowa. "That was Unitas," Lenny said. "Tough, committed, hard worker, throw with either hand, strong belief in himself—like in stone, like in ice. Even when he was hurt, he still pushed that body. He deserved to be different. He *was* different. He had character. He wasn't the All-American-looking quarterback like out of a movie. He had it inside."

(Lyles and Unitas's paths would intersect twice more. In 1958, Lyles would be the tenth player selected in the National Football League draft, the number one pick of the Baltimore Colts. A shy, sweet-tempered running back, number 26, would leave the team for several years. A mean, All-Pro defensive back, number 43, would return.)

A few days after John's final game at Louisville, a 20–6 loss to Eastern Kentucky, he went home for Thanksgiving, and at the Church of the Resurrection in Brookline (with Father Constantine Superfisky officiating), he married Dorothy Jean Hoelle. "Don't you think he's handsome?" she once asked her mother. "No, I don't think he's handsome, Dorothy, but I think if you marry him you'll never have to worry about where your next meal is coming from." Mrs. Hoelle had no way of knowing that within a year, John, Dorothy, and baby Janice Ann would be moving back into

Dorothy's old bedroom. (By the way, both of the promises Frank Gitschier made to Helen Unitas were kept. John went to Mass every Sunday, and he graduated.)

Draft day of 1955 fell on January 27. Except for the first choice overall, the order of selection was determined by inverting the NFL standings. The very first pick was the so-called bonus pick. From 1947 through 1958, each of the league's twelve teams would have a turn at the top, counting down by lot. In 1955, Baltimore's name was pulled and the Colts took quarterback George Shaw of Oregon. After the Cardinals selected Oklahoma end Max Boydston, the Colts in their regular slot drafted the Heisman Trophy–winning fullback from Wisconsin, Alan "the Horse" Ameche. The Pittsburgh Steelers went sixth in the first round, fifth in all of the others. In the first round they took Notre Dame tackle Frank Varrichione. They traded their second-round pick. In the third round, they took end Ed Burnett of Mississippi Southern. In the fourth round, they took center Fred Broussard of Northwestern State. . . . In the ninth round, the Pittsburgh Steelers took Johnny Unitas of Louisville. He was the 102nd player selected, right after the Packers took tackle Ed Culpepper of Alabama, just before the Rams took tackle John Witte of Oregon State.

In the twenty-eighth round, the 258th position, the Steelers drafted another local boy, Richie McCabe of Pitt, the skinny kid from North Catholic who had auditioned with John and passed the entrance exam. Still undersized, still tough, Richie would win a position in the secondary and have a nice career. Mailed a one-year, $5,500 contract, Unitas signed it immediately and sent it back. Of course, the agreement was predicated on his making the team. "Don't spend the money just yet," he told Dorothy. A year later, when the Steelers drew the bonus pick, they would take Gary Glick of Colorado State—a quarterback. He would end up a defensive back with the Baltimore Colts.

THREE

1955

"I think they're going to cut me tomorrow."

Good-bye, Pittsburgh—Hello, Bloomfield

On his first day in the Steelers locker room, as John recalled for Steve Sabol, "I asked the guy, 'Where are the whites?'—you know, the T-shirt and the athletic supporter and the socks, the undergarments you put on before your pads. He said, 'Oh, right over there on the floor.' I said, 'On the floor?' He said, 'Yeah, over there.' Here was this big pile of socks and athletic supporters and T-shirts. You rooted around in there until you found what you wanted. And I said, 'This is professional football?' 'It's the way *we* do it.' We went out and practiced and came back in. So, I just figured you took off your whites and threw them in a laundry hamper. 'No, no, you hang them up on a hanger and we turn a big fan on to dry them up for the afternoon's practice.'"

Unitas threw back his head and laughed. "That was Pittsburgh."

◆

"Pittsburgh was hard work, hard work, hard work," said Jim Kelly of East Brady. "My father worked three jobs at a time. He worked in the mills. He was a machinist. He did pretty much everything. If you checked his hands, you'd know what I'm talking about. He has those rough, sandpaper hands." "All of western Pennsylvania was blue-collar territory," said Joe Namath of Beaver Falls, "certainly in the forties and fifties, when the steel mills and the coal mines were going full blast." George Blanda of Youngwood said, "You turned to football so you could turn away from the furnaces." Babe Parilli of Rochester said, "The kids got out of the mills and the mines, but they stayed mills and mines kids."

"You saw what your father or grandfather had gone through," said Joe Montana of Monongahela, "how hard they had to work to make a living. People here took their sports pretty seriously anyway, so what better way out of the mills and mines than doing something you loved?" On a pogo stick, young Daniel Constantine Marino (interesting middle name, Constantine) bounced from block to block among the Italian, Polish, and Irish families in the Oakland section of town. The Marino house on Parkview Avenue was across from a church and adjacent to a bus stop that supplied the background music to his boyhood *(eeerrrr, screech!)*. "There aren't many players who can say they went to grade school, high school, and college all in the same neighborhood," Marino said, "but I did. It was literally a ten-minute walk from my home to the fifty-yard line at old Pitt Stadium."

Kelly, Namath, Blanda, Parilli, Montana, and Marino were all quarterbacks, of course. "Marino, Montana, and I sometimes joke," Kelly said, "that the reason western Pennsylvania has produced so many quarterbacks—Johnny Lujack to Marc Bulger—don't forget Bulger—is that all of our parents were brought up either on Rolling Rock or Iron City beer. Joe says Rolling Rock. I say Iron City [slogan: *It tastes like coming home*]. But I know the Marino and Montana families real well, and I know Dan and Joe were brought up on the same thing I was brought up on—and all of western Pennsylvania is built on—a work ethic that says, 'What you get out of something depends on what you put into it.'"

Parilli said, "I played for Rochester High School. Jim Mutscheller
—Bucky Mutscheller—played for Beaver Falls High, about three
miles away. We beat them my senior year—nineteen–nothing, I
think it was. But after the season, Mutscheller called me up to say,
'We want a rematch.' 'All right,' I said, 'come on down Sunday,
we'll climb the fence and play on our field. So, he brought his whole
team down, and so did I, and we climbed the fence and played another game." ("No way!" Montana exclaimed when Parilli's story
was passed along.) "We won again, this time by just a touchdown.
To me, that's western Pennsylvania. That's who we were."

They came not just from the smoke, the mills, and the mines,
but also from the dirt, the fields, and the river valleys. So many of
them were Catholics from Eastern European stock that there were
years when Notre Dame's football roster was almost completely
unpronounceable. Wherever he was from, even if his name was
Ditka or Biletnikoff, every western Pennsylvania athlete was also a
direct descendant of a 147-pound Irish fighter named Arthur J.
Rooney. From opposite ends of the standings, George Halas in
Chicago and Rooney in Pittsburgh were the indispensable pioneers
of the National Football League, who went in person to newspaper
offices to beg sports editors to publish the pro scores. Both men
had official at-bats in the golden age of sport. Halas, a Rose Bowl
MVP for the University of Illinois, was replaced in the New York
Yankees outfield by Babe Ruth. During a semipro football game,
Rooney once punted to Jim Thorpe. (He regretted doing it; Thorpe
returned the kick for the winning touchdown.) In 1920, the year
Halas stood on the running board of a Hupmobile in Canton, Ohio,
to proclaim a new league, Rooney won a place on the U.S. Olympic
boxing team. At his mother's request, he switched to baseball,
playing in the minor league systems of both the Boston Red Sox
and the Chicago Cubs. But his enduring love was horse racing.

As the musty old museum piece of a story goes, Rooney
bought into the NFL with his winnings from a big score at the racetrack. It's absolutely irresistible and totally untrue. "I've pointed

that out to a zillion writers," said Ed Kiely, who may be the best
public relations man who ever lived, but in this context is better
described just as one of Art Rooney's great friends. "They don't
want it to be a myth because it's so much more romantic to think,
Gee, he won the team." He bought the Pittsburgh team (at first
named the Pirates) on July 8, 1933, for $2,500. A saloon keeper's
son, Rooney was neither rich nor poor, but he could come up with
$2,500 in 1933 (the year John Unitas was born). The windfall at
the races occurred a full four years later, on August 8, 1937, a date
Tim Rooney (the third of Art's five sons) has no trouble remembering. He was born that day.

The exact amount of Rooney's score has never been told, but
a quarter of a million dollars may be a reasonable estimate. "I'm
never going to let you forget this date," Rooney told Giants owner
Tim Mara, himself a legal bookmaker. "I'm naming my new son,
Tim, after you." Beneath the myth, as usual, is a true story better
than the lie. Empire City, where the streak began, turned into
Yonkers Raceway. The Rooneys came to own it, and Tim Rooney
ended up the president. But in 1955, when Johnny Unitas was
looking for his whites, Tim was the Steelers' eighteen-year-old
camp manager in Olean, New York (where Art's brother, Father
Dan, served as athletic director at Saint Bonaventure). As the preseason was winding down, Tim wrote a marathon letter to his father about John ("Twenty-two pages," he said; "twenty-two sides
of a page, that is, in longhand"). It began, "Dad, there's a guy here
in camp who has not been given any chance at all. . . ."

◆

The Steelers' coach was a rock-headed German named Walter
Kiesling ("Keez," to almost everyone), who won his place in the Pro
Football Hall of Fame blocking and tackling for the Duluth Eskimos
and the Pottsville Maroons. Keez often said he preferred to be an
assistant coach, his natural position, but three different times

Rooney appointed him the boss. After manpower shortages forced wartime consolidations of first the Steelers and the Philadelphia Eagles (the Steagles) and later the Steelers and the Chicago Cardinals (the Carpets), Kiesling helped co-run the combined teams. In 1955, he was in the middle of a final, three-year hitch in solo charge, after which he would settle in again as the pinochle master who remembered every card but, as far as anyone could tell, had no firsthand knowledge of imagination, passion, or romance. "Keez was still there when I played for the Steelers in the late fifties," Jimmy Orr said. "He was on the defensive staff, running the projector one day. I had just left an offensive meeting and was leaning in the doorway watching the end of the movie. As the film ran out, the projector started going *clickety-clickety-clickety.* Then it went *flap, flap, flap, flap.* Everybody in the room was sound asleep, including Keez."

Compared to Kiesling, Woody Hayes at Ohio State had a devout and sentimental attachment to the forward pass. Wistfully, Pittsburgh was the last pro team to let go of the single-wing formation. When Keez was calling the tune, so many of the games opened with a direct handoff to Penn State alumnus Fran Rogel that the Steeler fans took to warming up before kickoffs by chanting, "Hi-diddle-diddle, Rogel's up the middle." Rooney rarely interfered with his coaches, and almost never fired them (or anyone else), but eventually he became so frustrated that he ordered Keez to launch a bomb on the first play. Jack Scarbath threw it; Goose McClairen caught it, and went eighty yards for a touchdown. But the Steelers were offside. The next play, they handed off to Rogel up the middle.

Besides Unitas, three other quarterbacks were at summer camp in 1955: the obvious starter, veteran Jim Finks, who was a brainy guy and a better player than people remember; Ted Marchibroda, John's original college opponent from Saint Bonaventure, who actually finished his collegiate career at the University of Detroit after the Bonnies dropped football on Father Dan's mournful watch; and Vic Eaton of Missouri, who was drafted two rounds and twenty-four places behind John. Marchibroda, an early-day Fran Tarkenton, had been the Steelers' number one choice in 1953, and though Ted spent the following season in the army, he made it to Olean for at least part of football camp each year and felt assured of the second spot. "Kiesling was an introverted guy," Marchibroda said, "who had very little correspondence with the players. It seemed all head coaches in the pros were more distant then, but he was more distant than most. I'm not sure Keez even knew that John was there. But to be honest with you, Finks and I hardly noticed him either. Later, when we had reason to think back, Jim and I talked about it. What had we missed? Neither one of us could remember a single thing John had done."

He wasn't allowed to do too much. During the exhibition season, he never took so much as one snap. His new number was 14. After practices, he tossed passes to the youngest Rooney boys, twins Pat and John, who were sixteen years old, and to defensive back Jack Butler, the only experienced player who seemed to be on Unitas's side. Pat Rooney said, "The veterans at training camp looked out for the veterans. They weren't interested in a college kid coming in and beating out one of their guys. In scrimmages, when Unitas did get in, they'd open the gates on him." (That charming phrase meant only brushing instead of blocking onrushing defenders.) "I grew up in the Munhall borough of Pittsburgh," said Butler, explaining why he was different, "about ten minutes from the center of town. I guess that's what made me gravitate toward Unitas. We were a lot alike. There were countless boroughs around the city: West Mifflin, Duquesne, Homestead . . . Each of them had its own mayor, its own town council, the whole bit. And each one had its own high school football team." Everybody had this thing in common that effectively delivered them all to the same place once a week. "Back before the mills closed, on Fridays and Saturdays, wow," Butler said, "look out." So Jack stayed after practice and ran pass patterns for "Clem." "I called John

'Clem' for Clem Kadiddlehopper [comedian Red Skelton's country cousin]; you know, just kidding around." He was a rookie, after all, and not too cosmopolitan looking at first (or last) glance. "But he could throw that football," Butler said, "and he was *accurate*." Pat Rooney said, "Your hands stung after you got done catching his passes, I can tell you that. Except for Elbie Nickel, who was pretty good, our receivers in those days were mainly blockers. But then, passing was contrary to Kiesling's philosophy of life."

Vic Eaton's bulge on John was that he was fleet enough afoot at least to think about playing some defensive back, and he could punt. "He *thought* he could punt," Pat said, "but we used to shag balls for him, too, and my brother John could punt the ball back to him over his head. Dad wasn't around to see any of this because he was at the racetrack trying to make enough money to keep the team going." As Art Rooney Jr. said, "In those days our father's big thing was survival." In Eaton, Kiesling undoubtedly saw a bargain-basement repertory player who at least theoretically could go both ways, and could even kick a little in a pinch. So Eaton was in and Unitas was out. "They weren't looking for any projects," Art Jr. said.

In what John always referred to as "the wet ball scrimmage," he quarterbacked one Saturday for both the first and the second teams, filling up the end zones with touchdown passes, scrambling twenty-five yards in the mud for a score of his own. "He knew he was in there only because the field was so bad and they didn't want to risk injuring the others," Butler said, "but he didn't care." Openers of the gates be damned, John willed both platoons up and down the swampy field. (Could the boys' memories be right? Was he really something like 34 for 35?) "Whatever it was, it was glorious," John Rooney said. That would be Unitas's valedictory with the Steelers. "We bused from camp to the final preseason game in Pittsburgh," said Butler. "Kiesling told us, 'After the game, if you want to bring your cars to Olean for the last few days, go ahead.' So I said, 'Clem, why don't you throw in with me? That way you can stay a couple of extra hours at home and we can still make it back for dinner.'" Marchibroda was also along. Ted may have been dozing in the backseat when John turned to Butler and said, "I think they're going to cut me tomorrow."

"'They're not going to cut you,' I said," Butler recalled. "'If they were going to do that, they would have done it in Pittsburgh, wouldn't they? They're not going to bring you all the way back just to cut you, not before they've had a real good look at you.' So we made it to Olean in time for dinner. We ate dinner. We finished. We walked back together to the dormitories. That's when he got the word." John Rooney knocked on Unitas's door and said quietly, apologetically, "Kiesling wants to see you, and he said to bring your book." As much to himself as to Rooney, Unitas murmured, "I can't be cut now. That was the best I ever played."

"They came down," John said, "and told me, 'Coach wants to see you. Bring your notebook so you can turn it in.' When I got into Kiesling's office, he said, 'We just can't carry four quarterbacks. It would be a luxury for that and you'd have to be able to do something else. We're going to have to let you go.' I got a little hot under the collar, and I just told him, 'You know, I wouldn't mind being released or being cut if I'd had an opportunity to play and I screwed up very badly. But you never gave me the damn opportunity to do it.'"

This was the sanitized version Unitas always repeated when describing the axe in Pittsburgh, but he told the sportswriter once, "I have to admit, I was really, really ugly with Kiesling. I called him every name I could think of. I regretted it, too. There was a job for a scout team quarterback to run the opponent's plays at practice. I swallowed my pride, went to the home opener, and hung around in the locker room, if you can believe it. [Assistant coach] Nick Skorich warned me, 'You better stay away from the old man for a while.' I took a bus out to the Hotel Schenley, where the team was staying, and stood around some more there, hoping for that fifty- or seventy-five-dollar-a-week job. Finally I came to my senses. Weeb [Ewbank] told me later that Skorich said I was just too dumb, that I couldn't keep the plays straight in the huddle, or some ridiculous thing like that. When

Weeb repeated this to Frank Camp, Coach Camp wanted to fight him. I can just see those two little guys rolling around on the floor."

(Two years later, the door to the coaches' office at the University of Louisville opened tentatively and a hat flew in. "I thought, What the hell's going on?" said Clark Wood. The hat belonged to Nick Skorich. "When I'm not sure I'm welcome, I throw my hat in first," he said. "If it comes flying back out, I just keep on going." Skorich was there on a scouting trip, "probably looking at Lenny Lyles," Wood said. "He was so apologetic about the way the Steelers had treated John, he said, 'Coach, I'm going to make it up to you. I'm going to go home and recruit you a player.' And he did. A good player, a Pennsylvania fullback named Ken Porco. He was a starter here for three years and cocaptain as a senior.")

"Great" could have been the title of Tim Rooney's twenty-two-page brief to his father. "How great Unitas was, what a great ball he threw, all of the great things he had done in the scrimmages, what a great guy he was in the dining room and around the halls, I just went on and on," Tim said. "We didn't just spend time with John, you know; he also spent time with us. Of course, I zapped Big Keez the way we always did, throwing a few more digs into him right at the end before finishing up by saying, 'Unitas is the best quarterback in camp, Dad.' My father got the letter, read it, said, 'That fresh punk,' and threw it in the garbage. Boy, I wish I had it today."

Pocketing the bus fare back to Pittsburgh ("Ten bucks," John said, "a nice, crisp ten-dollar bill"), he and a discarded lineman hitchhiked home together. ("A guy from Dayton, Ohio, a guard. Good hitchhiker. I got a note from him years later. He became a Catholic priest.")

"You probably heard this story from my father," said Dan Rooney, the old North Catholic quarterback. "After John got cut, my dad and I and Kiesling were riding along Route 51, either going to or coming from a funeral parlor, I can't remember which. I was driving, Keez was in the backseat, and I said, 'Dad, do you see that car in front of us? Do you know who that is?' 'No.' 'That's Johnny

Unitas.' 'Pull up! Pull up!' I caught John at the light and Dad rolled down his window. 'Hey, Johnny!' 'Oh, hi, Mr. Rooney.' 'I've heard a lot about you,' my father said, not mentioning that the ones he'd heard it from were my brothers, 'and I hope you get a chance. I hope everything works out. I hope you become a great star.' 'Thanks, Mr. Rooney,' John said, and we veered off in different directions. In the backseat, Keez growled, 'He'll never be anything.'"

"You probably heard this story," John Rooney said. "My father and I and Kiesling were riding up Grand Street—I was driving—and we stopped at a light. Unitas pulled up along the driver's side and called out to me, 'Hi, John!' I waved back. 'Who was that?' Dad asked. When I told him, he said, 'Catch up to him! Catch up to him!' Rolling down his window, Dad yelled, 'I hope you become the greatest quarterback who ever lived!' Kiesling didn't say a word."

Art Rooney Jr. said, "*I* was the guy driving the car. At least, that's what I tell Dan and John when they get to arguing about it, even though I know I wasn't. 'And I have proof!' I say. 'Because *Unitas* said I was the guy driving the car!' "

That part alone is a definite fact. Unitas *did* always say that Art Jr. was driving. By John's account, they were neither on Route 51 nor on Grand Avenue. They were in Ohio, outside Nippert Stadium at the University of Cincinnati. ("Cincinnati?" mused John Rooney. "Yes, it could have been Cincinnati.") And the occasion was a Colts-Steelers exhibition game won easily by the Colts, which makes the most sense. "I had a pretty good day," Unitas told the sportswriter, "and Mr. Rooney said some nice things to me, right in front of Kiesling. It was very gratifying." In all of the renditions, one detail never changes. Keez is wearing the same expression, a dyspeptic look of perpetual indigestion.

●

"Between leaving college and reporting to the Steelers camp," said big brother Leonard, "John had worked a construction job. But when the Steelers cut him, he came around and asked me, 'Is it all right if I drive the truck for a while?' 'No way,' I said. 'What do you mean?' He couldn't believe I was turning him down. 'If I let you drive this truck,' I told him, 'you'll end up a truck driver. Call Max Carey. Start writing letters. Hell, don't quit yet.' The first thing he wrote was a telegram to Paul Brown in Cleveland. I'll be damned if Brown didn't phone him."

Before Brown called John, he called Frank Camp. ("Some time later," Clark Wood said, "Brown called Coach Camp again to tell him, 'If you ever say anything to me in the future, I promise to believe it.'") Cleveland quarterback Otto Graham had retired following the 1954 championship game, a 56–10 Browns victory over the Detroit Lions. Neither of Otto's quarterbacks-in-waiting, Babe Parilli or George Ratterman, was wowing Brown, especially after Cleveland was beaten by the College All-Stars. For half a week, John was hugely encouraged. But less than twenty-four hours before the season began, Graham unretired. John's invitation to try out was put on hold. "Brown left me with the vague promise of a tryout someday," Unitas said. "Someday."

Meanwhile, two job openings came to John's attention: a pile-driving crew needed a monkey man, and a monkey crew needed a quarterback. He snapped up both positions. On the pile driver, he worked 125 feet in the air, covered with grease. Quarterbacking in the Steelbowl Conference was equally precarious. John joined the Rams of Bloomfield, an inner-city enclave on the east side of Pittsburgh. The opponents included the Pittsburgh Cubs, Arnold A.C., and the Nanty-Glo Blackhawks. "Basically, it was like pickup games," John said. "You know, you practiced maybe once a week. Half the guys didn't have full uniforms. You wore old army boots if you didn't have shoes, that kind of stuff." His new number was 45, an appropriate one for the first Thursday night game, when John played defensive back exclusively (and intercepted a pass) while watching player–coach–general manager–ticket salesman Chuck "Bear" Rogers direct the offense. "We didn't go by numbers," Rogers said. "We had some guys with three-digit numbers, I'm serious. Heck, I was a quarterback, too, and my number was *fifty*-five. The uniforms were striped, red and black, patterned on the University of Pennsylvania." The program roster read: "45 J. Unites [*sic*] B [for back]." "Of course, from the second game on, John was the quarterback," Rogers said. "I wasn't blind."

A beer salesman at the time, still distributing from the same stand forty-nine years later, Bear may have been the most important Pied Piper in the history of the sport. He even looked a little like a football. "Kids here played football year round," he said. "Growing up, we didn't do nothing else *but* play football. Supposedly, we'd start on Good Friday, but we never really stopped. Across the train tracks was a vacant lot and it just always was filled up with kids in huddles. Some parents wouldn't allow their kids to play football, but they played anyway, even if they had to sneak on the uniform at some other person's house, like mine. When we were eleven or twelve, a friend of mine's parents never had the slightest idea that he played football, until he broke his arm." For years Rogers ran teams out of his pants pockets for boys and men of practically every age and size, from the under-a-hundred-pounders all the way up to the Rams.

"In nineteen fifty-five, a guy who used to run the sporting goods store just up the avenue—you probably passed it on the way here, but it's not there anymore—told me a fellow by the name of Johnny Unitas had been released by the Steelers. I contacted John. We were one of the few teams that actually paid its players. Six dollars a game was the lowest, fifteen the highest. At first John got the six. By the end he was getting the fifteen, naturally. The full fifteen. We were undefeated."

They practiced at Dean's Field under the Bloomfield Bridge and played all of their home games (and some of the away ones) at Arsenal Park. "Sandlot" football was no lie. Both gridirons had more glass than grass. "They were good fields to play on," Bear said, "if you liked stitches." A few basic plays were installed at practices Rogers conducted once or twice a week. "If you missed a practice, I'd deduct three dollars," he said, "so some guys never got nothing." In the course of drives, John often knelt down in the dirt and drew plays with his finger. "'You go here and do this,'" Rogers demonstrated; "'you go there and do that; you stay in and block; you go in motion. On two. Ready?' You could just look at Unitas and know he was playing for keeps, but he had to win over the players on both sides, and it wasn't easy. The opponents laid for him because he had been with the Steelers. They made fun of his dreams, There was a wall about six or eight feet from the side-line. They'd try to run him into it. The word got out that he was still hoping to play in the NFL; so, after they knocked him down, they'd step over him and say, 'Welcome to the Steelbowl Conference.' He never retaliated. He just got up and dusted himself off."

In John's own huddle, there was some smirking at first. "Just being a college graduate set him apart," Rogers said. "The other players, some of whom had dropped in at schools like Bowling Green or Kent State, asked, 'What did you take, John? Basket weaving? Finger painting? Ballroom dancing? Come clean.' He'd just smile. From the sidelines, I could always tell when John had called a pass play, because Celender, number twenty-five, and Galioto, number twenty-two, would make faces. They were the halfbacks. Red Celender didn't like being kept in to block. These were all tough guys, you know, and they wanted to run, run, run. But he was tougher than they were. Once that was established on both sides of the line, everything was fine. Then, after the games, we'd all go over to Parise's restaurant on Liberty Avenue, a husband-and-wife hoagie joint across from Saint Joseph's Church. The players lined up in the basement to collect their six dollars, ten dollars, or fifteen dollars."

Once a year, the Rams played a game at the Allegheny County Workhouse, where the goalposts were painted on the side of a brick building. Rogers said, "I was our placekicker, too [why wouldn't he be?], and I'd boot the extra points, *boing,* right off the

wall between the painted uprights. They had an old-fashioned barber chair at the workhouse. Once, when the littlest kids played a
game there, I told them it was the electric chair. 'You better hope I
don't leave you here,' I said. We won that game, seven–nothing.
Anytime the Rams played at the workhouse, all of the convicts
would bet; cigarettes, you know. They were allowed to stand only
on the one sideline. When we'd file off the field into the dressing
room to go home, they'd slip us letters and packages to mail. Considering all of the guys in Pittsburgh who claimed that they once
played football with Johnny Unitas at the workhouse, you'd think
there were five thousand people on my team. Let me tell you, there
have always been a lot of claim jumpers in this town. Hell's bells,
sometimes we were lucky to have eleven."

This was not an exaggeration. Post-Unitas, Bear and the boys
started out once for a game in Ohio with just ten. "On the way
there, we stopped at a gas station, and the kid who filled our tank
looked pretty fit. I said, 'Do you play football?' He said, 'Yeah.' 'Will
you play today for ten dollars?' He got in the car." But in John's
time, the Bloomfield Rams always had a full complement of close
to thirty players. They were good. "Nobody's perfect," Rogers said.
"Here's one of the great mysteries of all time: We'd already won the
championship—maybe that's the answer—but we had one more
game at Arsenal Park. It was Thanksgiving Day. We were leading
by seven with twenty-eight seconds left when John stepped back
into the end zone and threw an interception that was returned for
a touchdown. The game wound up a seven–seven tie. I still can't
believe it. You know, somebody kicked a ninety-two-yard punt that
day. It just rolled and rolled on that concrete field." The ninety-
two-yard punt, he could believe.

Alone among NFL teams in 1955, the Baltimore Colts
(5-6-1) were desperate enough to hold regular Saturday tryouts
for Walter Mittys. "Our punter was an unusual character named
Woody McDaniel," Rogers said. "He was unusual because he had
money. His father was an insurance big shot. Woody got us our

policy when the Arsenal school wouldn't let you use the field without one. 'Is this a good insurance company?' I asked Woody. He
said, 'Yeah, but don't ever try to collect on it.' He used to punt the
ball so high, you didn't know where it was coming down. You had
to guess. I think he may have been the first one of our guys who
snuck up to Baltimore to try out. And that may have been what inspired my wife to write the letter."

Weeb Ewbank forever joked that John wrote the fabled "letter
from a Bloomfield fan" himself. "No, Roberta wrote it," Rogers said.
"We had a little two-room apartment after we got married and I can
still see her sitting there writing it. We were hoping to get a tryout
for one of our tackles, Jim Deglau. In response to Roberta's letter,
this guy calls up—Don Kellett, general manager of the Colts—and
says, 'Sure, we'll take a look at Deglau, but let me ask you something. Ever hear of a guy named Unitas?' I said, 'He plays for us,
too.' After we talked about John for a little while, I gave Kellett his
number." This was February of 1956. In what became a famous
"eighty-cent phone call," Kellett invited Unitas to visit Baltimore in
the spring so Ewbank could work him out a couple of months before training camp. John always enjoyed the legend of the fan's letter and the telephone call, but he never stopped believing that the
essential ingredient in the stew of events that delivered him to the
Colts was the history Ewbank had with Camp. ("Another small
piece of luck," John said, "was that offensive line coach Herman
Ball was in Pittsburgh when I was there and in Baltimore a year
later. I think he told Weeb that Nick Skorich was full of shit.") Split-
ting the gas money, Unitas and Deglau drove to Baltimore together.
"This may be a total waste of time," John said. For Deglau, it was.

●

Unitas probably never knew it, but Art Rooney quietly slipped into
several Bloomfield games to see John play. "Not all of them," said
Ed Kiely, the PR man, "but a few. The Chief and I talked about it,

and about him." Of course, Unitas couldn't possibly have known that the Chief was also a longtime benefactor of the Toner Institute and Seraphic Home for Boys. John Rooney said, "We kids were out there for different events all the time." In the city of Pittsburgh, every lifeline seems to cross every other one, over and over.

Cutting Unitas would become the Steelers' signature blunder. All teams have regrets of a similar kind, but in the space of just two years and a day, the Steelers passed up Unitas, Lenny Moore, and Jim Brown, which must be some kind of record. Rather than Brown, they drafted quarterback Len Dawson, which wasn't so bad, but then they traded Dawson to the Cleveland Browns, who cut him. As Bear Rogers said, "Nobody's perfect."

"In nineteen sixty-one or -two," Pat Rooney said, "I was in the army courageously defending my country at Fort Rucker, Alabama, when I briefly went AWOL to see the Steelers play an exhibition game against the Colts in Jacksonville [although it could have been Roanoke]. Before the game, I was walking underneath the stands and there was Unitas warming up. I didn't think for one second that he would remember me, so I just kept going. The ball whizzed right past my ear. 'What's the matter,' John said, 'don't you say hello?'" Unitas couldn't forgive Kiesling, but he never held anything against the Rooneys—because, from afar, he could feel them rooting for him, as gigantic an embarrassment as he would become. "How could we root against him?" Dan Rooney asked. "He was our guy. He was one of us."

He was Pittsburgh.

FOUR

"Go deep, Jim, and then loop back."

Baltimore

The leader, the captain, *the man,* was a defensive end with brilliantined black hair, Gino Marchetti, who, in the locker room before the games, paced and smoked like an expectant bear. He fought the Germans on the Siegfried Line at eighteen, *before* he went to the University of San Francisco. During World War II, Marchetti's mother was interned in a camp for Italians outside Antioch, California, even though she had two sons in the army. Gino's uniform number was 89.

Six lockers down—the Colts always dressed in sequence— sat Don Joyce (83), who was a professional wrestler in the off-season, as was Eugene "Big Daddy" Lipscomb (76), seven spaces farther along. Lipscomb, who never went to college, learned some of his football at Camp Pendleton in the Marine Corps but most of it from Marchetti. Another marine, Artie Donovan, number 70, leaned over at his locker, taping magazines to his shins for body armor—*Newsweek* on the left leg, *Time* on the right, appropriately. Artie's father, Arthur Donovan, refereed both of the Joe Louis–Max Schmeling fights in Yankee Stadium. The Donovans were from the

Bronx. Arthur Donovan killed his best friend in a drunken fistfight in the Bronx.

Sitting beside Artie was guard Alex Sandusky, 68 ("Nobody had the guts to wear sixty-nine," Sandusky said primly), a sixteenth-round draft choice from Clarion State Teachers College, who would be sent into his first pro game in the middle of the second quarter and start every game after that but one, for thirteen years. A postman's son, Sandusky had been an end when he boarded the Pittsburgh plane that brought him to Baltimore. But during the ride he met Notre Dame end Jim Mutscheller, yet another marine, and changed positions. Alex figured Notre Dame trumped Clarion State in any competitions for employment. Also, coming directly from Korea, Mutscheller had a look in his eyes that could bore a hole in a vault. It somehow made blocking even Leo Nomellini seem a cheerier proposition. (Babe Parilli would probably understand. Bucky Mutscheller was the high school kid from Beaver Falls who had called Parilli to request a rematch.) Mutscheller was the son of a workingman who was known by his neighbors as "the best bricklayer in Beaver County."

L. G. Dupre and Bert Rechichar (*wretch-it-char,* like choking on broken teeth), 45 and 44, sat side by side. As almost nobody knew, the "L. G." stood for Louis George. A happy-go-lucky halfback from Baylor, he came to be known as Long Gone Dupre. Next to Night Train Lane's, in Detroit, his was the best nickname in the National Football League. "Back in Texas City," Dupre told Gene Gregston of the *Fort Worth Star-Telegram,* "my daddy would take my brothers and me around from saloon to saloon, pair us off against each other in bare-knuckle boxing matches, and pass the hat. Made a pretty good dollar, too. That's why, when the fights break out today, I'm the only one in the league throwing jabs." Rechichar, an equally ready and even more willing defensive back from Belle Vernon, western Pennsylvania, preferred to be called simply Forty-four. In fact, he insisted on it. In the further cause of simplicity, he addressed everyone he was still speaking to by one name: "Peas." On the road Rechichar required his roommates (including Alex Hawkins, eventually) to keep the shower running in the bathtub when he was out. If any of the coaches happened to drop by the room, they were to be told, "Forty-four is taking a shower."

Rechichar wasn't the Colts' field goal kicker—that was Buck McPhail—but he was their strong-footed kickoff man. Goalposts were still on the goal line in the 1950s, and teams kicked off from their own forty-yard line. In 1953, the first year of the second coming of the Colts, head coach Keith Molesworth had been noticing how close to the uprights Rechichar's straight-on kicks were tumbling. In an opening day upset of the Chicago Bears, the inaugural game in Baltimore's Memorial Stadium, Molesworth let Forty-four close the half with the first field goal try of his life from an unheard of fifty-six yards out. That stood as the NFL record for seventeen years and forty-two days. It's still the record for anyone born blind in one eye.

Also cheek to jowl were numbers 36 and 35, middle linebacker Bill Pellington and fullback Alan "the Horse" Ameche, the NFL's Rookie of the Year. Pellington, a navy vet and an ironworker who helped build the Tappan Zee Bridge in New York, was the cruelest person and most wanton player on the team. He was known for gritty feats such as playing for an extended time with a broken arm. The truth was, long after the fracture had healed, he kept the cast for purposes of knocking opposing players unconscious. "Bill Pellington," Hawkins said, "should have been thrown out of every game he ever played, and most of the practices." "Pellington was nuts," Donovan said. "Even the officials were a little afraid of him. He got away with murder." In contrast, Ameche was the smartest, nicest, and most-civilized member of the team. He was a bridge player, an opera buff, and a distant relative of the movie actor who portrayed Alexander Graham Bell, Don Ameche.

Just a few more players down, after the fading greats Buddy Young (22) of Illinois and Billy Vessels (21) of Oklahoma, and the unremembered Jim Harness (20) of Mississippi State, sat the rookie quarterback, Johnny Unitas. "At Westminster, Maryland, where we trained," Donovan said, "I liked to come to work early. We had an assistant trainer named Dimitri Spassoff, a real Bulgarian bullshitter, who used to rub my feet and tell me humorous stories. I looked across the room and here was this new guy, this skinny little scarecrow, with a hot pack on his right shoulder. 'Who the fuck is that?' I said. 'That's the new quarterback,' Spassoff said. 'We got him from Pittsburgh, I think.' 'And he's already got a bum shoulder? Christ, he'll never make it.'" John's new number was 19. Though his college number, 16, had been available, he took the jersey that was handed him and said nothing. After Jack DelBello and Cotton Davidson, John was the third Colt to wear 19, and the last. Abruptly, Young would hang up number 22 before the regular season began. Vessels and Harness would pass their numbers on to Art DeCarlo and Milt Davis just one year later. Unitas would keep his forever. At the end of the row sat number 14, quarterback George Shaw, the star of the team, the bonus pick of 1955, the NFL Rookie Quarterback of the Year (and runner-up to Ameche among all of the freshmen), whose $18,000 salary was by far the highest in the room. After working out with Molesworth's successor, Weeb Ewbank, at Clifton Park in Baltimore, Unitas had signed a one-year contract for $7,000. Remembering the $5,500 pact that was never activated in Pittsburgh, he told Dorothy, "Try to think of it as a fifteen-hundred-dollar raise."

Donovan wasn't just a round man in the middle of the Colts' defensive line. He was also a circular figure at the center of the city of Baltimore. Eight years older than Unitas, Artie had worn the green and silver of the original Baltimore Colts, born the Miami Seahawks, who survived the demise of the All-America Football Conference in 1949 only to go out of business one year later, one horrible 1–11 year in the NFL. After half a cup of coffee with the Cleveland Browns, the leading remnants of the AAFC, Donovan played on with the New York Yanks, who became the Dallas Texans, who became the new Baltimore Colts. The franchise ricocheted from Dallas to Baltimore on January 23, 1953, but the birthday should be celebrated on March 25, the date five Colts, including tackle Mike McCormack, were traded for ten Browns, including guard Art Spinney and three defensive backs: Rechichar, Carl Taseff, and, most significantly, a granite-jawed Hungarian from Painesville, Ohio, Don Shula.

Roughly the same size ("roughly" is exactly the right word), Shula and Taseff had been college teammates at John Carroll University in Cleveland, and Paul Brown couldn't tell them apart. Only by the grace of one standout performance, a startling John Carroll victory over Syracuse in Cleveland Stadium, did either Shula or Taseff even get a look from the pros. When one afternoon at practice Brown barked, "Nice tackle, Taseff," Shula hopped straight up to shout back, "The name's Shula! *S-h-u-l-a!*" The whole industry would come to know it, and though he wasn't what you would call a great football player, Shula started at cornerback for four seasons with the Colts, through the end of John's rookie year. Later they would be bound together as coach and player; from John's perspective, not altogether happily.

It's an exaggeration to say Shula and Unitas were the same guy, but only a slight one. Shula was also the son of immigrants. He was also a Catholic who was a regular at Mass. As a boy, he also dreamed of playing football for Notre Dame. Instead, he played for a little Catholic college that, among its opponents, counted Saint Bonaventure, quarterbacked by Ted Marchibroda. Shula had a father he both liked and loved, a quiet, humble man. But Don's mother ran the household in Painesville. "Mom was a take-charge woman," he said, "and the biggest influence in my life." Shula and Unitas had the same attitude about work, the same competitive spirit, the same tunnel vision, the same stubbornness, the same bluntness. Shula was louder. He was that screamer John had always detested. "I'm about as subtle as a punch in the nose," Shula liked to say. Don was a much better student. His first two off-seasons in Cleveland, when he wasn't selling cars or working construction, Shula was taking mathematics courses at Western Reserve University, earning his master's degree, and planning a life as a high school football coach and math teacher. "Canton Lincoln offered me thirty-seven hundred and fifty dollars to coach and teach," he said, "but I just couldn't stop playing football yet. I played seven seasons in the NFL, making five thousand dollars in the first and ninety-seven fifty in the last. But we had more fun, I can tell you."

Was it true that Shula once stole a taxicab?

"I've been accused of stealing it," he said, "but I didn't take it home with me on the plane. Taseff, Pellington, and I had gone out after a game in Green Bay, to Chili John's or one of those places, for a late bite. We come outside the restaurant, and here's this taxi with the motor running and no driver. We honk the horn, but nobody shows. We honk it again. It's cold out, and by this time, Taseff and I are sitting in the backseat. Well, Pellington was kind of an impatient person, as you may remember. So Bill puts the cab-driver's hat on and drives us back to the hotel. We left the cab there, so we didn't really steal it. We just borrowed it. In the early years, there wasn't anything we *didn't* do. We did it all."

Before any of them were married, Shula, Donovan, Pellington, and sometimes Marchetti lived together in the Campus Hills section of Baltimore. "One year," Shula said, "we rented this completely furnished town house with very delicate furniture. In our spare time, we wrestled each other. The crystal in the dining room would shake and chime. Donovan would get into his stance and Pellington and I would try to knock him off his feet. You know how strong Dunny was. Nobody could move him. He was just so strong down in here and up in there. We'd be holding on and that furniture would be rattling." Donovan said, "Eventually I'd get to laughing, and they'd put my two legs over my shoulders and just whop the hell out of me."

Shula was one of the first players to notice—truly notice—John. "At practice, it'd be pass offense versus pass defense," Shula said. "That's when I started thinking, This guy's pretty good. I'm trying to cover Lenny Moore, who was a rookie too, and Raymond Berry. John was just starting to time up with these guys, and I wasn't good enough when Unitas had the ball." When Shaw had it, Shula was on firmer ground. "George was a rollout quarterback, not too tall (listed at six foot even, but honestly only five foot ten), very strong arm, nice runner, good guy. But he was just a good athlete trying to play quarterback. John *was* a quarterback." Because this was the era of thirty-three-man rosters, Ewbank also pressed defensive signal caller Shula into standby service as the "emergency quarterback," what Unitas might consider a third-stringer. So, in the process of memorizing all of the offensive plays and signals, Don had an even closer look at John. "In one of the exhibition games," Shula said, "Gino goes up to Weeb and says, 'Why don't you put Shula in?' Weeb says, 'Huh?' 'Put him in, get him a little experience.' So, he puts me in, I take the snap, fade back to pass, start to scramble, and the whole defense falls on top of me. I got up with a knockdown shoulder and had to come out. That was my one play at quarterback in my entire career." Within a year Shula would be dropped by the Colts and picked up by the Redskins. In a game at Washington, he was assigned to cover Berry one-on-one. "I didn't do very well," Don said sheepishly. Raymond caught twelve passes that day for 224 yards and two touchdowns. He and John were getting timed up all right.

◆

The first things they noticed about each other were their hands. During a high school game in Paris, Texas, Berry had badly broken the little finger of his left hand, and it had been dislocated so many times since then that it no longer worked with the others. John's right hand looked like it had been blown up by a .38 caliber slug, which, of course, it had. The first time Unitas and Berry shook hands, a connection was made. It is not too strong to say that they became a team within a team. "Raymond's hands caught my attention even before we met," John told Cameron Snyder of the *Baltimore Sun.* "All through the offensive meetings, he would be squeezing a pink blob of clay in each fist [this being the decade of McCarthy, Kinsey, Presley, and Silly Putty] and he carried a football with him everywhere he went, even to meals. You know, Raymond didn't catch that many passes as a rookie starter the year before [thirteen in twelve games, none for touchdowns] but he looked like a receiver to me."

Past the point of eccentricity, Berry was a details man. He searched and searched for just the right pair of football pants; and when he found them, he never entrusted them to the equipment men again. Raymond insisted on washing and ironing the pants himself. To him, the fit was crucial, and every crease held a particular significance. Berry carried a bathroom scale with him on the road, to monitor his weight precisely. He scouted the sunlight at various times of day. He had a pile of football shoes with all manner of cleats, including an especially uncomfortable pair with longer "mud" cleats over just the balls of the feet, which would someday come into play in New York. As nearsighted as Mr. Magoo, Berry wore horn-rimmed glasses off the field, and contact lenses on it. They made him look startled. On the West Coast, he added sun goggles that owed something to the Creature from the Black Lagoon. "The sun in December moved in such a way," he said, "that for about a quarter, it was blinding. I arranged to design dark glasses that snapped on my helmet. They worked, too."

From the day they met, Unitas and Berry regularly stayed after practice to pass and catch. "When Weeb saw what we were doing," Berry said, "he told me kind of quietly, 'Keep working with this

Unitas.' Looking back, I wonder if Weeb didn't already know." In one of their earliest sessions, Berry was running "little L-patterns," square-ins, and John asked him, "What if a linebacker got right up on top of you?" "It hasn't happened," Berry said. "What if Joe Schmidt [of Detroit] is standing right there? What would you do?" "I guess I'd give him an outside fake like this, try to make him come after me, then jump underneath him like this." John nodded. Neither of them mentioned or thought of it again for more than two years, not until Berry crouched down in his stance on the left side of the line with a minute and a few seconds to go in a game the Colts were losing, 17–14. Raymond looked up and there stood the linebacker. But it wasn't Joe Schmidt of the Lions. It was Harland Svare of the New York Giants. Berry glanced over at Unitas, who smiled.

Like John, Raymond had been an undersized boy with an oversized ambition. Berry said, "I was just a kid who grew up loving football and wanting to play real bad, who saw a movie about Crazy Legs Hirsch and got a vision in his mind about being a professional football player, who happened to end up in Baltimore in the time of Unitas. This is not your average experience. It defies all of the odds." His father was a high school football coach in east Texas, where the high school coach was a larger figure than the mayor, when football was considered a hard game that taught hard lessons that could not be learned anywhere else. "I was slow developing physically," Raymond said. "During World War Two, boys were often moved up a grade to get them out of high school quicker, and I was a sixteen-year-old senior who was five foot eleven and weighed a hundred and fifty pounds. That was the first year I started on offense. I called the plays. My dad believed his players could think. He was a very independent man himself. Every year he assessed who knew the most about the game. It wasn't necessarily the quarterback. It might be a center. It might be a fullback. In my case it was a left end. So, I called the plays."

Berry's hope, not surprisingly, was to land in the Southwest Conference, but he had to muscle up for a year in junior college before, out of respect for his father, Southern Methodist University took a flier. It was a long climb there, too. "But I was elected co-captain my senior year. That's when I got into taking notes and studying film. I played in the East-West game. My junior season had been my fourth year in college, and the Colts had drafted me that winter in the twentieth round. So, they owned me when I got out the next year." Thirteen rookies made the club, which was almost ridiculous. In Shula's first year with the Browns, he was the only rookie who made the traveling team; Taseff made the "taxi" squad (fittingly). Thirteen rookies may have been a record. "That's the only reason I made the team," Berry said. "I was one of the thirteen. I didn't have the slightest clue how to be a pro receiver."

Berry didn't even know what a zone defense was. He said, "Some players have this gift—a few do, most don't—that I call 'quality of growth.' Coaching staffs in those days were pretty limited. It was really just swim or drown. I kept reading how pitiful I was and that I was going to be replaced. But I studied every film that came in the door. I'd say I was completely self-taught, except I wasn't completely alone. I had Unitas. Where I was more of a trial-and-error guy—you know, study, study, study, study—John was more of an instinctive player. He had an amazingly organized mind, a fabulous memory. 'This is open? Okay. I'll get to you. How long before this will work? Okay. You're on my list.' He'd wait in the pocket until the absolute last second, deliver the ball right on the money, and get smashed in the mouth. Then he'd call the same play over again and hold the ball a little longer this time and get smashed in the mouth even harder. The bridge of his nose would be split. His mouth would be full of blood. Do you think he cared? John would have been a great middle linebacker."

On Berry's very first pro play in 1955, on George Shaw's very first play, on Alan Ameche's very first play—a play called Fifteen Sucker—a guard pulled right to suggest a sweep, and, exactly according to plan, the Chicago Bears' defense flowed in that direction. But Shaw handed off to Ameche punching straight ahead, and the Horse ran seventy-nine yards for a touchdown. On the very first play. "It was a play that was in everybody's offense," Berry said. "You ran it all the time for a yard or three or four. In an entire career, the truth of the matter is, that play was going to break into the secondary one time. But you had to block downfield as if it was going to break every time. Because if you didn't go absolutely full speed for the man you were supposed to block, if you looked back first to see if it broke, you'd never get there in time. Who was responsible for blocking the free safety on this play? Me. Well, of course you're going to go full speed on the very first play of your very first game. You're not tired yet. You're not realistic yet. You're not cynical yet. You're not playing the odds yet. I had no idea Alan had broken into the clear until I saw the safety's eyes light up just before I hit him."

Fifteen Sucker wouldn't break again for about three years, not until Unitas called it as an audible on the Giants' forty-two-yard line in overtime at Yankee Stadium. "I was tired," Berry said ruefully. He had just caught a pass for twenty-one yards, his eleventh (second-to-last) in the game. "What's that old saying? 'Fatigue makes cowards of us all.'" Ameche gained twenty-three yards on the play, but if Berry had done his job, the game could have ended right there. Nobody in the stadium knew it except Raymond and John. "He didn't say a word as we huddled up," Berry said. "He just looked at me as if to ask, 'Where were you?' But then he smiled as if to say, 'Don't worry about it.' Johnny U."

The Colts always ended training camp with an intrasquad celebration in Baltimore, Colt Nite, a benefit for the Baltimore Police Boys'

Clubs where every seat in Memorial Stadium went for a dollar. It amounted to a dress rehearsal for the season, except that 38,447 people were sitting in the theater. For most of John's first Blue-White game, he was pitted straight up against Shaw in a misty rain. George outran John, and all of the running backs, too; John outpassed George (fourteen of twenty-four, for 288 yards and three touchdowns). The final score was 20–20, just like hindsight, and the headline and deck in Tuesday morning's *Sun* read, "UNITAS STARS FOR BOTH TEAMS, SCORING FINAL POINTS OF 20–20 GAME. Discarded Steeler Quarterback Leads Whites to 20–14 Advantage, Then Joins Blues in Drive for Late-Tying Touchdown." Citing a fifty-one-yard rainbow to Berry, Coach Ewbank said, "A lot of guys can throw deep; Unitas can *pass* deep." Looking back, the guard, Alex Sandusky, said, "It was *some* performance, it really was. I hadn't hardly noticed John before that. I noticed his *car*. It was green but blew blue smoke out the back. If Unitas ever drove past you, you'd cough like a dog for about ten minutes."

The halftime entertainment at that Blue-White game featured a footrace between a renowned Kansas miler named Wes Santee and a relay team of ten Colts, including Taseff and Pellington, running 176 yards each, handing off a football instead of a baton. Santee's 4.22 time wasn't horrible, considering the mud, but he lost by a stride. The mood was right for a county fair or a picnic. Mutscheller beat Berry and all of the other ends in a 100-yard dash. Rechichar won a placekicking contest. The barrel throw—four quarterbacks competing—went to John. (A lot of guys could throw deep; Unitas could *pass* deep.) Finally, with linebacker Joe Campanella's three-year-old son bouncing on his shoulders, Alan "the Horse" Ameche galloped a ceremonial lap around the field and became the first human being ever invited to run in the Pimlico Special.

Another young tradition was the opening exhibition game against the Philadelphia Eagles in a high school stadium at Hershey, Pennsylvania. On August 11, 1956, in front of an essentially sold-out Hershey crowd of 17,575, John at last made his NFL debut. That morning, high school freshman Ernie Accorsi caddied eighteen holes—doubles—to secure the $2.50 price of admission. Growing up in Hershey, Accorsi felt no overpowering affection for the Eagles, to say the least. He had been one of 10,031 spectators at the first Colts-Eagles exhibition game in 1954, when Baltimore won, 10–0, thereby becoming Ernie's team. The Colts had never recorded a winning season, but hopes were high in 1956. "We were all excited by George Shaw," Accorsi said. "He had been the rookie sensation, scrambling all over the place. I'm sitting on the Colts' side with my best friend, and I'm happy, they're winning [they ultimately won, 24–13], and then suddenly they take Shaw out and put in this awkward-looking number nineteen with rubber bands on his sleeves. The public address announcer pronounces his name, '*YOU*-knee-*tASS*.' What is this? I'm fourteen and I'm bitching. But a man sitting close to me says, 'Calm down, kid. You should have seen this guy in the Blue-White game.' I did calm down. I watched him closely. I wasn't a scout [though he would be, with the Colts] or a general manager [though he would be, with the Colts, Browns, and Giants]. I was just a kid. But I'm telling you, he threw lasers all over the field."

Halfback Lenny Moore, the number one pick from Penn State, the eighth man taken in the draft, had come to Hershey directly from the College All-Star Game in Chicago. Moore owned a miniature Bible that he read along the way. He was daunted enough to tuck it into the pouch behind the right thigh pad of his football pants, where it remained the rest of his career. "I didn't know any of the plays yet," Moore said, "so I got in only on special teams—Buddy Young talked me through it. For most of the game, I just sat on the bench and watched. I couldn't believe what I was seeing." It seemed to Moore that absolutely nothing was illegal. "Chuck Bednarik and another Eagles player didn't just tackle Ameche out of bounds. They carried him out of bounds and slammed him against a table behind the bench. I said to myself,

Man, I can't do this. There were guys beating on guys like you couldn't believe. I thought, Am I strong enough to take this kind of punishment? I had my doubts." Sitting next to Marchetti on the bench was a rookie tackle. "I forget where he was from," Gino said, "but I think his name was Seals. He looked at me and asked, 'Is it like this all the time?' I said, 'Hell, no. Wait until the league games start. Wait until the season starts.' Honest to God, I never saw him again. The middle of the night, we go back to Westminster. Next day, no Seals. Gone."

A month later, the Colts remet the Eagles for a second exhibition game in, of all places, Louisville. As coincidences went, this one ranked right up there with Bernie Crimmins being a Louisvillian. Long before Don Kellett made the eighty-cent phone call to Unitas, the general manager had already struck a two-year deal to play first the Eagles and then the Cardinals at the new Fairgrounds Stadium in Kentucky. Later, probably because of Unitas, the agreement was extended a third year to include an exhibition game with the Giants, one of what turned out to be *four* meetings between the Colts and the Giants in 1958. Before the Blue-White game of 1956, newspaperman–turned–publicity director John Steadman (about to turn newspaperman again) went to Unitas's room at Western Maryland College to tape a local-boy-makes-good feature intended for the use of Kentucky radio stations in September. After they finished the interview, Unitas asked Steadman, "Do you think I'll still be here then?" The morning after the Blue-White game, Steadman tapped on the quarterback's door. "I think we'll be able to use that recording all right, John," he said softly.

In the interest of public relations, Ewbank started Unitas in Louisville. Then Weeb turned over the running of the game, essentially a controlled scrimmage, to his assistant coaches. For a fee of $15, John's old friend and college teammate Bob Bender kept statistics in the press box. "There had already been a couple of dropped balls," Bender said, "when John threw about a fifty-yard pass to Lenny Moore, and Moore booted it. I jumped up and shouted, 'Goddamn it!' I'm ashamed to say, I also said something derogatory about Moore's color. The guy sitting next to me took offense, but I was just so frustrated. 'I'm sorry,' I said, 'but how's Unitas going to prove he should be their quarterback if they keep dropping the ball?' He said, 'What do you mean? They've got Shaw.' 'Hell, Shaw won't have the job long,' I said, 'once they see what John can do.' The guy left his seat at halftime and didn't return. It wasn't until later that I found out it was Weeb Ewbank."

●

Opening the season against Chicago at Memorial Stadium, Shaw completed all but one of his first fifteen passes as the Colts beat the Bears by a touchdown. The following week, Baltimore lost at home to Detroit, and after a loss to Green Bay in Milwaukee, the Colts brought their 1–2 record to Chicago's Wrigley Field, where everything changed. Leading 20–14, the Bears tried a wishful field goal that died four yards short. Catching everyone flat-footed, Carl Taseff scooped up the ball and ran ninety-six yards for the go-ahead touchdown. A good description of Bear games in those days is that, in the locker room afterward, Taseff couldn't recall scoring the touchdown or anything else that happened. "The only thing I remember is running head-on into Perry Jeter," he said. "How did we do?" Not so good. Shaw was driving the team across the fifty-yard line when he was buried under a pile of Fred Williams and George Connor, and the ligaments in his right knee popped. Offensive tackle George Preas told Steadman, "It sounded like a Venetian blind." Artie Donovan said, "The Bears had been after Shaw for a while. The year before, Connor broke George's face mask on a blitz. Shaw stumbled over to the sideline and asked Dick Szymanski, 'How do my teeth look?' 'It's hard to say,' Sizzy said. 'They're not there anymore.'" This time, as Shaw was dragged off the field, Unitas ambled on.

John's first of 5,186 passes was a short throw into the right flat that Chicago cornerback J. C. Caroline timed exquisitely. Intercepting the ball in his longest stride, Caroline returned it fifty-nine yards for a touchdown with Unitas and Ameche giving feeble chase. The rest of the game was a Gothic nightmare of botched handoffs and fumbles. John and his ball carriers were so unused to one another that, when he wasn't bumping into them, they were crashing into him. The final score was 58–27. "That would be enough to rattle anybody, wouldn't you think?" Berry said. "Do you know how much that affected him? I don't think it affected him at all." For the record, in the midst of this debacle, John threw his first official touchdown pass, thirty-six yards to Mutscheller.

The football writer for the *Sun,* Cameron Snyder, was a two-fisted, burly, and opinionated little man who once had to be restrained from punching Burt Lancaster. Though drinking was known in his profession, Snyder wasn't a heavy drinker, just an interesting one. He never ordered the same cocktail twice in a sitting. He would have a martini, then a Manhattan, then a gin and tonic, then a vodka tonic, then a Rob Roy—all the time insisting that the bartender not change the glass. One night, observing this spectacle from the other end of a hotel bar, Lancaster became fascinated and wandered over. He made the mistake of touching Cameron's glass.

"I'm kind of an obstinate guy," Snyder said, "and I guess it took me a little longer than most to believe in Unitas. I knew he could throw the football. Steadman used to say, 'I spend all of my time building him up, and you spend all of your time knocking him down.' After that Bears mess, I went to Ewbank in the locker room and kind of snorted, 'Not a very auspicious start for Unitas.' Weeb looked at me and said, 'He went in icy cold, but did you see how he stood up to it? Did you see how tough he is, Cameron? He wasn't in sync with our guys and they weren't in sync with him. But there were a lot of missed blocks, too. I'll tell you something, I'm more impressed with Unitas now than I was before.' I thought—I may have even said—You're out of your mind!"

"We're on the bus after the game," Mutscheller said, "waiting to go to Midway Airport. You can imagine how tense the atmosphere was on that bus. Now we're one-and-three. We just got annihilated by the Bears, and we lost Shaw in the bargain. I happened to be sitting behind John and a writer for the *Evening Sun,* Walter Taylor. I couldn't help but eavesdrop on their conversation. It was the first time I can remember ever hearing John talk. He was explaining to Taylor all of the things that went wrong, exactly why they went wrong, and exactly how he planned to correct his mistakes. I couldn't believe how cut-and-dried and matter-of-fact it all sounded. He was completely undismayed, perfectly confident about everything he was going to do. Jeez, his first pass in the NFL is intercepted for a touchdown, and he's sitting there saying, *I'm going to do this, and we're going to do that, and this is what's going to happen next, and here's what's going to result eventually.* That's when I thought to myself, Who *is* this guy?"

"On the way to the airport," Donovan said, "the highway flooded and the bus broke down. A few of us stripped to our underwear and pushed it out. It wasn't a very good day." In his game story, Taylor included no quotes from his conversation with Unitas. Instead of looking back, he concentrated on the upcoming "tilt" between "the Ewbankmen" and "the Wisconsinites" from Green Bay.

General manager Kellett decided they'd better call Gary Kerkorian, a Stanford quarterback who had started for the Colts in 1954 but, loath to sit around behind Shaw (especially for these salaries), had quit football to enroll at Georgetown Law School in Washington. Really, this decision was the one that presented John his pro chance. "What can I offer Kerkorian?" Kellett asked Ewbank. "Money," Weeb said. "No, seriously, what can I promise him?" "Money," Weeb repeated. The next day, when the banner headline in the *Evening Sun* read, "Colts Hope Kerkorian Will Check Tailspin," Ewbank pulled Unitas aside in the clubhouse and whispered, "Kerkorian is coming in as the backup. Don't worry." Before the Packers visited Baltimore that Sunday, Weeb and John sat together at a large desk—it might as well have been a school desk—and pared down what was already a comparatively simple offense. In a cautious but clean performance, Unitas threw just sixteen passes against Green Bay and completed half of them, two for touchdowns, including a forty-three-yarder to Berry. This time taking John's handoffs in the stomach instead of on the hip, Lenny Moore put together two sparkling touchdown runs of seventy-two and seventy-nine yards, and the Colts won, 28–21. Years later, at his home in Oxford, Ohio, Ewbank told the sportswriter, "I taught John quite a bit the first couple of years. I think he'd tell you that himself. Then he started to teach me."

In a stroke of almost unbelievable luck, the next game, against the Redskins in Baltimore, was put off until the end of the season. Navy and Notre Dame had booked Memorial Stadium for Saturday, November 4, and the fine print in the contract forbade the scheduling of any other football games within forty-eight hours. So, John and Weeb had two full weeks at the desk to restore the playbook and prepare for a game at Cleveland, an especially important stop to Ewbank. Though Paul Brown's players were proliferating as head coaches throughout football, any assistant coaches who walked away from Brown were forever encased in icicles. This was Ewbank's first game opposite his old boss. Weeb was frantic to win, and John knew it. Incidentally, to this point in their brief history, the Colts had played twenty-six road games and won a grand total of three. Trailing Cleveland 7–0 when the Browns fumbled on their own thirty-five-yard line, Unitas went thirty-four yards on a quarterback keeper that Browns fullback Ed Modzelewski said "was like watching a crazy man running through a burning building. Would you want to get in his way?" Marchetti's red-dog rush of Babe Parilli led to a second Colt score ("and to my exit from Cleveland," said Parilli), and Moore contributed another seventy-yard dance in the broken field. After the Colts won, 21–7, Brown refused to shake Ewbank's hand.

The Los Angeles Rams were beaten in Baltimore (as John completed eighteen of twenty-four passes, for 293 yards and three touchdowns), but including back-to-back games on the West Coast, the Colts mostly lost the rest of the way. "When it came time to play that postponed Redskins game," Cameron Snyder said, "everybody in town knew Weeb's job was on the line." It was an odd-feeling game, the only one scheduled in the league that day, two days before Christmas, in the buffer week between the end of the season and the championship game. "It was a lousy, rainy day," Mutscheller said, "and we were driving toward the open end of the horseshoe in Memorial Stadium. I caught a pass, got hit, and fumbled. I *never* fumbled. Here I go, I thought. I'm gone for next year. Me and Weeb both." With fifteen seconds left in the game, the Colts had the ball on their own forty-seven-yard line, losing 17–12. "In the huddle," Mutscheller said, "John didn't call a play. He just gave the pass-blocking numbers, and told me, 'Go deep, Jim, and then loop back. It'll be there.' I was split right. I ran as fast as I could to the goal line, turned, and came back a step, and there it was. Three Redskins and I jumped like basketball players going up for a rebound. I don't know how, but I tipped the ball [or it bounced off Norb Hecker's head] and then caught it on the way into the end zone as the gun went off. We won, nineteen to seventeen. That was my first moment in the sun [though without the sun]. Because no other games were played that day, and the weather was so bad all over the East, everybody was watching. I got a million phone calls."

Ewbank's and Mutscheller's jobs were saved. Unitas's position was officially secured. It had been unofficially secured six weeks earlier when, walking through the clubhouse, equipment man Fred Schubach had wondered aloud when Shaw would be coming back, and Marchetti replied, "Shaw ain't coming back."

John's 55.6 passing percentage for the season (110 completions in 198 attempts, for 1,498 yards and nine touchdowns) was the best by a rookie quarterback in the thirty-seven-year history of the NFL. As obstinate as ever, Cameron Snyder told Unitas, "It looked to me like you underthrew that last pass." John laughed and said, "Looks don't count." Although Gary Kerkorian connected on the only two passes he had been asked to throw, for fifty-nine yards and a touchdown to boot, he would resume law school in the fall, bequeathing his number, 18, to returning sub (and punter) Cotton Davidson, who didn't bother to request his old jersey. Donovan said, "I guess Kerkorian was a pretty good guy, but I wasn't sorry to see him go. In nineteen fifty-four, when Gary did some of the kicking, too, he missed five field goals inside the twenty-yard line, and we lost to the Forty-niners, ten–seven. I never forgave the son-of-a-bitch for that."

By the way, Gino was right. Shaw did not come back. But he did return, first to hold the ball for Colt placekicker Steve Myhra against the Giants in 1958, then to hold it for Giant placekicker Pat Summerall against the Colts in 1959. In 1982, Shaw would be immortalized in the cult movie *Diner,* whose central love interest was the one between the city of Baltimore and its football team. The picture is set in 1959, when a young bride-to-be, Elyse, has to pass a test on the Colts before her fiancé, Eddie, will clear her to walk down a blue-and-white aisle to a "tasteful" rendition of the fight song.

Those were also the colors of Forest Park in Baltimore, where the filmmaker Barry Levinson went to high school. With a gang of young Colts fans, Levinson made summer pilgrimages to Westminster, Maryland. Sitting together on a grassy slope, the diner guys—the real ones—were eyewitnesses to the birth of the two-minute drill. "After the other players left the field," Levinson said, "Unitas and Berry stayed behind. Raymond would run in one direction and John would throw in another. But suddenly Berry cut to a certain spot, and there was the ball. Up on his toes he caught it, dragging his feet as he went out of bounds. We kept watching as they did this over and over. Going left. Going right. Pass, cut, catch, toes, out of bounds. It was extraordinary. The precision."

The true-false section of the test ended with the trick question "Was George Shaw a first-round draft choice?" (No. He was the bonus pick.) Other questions:

"Before the Cleveland Browns joined the NFL, they were in another league. What was it called?" (The All-America Football Conference.)

"Buddy Young played for a team that no longer exists. What was the name of that team?" (The New York Yankees Football Team.)

"What was the longest run from scrimmage by a rookie in his first game?" (Seventy-nine yards by Alan Ameche on his first play from scrimmage as a pro.)

"The Colts signed him, a Heisman Trophy winner, but he decided to play in Canada. Now, however, he plays for the team. What's his name?" (Unfair question. By 1959, the movie year, Billy Vessels was as "long gone" as Elyse's incorrect answer: L. G. Dupre.)

"The Colts had a team here, lost the franchise, then got one from Dallas. What were the colors of the original Colts team?" (Green and silver.)

The Colts of 1956 were much better than their five wins and seven losses, but they didn't know it yet. As a matter of fact, they were only one great pass blocker away. In Moore, who succeeded Ameche as the NFL's Rookie of the Year, they had the most explosive offensive weapon in the league. Nobody noticed, of course, but with that fifty-three-yard heave to Mutscheller, John had passed for a touchdown in three straight games. Come the opener of 1957, he would throw another touchdown pass to Mutscheller, one to Berry, and two to Dupre. A hundred and two touchdown passes later, on December 11, 1960, the streak would end at forty-seven games in a row.

The original coach of the original Colts was a former Green Bay quarterback named Cecil Isbell, whose Raymond Berry had been the stately Packer end Don Hutson. In 1941 and 1942, Isbell threw touchdown passes in twenty-two consecutive games, to set an NFL record that lasted sixteen years. John broke it, and broke it, and broke it, and broke it . . . twenty-five times.

FIVE

1956

"Do you need anything? How can I help? What can I do?"

Learning It Together

"There was no crash of thunder early on," said Lenny Moore, "when I thought to myself, This is going to be the great Johnny U. No. I could see that he was improving. But *I* was improving. *Raymond* was improving. Nobody really singled John out yet as being the reason we all were improving. But he was the reason. John was the first one of us to think in terms of being world champions, I know that. He *made* us rally around him. We didn't have a choice. Going into the second half of our rookie year— John's and mine—I had started to settle in. Hey man, I thought, you can handle this after all. One morning before practice, J.U. looked over at me and said, 'You're feeling pretty happy with yourself, huh?' You see, he could read your mind. I told him, 'I know I've still got a lot to learn.' He smiled and said, 'Let's learn it together.'"

◆

Wilbur "Weeb" Ewbank swore he was five foot six, but nobody on the team believed him. Weeb also insisted he had been a quarterback (only John believed that), a middle infielder, and a basketball *forward* at Miami University, just across the state line from his boyhood home of Richmond, Indiana. Like almost everyone who ever went to school there, Weeb resented the clarifier "Miami of Ohio." Under the alias Shorty Thomas, Weeb played semipro baseball all through college. Already married by then, he needed the cash.

A former aide to Paul Brown, Ewbank wasn't nearly as quick on the trigger. Brown once fired a terrific player, the mountainous tackle Doug Atkins, for belching during a team meeting. Bert Rechichar wasn't Paul's type, either. But Ewbank never cashiered anybody, even Rechichar, until he was positive he had a superior replacement. "He started to get rid of Forty-four a bunch of times," said Buzz Nutter, the center. "One morning at training camp, I ran into Weeb in the hallway. I said, 'You look like hell, Weeb.' He said, 'I didn't sleep so good. I kept dreaming Rechichar was back.' When we went out to practice, I swear to you, there he was, sitting on the hillside. The trade had fallen through. Bert had failed his physical or something. He was back."

Rechichar was famous for staying up all night, but only once did he do it in Unitas's company. "We roomed together in Los Angeles just one day near the end of the fifty-six season," Rechichar said, "so he could teach me the middle guard position. Somebody was injured—it might have been Pellington, I don't know—and even though I weighed only about two fifteen, I was usually the guy who filled in for everybody. All through the night, John drew up different formations, telling me where I was supposed to drop back to, and so forth. The Rams' quarterback was a kid named Rudy Bukich. 'Always watch the quarterback's eyes,' John said. 'Nine times out of ten, he'll telegraph the play.' I never did get to see the film of that game, but I had a pretty damn good day there."

One of the times the Colts started to unload Forty-four, he had a chance to try on a Cardinals uniform and actually played in an exhibition game *against* Unitas. "It's a lot different watching him warm up before a game," Bert said, "when you're standing on the other sideline. He'd just sling that ball out, kind of flick that wrist. He'd throw his right hand straight out, like he's really putting a damn curve on that ball or making it sink or something. Did you ever watch him do that? During the game, John winked at me once because he knew that I knew what the 'live' color was when he checked off. He didn't seem to mind that I knew exactly what was coming. I could hear Weeb on the bench yelling to the rookies, 'Don't turn your back on Rechichar, he'll take a whack at you!' I hit this one poor kid so hard, his damn eyeballs read '*Tilt*.' The next thing you knew, I was a Colt again."

The way Rechichar looked at it, John's instructions in Los Angeles represented no more than a fair exchange for a bit of tutoring Bert had provided free of charge to a Colt quarterback named Fred Enke in 1953. "We were getting murdered by the Eagles in Philly," Rechichar said, "when Shula and I decided we'd had enough of it and put ourselves in on offense. 'Pay attention, Peas,' I told Enke, 'here's where Forty-four's going to be wide open.' We drew the damn plays up on the damn ground in the damn dirt. Enke threw me three passes in all, for a hundred and fifty-one yards. Shula was my decoy, you understand." You could look it up. Rechichar indeed had three receptions that Sunday (November 15, 1953), the longest one covering sixty-six yards, for a total of 151 yards and two touchdowns. The decoy, Don Shula, caught a solitary pass for six yards.

Obviously, pro football wasn't quite the science then that it has become. John's original pro center, Madison "Buzz" Nutter, can speak to this, too. "To tell you the truth, I never played with Johnny Unitas," he said. "Johnny Unitas played with me—and he had cold hands, too." A mechanic's son, Nutter grew up in Huntington, West Virginia, and just like John's, his edges were smudged with coal dust. In what would be a scandal today, Nutter practiced with the Marshall College football team for a full six weeks during his senior year of high school, and then went to VPI instead. Though Buzz weighed scarcely two hundred pounds, he stood six foot four and was drafted by the Washington Redskins in the twelfth round. George Preston Marshall owned the team then. Curly Lambeau was the head coach. Titans walked the earth.

To get to the Redskins' training camp at Occidental College in Los Angeles, Nutter naturally took the train. Nothing he ever did in the NFL, and he did quite a lot, stayed with him like that ride. The thrill and wonder of the whole country flying by the window helped take Buzz's mind off Les Bingaman, who played for Detroit. All middle guards were persons of interest to rookie centers, but Bingaman was a special concern. "I heard he weighed four hundred pounds," Nutter said. "The Lions coach, Buddy Parker, swore it was closer to four twenty-five." As a matter of fact, these were gross exaggerations. Though Bingaman did have a head like a nineteen-inch television set, housed in a customized silver helmet that may once have been a brewery vat, he was eventually weighed by the Ypsilanti Farm Bureau and found to be a mere 349.

"As it turned out," Nutter said, "I needn't have worried. I didn't make the team. Alex Webster and I were the last two players cut. Alex went off to Montreal to play for the Alouettes." (A fierce ball carrier from North Carolina State, Webster would run into Nutter again, in New York.) "Marshall himself told me, 'You can come back in a year. In fact, we'll sign you up for next season right now.' He whipped out a contract he just happened to have on him. 'Mr. Marshall,' I said, 'I'm going to play somewhere next year, but it ain't gonna be here.' So, Unitas was dumped by Pittsburgh. I was dumped by Washington. Donovan, Pellington, and Rechichar were all dumped by Cleveland. It seemed most of us were dumped by somebody. In the only pep talk Weeb ever gave that made any sense, he went around the room pointing out all the different teams that didn't want us." This was in Yankee Stadium.

The Colt players who were present in 1954 all tell the story of the day Weeb asked the team to help him execute *his* final cuts. "That was in the Pikesville Armory, our last practice before the season started," Jim Mutscheller said. "I was one of the ones voted on. Six players were asked to leave the room. Four would be kept, two would be axed." ("Can you imagine Paul Brown or Buddy Parker," Nutter said, "calling for a vote on who goes and who stays? Weeb was a pisser.") Rechichar threw out the first name— "That son-of-a-bitch ain't going to help us any"—and Weeb went, "There's one." Somebody nominated Mutscheller, but Marchetti intervened. "Naw, he's my backup," Gino said, and Jim was saved. Indeed, when a hot appendix sidelined Marchetti for all of one game, Mutscheller went in for Gino, and the six-foot, 190-pound defensive end was born.

The day Mutscheller left Notre Dame, he wasn't certain that he wanted to play professional football. In fact, he was pretty sure he didn't. Both of his knees were complaining, loudly. "I signed a contract with the New York Yanks," he said. "Cecil Isbell signed me. I figured, Okay, I'll sign. What difference does it make? I'm not going to play." He went straight into the Marine Corps, entering officers' candidate school at Quantico, Virginia. The classic fifties book and movie *From Here to Eternity* was about an army boxer who didn't want to box. Though Jim's experience was less cinematic (no knife fights with Ernest Borgnine), the same kind of majors and colonels were involved, applying a similar pressure. "You will play football for the marines," they told him, and ultimately he did. "Every day I got up at five in the morning to go out in the field and learn all the stuff a platoon leader had to know. Then, at three in the afternoon, a few of us would be airlifted by helicopter to football practice. They'd feed us a quick meal and bus us back just in time for bed. I did that every day."

The air force had the best service team at the time. It was so good that a congressional investigation was under way. But the marines weren't bad either. Bud Carson, who later coached in the NFL, was one of Mutscheller's teammates. When the entire division was shipped to Korea, a few riflemen paused in Japan for maneuvers and football practice. Jim's orders were simple: "You people will beat the air force; do it." And they did. "Two days after the Rice Bowl," Jim said, "boom, we're in Korea." Their leading ball carrier, a Mississippi halfback named Gene Stewart, was killed there. But somewhere on the DMZ, Mutscheller finally conceded the point to himself. He was a football player.

●

Though Ewbank could be decisive at important junctures (witness the Kerkorian matter), his tendency to become flustered and tongue-tied under pressure combined with his cartoon build and fondness for pregame oratory to make him a figure of fun among the players. They all told Weeb stories. "Weeb was scared stiff of thunder and lightning," Artie Donovan said. "Sometimes, just by looking up at a dark sky, you might get him to call off practice. Years later, when I referred to Weeb as a 'little weasel bastard' in my book, he called me up. 'What's the idea of calling me a weasel bastard?' he asked. I said, 'Weeb, I meant it affectionately.'"

"Unitas comes over to the sideline," Don Shula said, "and asks Weeb, 'What have you got?' And Weeb says, 'Run something from all-left-flank-right'—he gives him a formation! John says, '*What?*'"

Alex Sandusky said, "We're in the huddle late in a game. It's third down, three or four yards to go. We need a TD. And here comes a play from the sideline; you know, a message from God. 'John, Weeb says to get the first down.' We're all trying not to laugh, but holy hell. Weeb sometimes would actually send in the play 'Tell John to score a touchdown.'" Unitas laughed along. "'Do you have anything for me?' I asked Weeb during a time-out. 'Nope.' 'Does anybody else?' He checked with his assistants. 'Nope.' 'Nope.' 'Nope.' 'Honestly,' I said, 'I don't know why I even come over here.'" But the truth was, Unitas understood Ewbank. There were plays to get first downs and there were plays to get touchdowns. John knew what Weeb meant.

They started out laughing at the coach, but as the players grew closer, the laughter was spread around, even to John. "Always, at some point in the game," Sandusky said, "Unitas would come up to you and say, 'Do you need anything?. . . Should we run a draw play to get this guy off your ass?. . . How can I help?. . . What can I do?' At the same time, one of us might say, 'Hey, John, a trap should work pretty soon.' He'd inventory it. Invariably he'd get around to using it. Of course, we did all of our talking before the huddle formed. Unless he asked you a question, only John spoke in the huddle." "That was his cathedral," Alex Hawkins said. "The last guy to break himself of talking in Unitas's huddle was Dick Szymanski. Sizzy finally shut up after John started kicking him in the ankle."

Sandusky recalled a game against the San Francisco 49ers in Baltimore, where John's first pass was intercepted by Abe Woodson and returned for a touchdown. "On our second possession," Sandusky said, "after a play or two, they intercepted another pass and kicked a field goal. Now we had the ball a third time and we were backed up against our own goal line. John asked, 'Anybody need any help?' and Szymanski said, '*You do!*' With that, everybody started laughing, John most of all. We had to call a time-out to get ahold of ourselves. But you know, we won that game."

The coach's Tuesday Rule (originally Paul Brown's Tuesday Rule) was the biggest joke of all—that and the superstitious fling Ewbank was having with Roman Catholicism. "According to Weeb's Tuesday Rule," Yvonne Ameche told NFL Films, "the players weren't supposed to have any intimacies after Tuesday. Everyone always said that was the worst-kept rule in the league." "All of these young men in their twenties," mused Raymond Berry. "Do you think a rule like that is going to have any effect? I don't think so. I think that was just a figment of Weeb's imagination." Though a non-Catholic, Ewbank spent the team's hottest stretches on his knees alongside his Catholic players at Sunday morning services. He did this for the same reason that, throughout streaks of good play, he would never consider pacing the sidelines in anything but his lucky brown suit. "We had about twenty-two Catholics," Donovan said. "No good Catholics, but Catholics." Donovan, Marchetti,

Ameche, Mutscheller, Sandusky, Szymanski, Shula, Taseff, Unitas, Joe Campanella . . . the Colts were so Catholic that, it was said, Nutter converted just to be a good teammate. "On Fridays in training camp," Buzz recalled, "Weeb would get up at the meal and say, 'Oh, I talked to Monsignor What's-His-Name, and I got all of you guys a special dispensation so that you can eat meat.' Bullshit! Weeb never talked to a monsignor in his whole goddamned life!"

In a *Sports Illustrated* profile of Big Daddy Lipscomb, Bill Nack relayed a story from assistant coach Charlie Winner that revealed both Lipscomb's sense of mischief and his religious affiliation: "Winner remembers the day Lipscomb was bent over a table about to have his prostate checked by a team doctor, when he looked around and saw that the doctor was slipping a rubber sheath on his finger. He asked the doctor what that thing was. 'A prophylactic,' said the doc. 'Take that thing off,' the player deadpanned. 'I'm a Catholic.'"

Winner was Weeb's son-in-law. Charlie had been a heady quarterback for Ewbank at Washington University in Saint Louis, but most of the Colt players thought of Winner as a son-in-law. (Only Unitas knew he was a teacher.) Sandusky said, "We're all at church in Detroit, eight o'clock Mass, and Weeb and Charlie are sitting together in the front pew. Seated on the other side of Weeb is the ventriloquist Jerry Mahoney. Do you remember him? Wait a minute, Jerry Mahoney was the puppet, wasn't he? [The ventriloquist was Paul Winchell.] Anyway, whatever his name was, he's sitting right next to Weeb. In the middle of Mass, Donovan yells out in that Bronx voice of his that bounces off the walls of the church, 'Hey, look everybody, it's Jerry Mahoney!' And George Shaw, another non-Catholic by the way, says, 'Yeah, and he's got his dummies with him.' The whole team broke up into hysterics."

All of these young men in their twenties were serious about the game of football. "Between Bill Pellington and Don Joyce and Tom Finnin," Nutter said, "if an arm was sticking out of a pileup, it didn't matter what color the jersey was, somebody was going to run over there and jump on it with both feet. In a Blue-White game—an intrasquad game!—I heard Pellington shout, 'Goddamn you, Sandusky, if you hold me one more time, I'm going to kill you!' The next thing you knew, Alex was standing there with his teeth in his hands." Sandusky gave Nutter a look of abject disgust and said calmly, "That son-of-a-bitch knocked my front teeth out." In an intrasquad game.

Sandusky worked for Westinghouse in the off-season. They all worked for somebody. John sold paint for the Farboil Paint Company (mostly to industries; a former employer, Bethlehem Steel, was his best customer). Sandusky said, "I worked *during* the season, too. We might be playing a game in Chicago on Sunday, but by seven o'clock Monday morning I'd be back on the production floor at Westinghouse. Around eleven, I'd leave to go to practice. Then, a lot of the time, I'd come back." Mutscheller was an insurance salesman. "The office was downtown," Jim said. "Going to and from work, I'd stroll the sidewalks of the city, just talking Colts football with the fans." Marchetti worked in iron, "in a hard hat," he said, "at Sparrow's Point. I'd climb up onto building beams—not w-a-a-ay up, if I could help it. Some guys would walk across the beams. I'd bump along on my butt, what we called 'assholing' it."

Rechichar had the best side gig of all. "Forty-four was the king," Nutter said. "For a while there, because he kicked that long field goal, Bert *was* the Baltimore Colts. The day he did it—I'm not certain of this, but I think even before he left the stadium—the McCarthy–Hicks Company hired him to sell liquor. Bert's assignment was to go around to every bar in Baltimore every damn night and get as drunk as he could with everybody in town. He was a wild man, crazy. Bert had a big Lincoln Continental, and Buddy Young was his chauffeur. 'Peas, get the car,' he'd say after practice. He called Buddy 'Peas.'" After lighting up a cigar only slightly smaller than a pool cue, off Bert would go to get loaded with Peas in the service of McCarthy–Hicks. Nobody knew for sure whether Rechichar was a bookmaker and numbers runner, or just a friend of bookmakers and numbers runners. That's what worried Weeb. Hawkins said, "Bert carried every cent he had, sometimes as much as eight or ten thousand dollars, in his pockets. Forty-four never had a checking account. He wrote all of his phone numbers on the lamp shade by his bed. Bert was different."

The time was different. The players lived next door to the fans, literally. There wasn't a financial gulf, a cultural gulf, or any other kind of gulf, between them. Except for a dozen Sundays a year, the Colts were occupied in the usual and normal pursuits of happiness. "I remember when Alan and I bought our first row house," Yvonne Ameche said. "We paid eight thousand dollars for it. John Unitas came over and laid our kitchen floor. Everyone pitched in, painted and helped us get that little row house ready." In Unitas's first off-season, a Colts basketball team was formed. Of course, he was the playmaker. "He could pass a basketball, too," said Mutscheller, who was among the best shooters. In his teens back in Beaver Falls, Bucky once performed in a charity game against the Harlem Globetrotters. Marchetti, Pellington, and Sandusky comprised what could fairly be called a physical front court. Nobody remembers any of their feet ever actually leaving the floor. They played against the Eagles in the preliminary to Wilt Chamberlain's fabled hundred-point game in Hershey, Pennsylvania. "We were amazed by the size of him," Marchetti said, "but we missed the hundredth point. We were in the bar long before then."

"Over just sixty days," Mutscheller said, "the Baltimore Colts basketball team played forty games against high school alumni associations and other groups and clubs from, say, the Eastern Shore or Delaware." What did the players get for it? "Probably ten bucks." Twice they faced the Eagles in prelims before NBA games in Philadelphia's Convention Hall. On those occasions, they were guaranteed $300. All of thirty bucks a man. But it helped tighten their connections to each other and to Baltimore. In an annual visit to every locker room in the league, the Philadelphia-based commissioner of the NFL, DeBenneville "Bert" Bell, emphasized the virtue of community. "He told us," Jim said, "that if you're going to play professional football in a town, you have to live in that town, really live there. 'Otherwise,' he said, 'don't play.' A lot of us took that to heart." Bell always signed off by reminding the players, "If you have any problems, boys, whatever they may be, call me collect—night or day—at Mohawk four, four-four-hundred."

"Let's face it," Nutter said, "the world was different then." By the way, was the story true? Did Buzz really convert to be a good teammate? He smiled softly. "My wife, Carol, was a Catholic," he said. "On her deathbed she asked me to become one, too. A couple of months before she passed away, I was baptized. That was seven years ago next week. No. Tomorrow."

So it *was* true. Buzz *did* convert to be a good teammate.

—◆—

Lenny Moore came from the railroad town of Reading, Pennsylvania, where a "slack" bag with a black hole in the bottom could be found on Lenny's porch, too. His boyhood idol was Glenn Davis of West Point, a halfback. "When I was a kid," Moore said, "I went to the movies every Saturday. It cost a dime. But I barely watched the feature, man, because I'd be waiting for the *Movietone News* to come around again, for the sports report and those little reels featuring Doc Blanchard and Glenn Davis of the Army team. 'Mr. Inside and Mr. Outside.' Davis was Mr. Outside. Really, *I* was Mr. Inside. I'd sit in that theater . . . all . . . day . . . long. Then I'd get my football and go down to a little vacant lot near home and imitate all of the great moves I'd seen, pretending I was Glenn Davis."

As Penn State seldom threw the ball, Moore wasn't certain he could catch it in the pros. But Lenny knew he could run. He wasn't just fast. "I was slippery fast," he said. Because Nittany Lions coach Rip Engle distrusted low-cut cleats and Moore felt hamstrung in high-tops, Lenny took to winding adhesive tape around his ankles and over his low shoes. Besides giving him support, this highlighted his moves and put his cuts in italics. It also prompted the nickname Spats. Every memory of Moore, like every one of Secretariat, starts with a flash of white feet. Lenny was a high-stepper and a glider anyway, who could sail through the smallest openings just by rocking sideways. But in Lipscomb's view, Spats was a wholly inadequate sobriquet. Searching for something more modern and kinetic, Big Daddy picked up a newspaper in 1957 and found it. The day after the Soviet Union launched the world's first satellite, Lenny was rechristened Sputnik, which Unitas shortened to Sput.

"He'd say, 'Come on, Sput, stick your head up in there. That was your man.' I'd say, 'Sorry, John. Won't happen again.' Weeb wanted L.G. and I—all of the backs, really—to learn the wide receiver position, too, just in case. 'If a receiver goes down,' he said, 'I don't want to be left shorthanded.' This was what led to me becoming a flanker and Mutscheller to becoming a tight end, and to the whole game changing." Lenny was catching the ball well enough, especially on the slant passes. So, he was surprised and a little annoyed when Berry pulled him aside one afternoon to say, "We're not getting everything we can from you." "I thought, What the hell is he talking about? 'You're going to have to get more involved in the offense,' Raymond said. 'Hey,' I told him, 'John's the one calling the plays.' 'That's not what I mean. John's not going to throw to you if he doesn't have confidence in you, and he can't have confidence in you if you haven't worked with him. Lenny, John won't ask you to stay after practice. You've got to do it yourself. He has to know that after three and two-tenths seconds, *this* is where you're going to be. You've got to time it up with him. It's like music. The same beat has to be playing in all of our heads.' From then on, I stayed out after practice. Not like Raymond. Nobody did it like Raymond. But enough to win John's confidence. 'Sput, you've got to come off that break just a half a beat quicker,' he'd say. 'Okay, John, I'll try.'"

Unitas might ask, "What do you have?" and Moore might reply, "I can do the slant-takeoff-sideline. That's there. I'll see what else we got going later on." "Okay."

"John wouldn't necessarily call it right away," Lenny said. "He'd file it in the back of his head. Raymond would come in and say, 'I can do a Z-out pattern. I can do a Q.' Most of the time, John would go right to what Raymond suggested. But sooner or later he'd turn to me and ask, 'Do you think we can do that thing now?' 'Yeah, it's still there, John, provided I'm allowed to flank out wide.' Sometimes he'd get on a roll, and just start reeling off my whole list. The angle-ins, the angle-outs, the angle-out-in, the angle-out-loop. As soon as I'd start to make my plant, I knew the ball was already in the air. I'd turn around and, wham, it would be on top of me. Three and two-tenths seconds."

Moore never stopped being astonished by how much of the field John could see, even under the worst duress. "There were thirteen seconds left in Wrigley," Lenny said. "The Bears were leading us by three, and we were about forty yards away. It had been a brutal game, typical Bears game. Alex Sandusky had to reach down into the mud to pack off John's bloody nose. His upper lip was shredded, too. He was a mess. The trainer, Eddie Block, had put Band-Aids all over his face, but they weren't staying on. We get in the huddle and John says, as casual as anything, 'Sput, you know sixty-six?' 'Yeah, an angle-in, at twelve yards, out of, like, the sixty-two series.' 'Right. I want the line to give me the sixty-two blocking protection, but I want you to give me the sixty-six takeoff with a good look to the inside, like you're poised for a quick hitter. I'll make a real big pump. You make a real good head turn. Plant hard, then break to the outside and take off.' Sure enough, the fake drew the defensive back inside. J.U. laid it right out. Six points. Man, I damn near ran the football straight into the brick wall. I mean, with everything that was spinning around him at that moment, how in hell could he think of a play that we don't ever run? He had told me not just what to run but how to run it. That should have been coming from me to him. He had been watching my man all game long, and waiting. He knew exactly what my man was going to do when it mattered. He saw him clearer than I did. I can't tell you how many games came down to a play like that." Moore's "man," by the way, was J. C. Caroline, the interceptor of John's first pass as a pro.

One of the most memorable touchdowns Lenny ever scored was on a last-minute catch against Dick "Night Train" Lane in Baltimore that only seemed to beat Detroit. By order of Ewbank, the Colts normally avoided Lane, which somewhat insulted John but was more than all right with Lenny. "Train would beat your head in," Moore said. "All he really seemed to care about was that lick. Either that or the clothesline. His wingspan was unbelievable. You couldn't fool Train with little bitty footwork and then break out or break in, because of that wingspan. His recovery was just too tremendous. Getting him to turn even slightly was difficult, and forget about anything beyond fifteen yards. That would be way out of John's and my time frame. I was a little afraid of Train, to be honest with you. If you went anywhere near him, he was going to deliver a blow, and he made sure you knew it was coming. Whether you caught the ball or you didn't, you were definitely going to get the hell knocked out of you."

Typically, Berry prepared schematics on defensive backs. In the locker room before that Lions game, Raymond spread out a large sheet in front of Moore that looked like the plat of a house. "He told me, 'I've been watching the films, Lenny, and Night Train never lines up twice the same way. That's what's confusing the receivers, but don't worry about it. The sideline is here. When you come off the line of scrimmage, try to even yourself up as much as you possibly can, so that you're not leaning either left or right, and then run straight at him. He's got to point his feet one way or the other. When he does, you should be able to blow by him going the opposite way. And if you're quick enough, that elbow he throws will just miss you.'" It just did. Lenny laid out in the end zone like a swimmer leaving the starting block, catching the back half of the football as Night Train caught the back half of him. Nobody who saw it could quite believe it, especially Lane. "Did the motherfucker catch that ball?" he asked the official, Tom Kelleher. "I don't know if the motherfucker did," Kelleher said, "but number twenty-four did. Touchdown!"

Tumbling out of the stands to press against the sidelines and prepare to celebrate the latest Unitas comeback, Baltimoreans had a closer than usual view of a good Detroit kickoff return and a last-second pass that won the game for the Lions. The quarterback who turned the tables that day was a Michigan State product they would come to know much better, Earl Morrall.

•

In the 1950s, a National Football League that was 70–80 percent black could not even be imagined. Black players, even black coaches, had dotted the league in its pioneer days. But from 1934 through 1945, by "gentlemen's agreement," blacks were excluded entirely. For the full length of the fifties, and two years after that, the Redskins maintained the ban, prompting *Washington Post* columnist Shirley Povich to observe tartly that the team's true colors were "burgundy, gold, and caucasian." Proving he was a double threat, owner George Preston Marshall responded, "When Povich was circumcised, they threw away the wrong piece." With a half dozen blacks on their thirty-three-man roster, the Colts of the late-fifties qualified as progressive. "The white Colts lived in Towson, Baltimore County," Moore said. "The black Colts lived in the inner city, downtown. We all went a little wild downtown. I did. I lost my first marriage to downtown." Of course, any man walking around with a black face in any era knows a great deal about racism, but Moore knew less than Lipscomb, Sherman Plunkett, or Buddy Young. Growing up, Lenny had the benefit of two loving parents. Unlike Lipscomb, Moore did not carry crime scene photographs in his back pocket, of a murdered mother knifed on the street.

"Big Daddy and I were in a cab when we first came to Balti-more," Lenny said. "At that time, the team worked out at the

Pikesville Armory. We didn't have a car. So we cabbed together to practice, after which we'd head down to Pennsylvania Avenue, to the places where we were welcome, and get our dinner down there. You know, Big Daddy was a very funny guy most of the time. He had a great sense of humor. Daddy could really get you laughing. But all of a sudden, sitting next to me in the back of the taxi, the big man [six foot six, 288 pounds] started to cry. Pretty soon he was crying like I don't know what. 'Hey man, what's wrong?' 'Ah, the Daddy don't feel so good.' 'Are you hurt? Do you want to go to the doctor?' 'The Daddy ain't right, man.' 'What is it?' I asked. 'It's just life,' he said. That wasn't the last time he cried in front of me. Little by little, I got to know Daddy's background and to understand what he meant by 'It's just life.' He meant, 'It's just being a black man. It's just being afraid.'"

Moore later wrote a letter to Red Smith of the *New York Herald Tribune* and asked the legendary sportswriter what he knew about black football players in the earliest days of the league. "Red wrote back that they were looked on as 'curiosities.' That's the exact word he used. It rang in my head." Smith pointed Moore to Dr. Edwin Bancroft Henderson of Howard and Harvard Universities, a onetime basketball star for a fabled Washington YMCA team, the 12th Streeters. In 1939, Henderson wrote a book titled *The Negro in Sports*. Lenny read and reread it. He said, "I also contacted Fritz Pollard, the first black in pro football"—also the first black *quarterback* in pro football and the first black *head coach* in the NFL, with the Akron Pros in 1921. "I wanted to hear from their own lips exactly how it was. Pollard told me about an all-star team he put together to play George Halas's Decatur Staleys in Chicago. Paul Robeson was on it. The final score was nothing–nothing. Listening to Fritz, it all came alive for me. Talking about Halas, he said, 'That no-good something-something-something.' Man, I was laughing." Through the Chock Full o' Nuts coffee company, Lenny reached Jackie Robinson. "He gave me all of his numbers. 'Call me,' he said, 'anytime.'" Robinson's first piece of advice stunned Moore and broke his heart. "He told me, 'Don't worry about the people who hate you to your face. Be more careful of certain folks who you may think are in your corner but, behind your back, are talking against you.' Who could that be? I thought. 'Buddy Young,' Jackie said. Oh, man."

Abruptly, Claude "Buddy" Young retired from the Colts and from football just before the real games started in 1956. Truth be told, most of the old stars whose "retirements" had been timed this way were fired. But if he wanted it, Young could have had a tenth season of pro ball, which would have been an amazement for a five-foot-four, 170-pound runner. Buddy was the son of a Midwestern railroad man whose name was not George but who was called George because, for the convenience of white travelers, all of the black porters went by George. Buddy's father worked his way up to a tuxedoed waiter's position on the Portland Rose—the run between Illinois and Oregon—and Buddy sometimes rode along in the club car drinking free Coca-Colas.

From his high school days in Chicago, Young was known for an incredible and uncompromising pride. When the coach of Englewood High said he was too pint-sized to play football, Buddy transferred to Phillips High and scored four touchdowns against Englewood. As a freshman at the University of Illinois, on his first play from scrimmage, Young ran sixty-four yards for a touchdown against Iowa. On his second play, he scooted thirty yards to score again. Before the season ended, he had registered two runs over ninety yards, another over seventy, and thirteen touchdowns, to equal Red Grange's 1924 record. Bill Stern, the radio fabulist, called Buddy "the fastest thing in cleats." He was also the fastest in spikes. Grantland Rice wrote, "Buddy Young couples grid talent with an ability to flit one hundred yards on a cinder path." He was the national collegiate champion of both the 100- and the 220-yard dashes, and he tied the world records for the 45 and 60. On top of that, he was the Amateur Athletic Union's 100-meter champion. Track people called him the Bronze Bullet.

Although everybody knew Moore was there to replace Young, Buddy was uncommonly generous to Lenny. "At Hershey and in the other exhibition games," Lenny said, "I'd be waiting under a kick and he'd be gently talking me through it. He taught me a lot of things, everything that he could. At first, I didn't believe Jackie when he said Buddy was badmouthing me."

Only those who knew Young well weren't surprised when he just stood up one day and quit. He became a leader in Baltimore's black community, eventually a minority liaison with the league. "There were functions where the black Colts went," Moore said, "you know, in our parts of town. But I was never invited. I'd read about them later in Sam Lacy's column in the *Afro-American*. The community started looking at me like, 'Who does he think he is?' I tried my damnedest to figure it out. Finally, Lacy and others told me it was Buddy who didn't want me there. The only thing I can think of is that I reminded him of what he no longer was. Or maybe he felt I was trying to make the people of Baltimore forget him. But nobody who ever saw Buddy Young could ever forget him. Of all the slights, that's the one that really hurt."

Some of the slights were indeed slight. "Sure, watermelon humor in the locker room, minstrel jokes, kidding on the square, you know," Lenny said, "no big deal, man. There were Colts I couldn't care less about and there were Colts I loved: Raymond Berry, [linebacker] Don Shinnick, Alan Ameche, Andy Nelson . . . You know, Nelson is a Memphis guy. Speaks with a drawl. Killer tackler at defensive back. Cut you in half, man. But there are some guys you can just look in their eyes and tell they're all right. That's Andy Nelson. Of course, we all knew that Marchetti had stood up for Ollie Matson at the University of San Francisco. Gino is the stand-up guy of all stand-up guys. And everyone will tell you, he was the heart and soul of the Baltimore Colts."

Where did Unitas stand? "I wanted to know John," Moore said after a moment's thought. "I wanted to have a relationship with him. I wanted to know that guy who came out of his home every morning, wherever he was going, whatever he was doing. That's the guy I wanted to meet. I never met that guy. I would have loved to have known him personally. I mean, we respected each other to the highest. I think we did. I know *I* did. But that didn't move itself into the area where I wanted it to go. Nelson and he were buddies; they figured to be—I mean, as much as anyone could be buddies with John. So, that said something good right there. And I certainly don't have anything bad to say about him. I liked Johnny U. But I wanted to love him, and he wouldn't let me. In later years, when we'd see each other, the greeting would always be very, very warm. 'Hey, J.' 'Hi, Sput.' Sometimes we'd hug. But we never talked."

"Maybe that was as far as he could go," the sportswriter said. "Maybe he didn't know the words."

"Maybe so. I hope so. I wanted so much to get to a place where we could love each other."

At the end of John and Lenny's rookie season, Moore went without him to the Pro Bowl in Los Angeles. John would make the next ten in a row, and under its co-MVP system (a lineman and a back), Unitas would be named the game's top back three times. On Saturday morning, as Lenny was stuck in the lobby traffic of the headquarters hotel, the Pro Bowl committee emerged from a conference room and Moore saw a face he recognized. As if Night Train Lane were chasing him, Lenny ran an angle-in, an angle-out, an angle-out-in, and an angle-out-loop, to break into the clear. He sprinted up to the man and introduced himself. "You're the reason I'm here," Lenny told him, and then he told him why. It was "Mr. Outside," Glenn Davis, the star of the *Movietone News*.

SIX

1957

"When it matters, I'll be on your side."

Coming to the Top

By 1957, the bonus pick lottery was down to two teams: the Green Bay Packers and the Chicago Cardinals. The Packers were in luck and chose quarterback Paul Hornung of Notre Dame. Jim Brown of Syracuse went sixth to the Cleveland Browns. Selecting two slots later, the Colts drafted All-America offensive tackle and linebacker Jim Parker of Ohio State. Weeb Ewbank insisted on Parker. Weeb knew Columbus; he had one or two acolytes hidden in the weeds there. General manager Don Kellett had argued for Baylor runner/receiver Del Shofner in the first round, and because Kellett was thinking of UCLA linebacker Don Shinnick in the second, he asked Weeb, "Are you figuring Parker for linebacker?" (That's how Parker's college coach had advertised him.) "Parker will be the left tackle," Weeb said flatly, "replacing Ken Jackson." Kellett was dumbfounded. When was the last time Ohio State coach Woody ("three yards and a cloud of dust") Hayes produced a pass blocker? But Don figured it was Weeb's call, if not his funeral. The coach didn't say that Parker would become the best tackle in the NFL, later the best guard, the first full-time offensive lineman in the Pro Football Hall of Fame, and the most honored pass blocker in history. But Weeb seemed to know it, all of it. "I made Jim a project for Johnny Bridgers," he told the sportswriter years later. "Bridgers was a line coach from somewhere in Alabama. He had a kind of dry, Southern sense of humor. Quite naturally, he enlisted the help of Gino."

By the third week of training camp, Parker was the best run blocker any of them had ever seen. As good as Alex Sandusky, Art Spinney, and George Preas all were, none of them weighed even 240 pounds. Parker was half again if not twice as quick, and getting on to 275. During and after practice every afternoon, Bridgers and Parker worked on pass-blocking fundamentals. Finally, examination day arrived. Bridgers laid out a pattern of tackling dummies to hem Parker and Marchetti in on one side of the line and the other. It was a little like Frank Camp's old hamburger drill. In effect, Jim and Gino were going up against each other in a corridor, or a phone booth. Bridgers asked John to call out a signal and backpedal seven steps. Though excused for the day, none of the other players went to the locker room. The whole team lingered to form a circle around this unusual scene.

On the first rush, Parker tried to block Gino too high, and Marchetti (six foot five, 240 pounds) went right between Jim's legs to John. "You've got to get much lower," Bridgers told Parker. So, Jim crouched down, closing his wickets this time, not taking any chances. Pressing his palms on Parker's dipped back, Gino leapfrogged over him to Unitas. "Try to relax, Jim," Bridgers said. "Take a deep breath. Find your balance." On the third play, Parker half stood up and half listed over, looking as lost as a man on a ledge. Like a thunderclap, Marchetti grabbed two fistfuls of Parker's jersey and tossed him aside. "Now what do I do?" Jim asked the coach from the ground. "Just applaud," Bridgers said. Of course, everyone laughed. In many of the accounts—and all of the old Colts tell some version of this story—Artie Donovan is the one who says "Applaud," or, "If I was you, Jim, I'd just applaud." It *could* have been Donovan. He was there. They all were. Parker was humiliated.

"The last exhibition game was against the Saint Louis Cardinals," Jim said. "I believe it was the Saint Louis Cardinals. [Close. They were the Chicago Cardinals still, but the game was in Saint Louis.] It was an away game, I'm sure of that, and then we came home to Baltimore to open the season against Detroit. I'm positive it was Detroit. Late in the exhibition game, my man got to Unitas a couple of times in the same series, and John said, 'If you can't block him, I'll take your ass out.' 'What did you say?' 'I'll take your ass out.' 'Well,' I said, 'that won't be necessary. I'll take my own ass out and save you the trouble.' So, I went and sat on the bench. Weeb was running up and down the sideline. 'Where's Parker? Where's Parker?' I was sitting there scrunched up like this, hiding under a jacket with a hood over my head. 'He's over here!' somebody yelled. 'Get your ass back in there!' Weeb screamed. I said, 'I can't. Unitas took me out.' 'Unitas doesn't have any say-so! I'm the fuckin' boss!' 'Well, you better tell *him* that,' I said, 'because I'll put my foot in his crooked ass real quick if he ever speaks to me like that again!' 'Get in there!' So, I went back on the field and I walked straight up to John and said, 'If you ever talk to me like that again, I'm going to break both of your skinny-ass legs.' All he said was, 'Do your job, Parker. You and I'll talk later.'"

That was a Saturday. They didn't have their talk until Monday, six days before the opener. "We went into a little boiler room at Memorial Stadium," Parker said, "away from everybody else. I was waiting for him to say something first, and do you know what it was? He said, 'What kind of guy is Woody Hayes?' 'Good guy,' I said. 'Tough guy?' 'Oh, man.' 'Did he ever embarrass you?' 'Every fuckin' day,' I said. 'What was the most embarrassing thing he ever said to you or did to you?' I told Unitas exactly what it was. It was the last time we were together, as a matter of fact. Woody, Ann, their son Steve, and I were at dinner in a restaurant. Woody went to the bathroom, and while he was gone, I ordered a beer. I had graduated. I was a grown man now. I was a married man. 'Goddamn it!' he said when he came back to the table. 'You don't drink in front of me!' Everybody in the place was looking at us. He picked up the beer and poured it out. 'All right, Coach. I'm sorry. I made a mistake. I won't do it again.' Unitas asked why I took that from him, and I said we'd been through a whole lot together. John said, 'You and I will be going through a whole lot together. I'll make you a deal. I'll take a few hits from your man if you'll take a few hits from me. I promise you, when it really matters, I'll be on your side.' 'I'll be on yours,' I told him. We never had no trouble after that. He called me the Perfessor. I called him Johnny U."

●

They won the home opener against Detroit, 34–14. John threw four touchdown passes, but the postgame statistic that jumped off the page was on the defensive side of the ledger: the Lions had been held to twenty-three yards rushing. "Probably in every sport, but definitely in football," Raymond Berry said, "it starts with defense. From the very beginning in Baltimore, we never had just an average defense. Donovan was like an anchor in the line. He was important. But the key to the defense, the key to everything, was Marchetti. Gino was equal to two or three people coming after the quarterback." Donovan said, "The offensive players may not want to hear this, but I think they drew their strength from Gino just as much as we did. By nineteen fifty-seven, Unitas had taken complete charge of the offense, but if you want to know the God's honest truth, the offense still had a ways to go to catch up to us."

After the Bears were beaten in Baltimore and the Packers were crushed in Milwaukee, the franchise that had never posted a winning record was off to a 3-and-0 start. "Parker was on that Big Butt team, too," Buzz Nutter said, "that went into the game for extra points and field goals. He'd be right there between Donovan and Sherman Plunkett. One time after a kick, Jim came racing off the field as fast as he could run. It was funny as hell. Now, I couldn't wait to see the films on Tuesday. Sure enough, Parker cold-cocked somebody and took off for the bench. He was catching on to the pro game real quick." The sight of Parker out ahead of a running play was something that almost had to be seen live, and at least once was invisible on film. "He wouldn't just hit the linebacker," Nutter said, "he'd knock the son-of-a-bitch right under the dirt." Jim Mutscheller said, "The most amazing piece of film I ever saw was of Parker blocking Joe Schmidt, Detroit's middle linebacker. Schmidt was a hell of a player. It was a trap play up the middle, where the weak-side tackle is coming for the middle linebacker, and the middle linebacker tries to step up into the hole first. Here's Parker picking up speed and there's Schmidt stepping in to make the play. And all of a sudden, Joe disappears. Completely disappears. Weeb ran it back, it must have been, a hundred times. 'Where the hell is Joe Schmidt?' he kept saying. It was like Jim had eaten him. Every now and then, Weeb would bring that movie back out and show it again. It was a classic."

"I'm going to tell you," Lenny Moore said, "I laid right there on Parker's hips. If you got Parker, you had a chance to get me. He was unbelievable and he just kept getting better. Gino helped Jim with his footwork. Big Daddy taught him how to balance himself. Daddy loved him; he called Jim 'Moobie-Foobie.'" Ewbank set Parker up with his own projector and a stack of films that focused on the Giant tackle Roosevelt Brown. "As far as Weeb was concerned," Moore said, "Brown was the best offensive lineman in the business. He had perfect balance, perfect position, perfect technique." "Ten o'clock at night, we'd go down into the basement, just Rosey and me," Parker said, "and I'd come back up around two. I had a big old notebook in which I wrote down every little thing he did. Roosevelt Brown was a Morgan State guy, you know. He didn't play for Earl Banks, I don't think. He was there before Earl Banks. Rosey never knew it at the time, but he broke me into professional football. He was such a beautiful, beautiful football player."

Lipscomb often dropped by Parker's house in the morning, sometimes as early as four-thirty. Famously, Big Daddy suffered

from insomnia. "We'd work out together in Druid Hill Park," Jim
said. "He was in great shape for a guy who drank like a fish. He
loved Seagram's VO. He'd drink two fifths of VO and he could still
outrun me. I never saw anything like it." Lipscomb was born in Alabama, but everything about him was from Detroit, where his
mother, Carrie, wasn't just murdered, she was slaughtered, at a
bus stop. "Eugene" was eleven at the time, already six foot four,
220 pounds. "I was a freak," he told Lenny Moore. Lipscomb
played a little ball at Miller High in Detroit but quit school a year
early to join the marines. Pete Rozelle, then the public relations director for the Los Angeles Rams, later the commissioner of the
NFL, saw Lance Corporal Lipscomb in a game at Camp Pendleton
and signed him to a $4,800 contract. After three spotty years, over
Labor Day weekend in 1956, the Rams let Big Daddy go for the
$100 waiver price. By virtue of its abysmal 1955 season, San Fran-
cisco had first call on him and exercised it by wire. But because of
the holiday, the telegram arrived at Bert Bell's office two days late.
Meanwhile, the team with the second-lowest standing, Baltimore,
had registered its own claim by telephone. After a small rhubarb,
Bell found for the Colts.

   "Printed on the roster, across from Lipscomb's name," recalled Baltimore broadcaster Chuck Thompson, "was the designa-
tion 'No College.' One of our very best play-by-play men, Joe
Croghan, misread that as an abbreviation for 'North College.' It
was an entirely innocent mistake on Joe's part. But some of the
meaner players, Bill Pellington for one, made a big joke out of that
and wouldn't let it go. Big Daddy, who was already the most insecure individual you'd ever want to meet, was devastated." Years
later, in a radio interview, Unitas told Pittsburgh newspapermen
Al Abrams and Pat Livingston, "John Steadman probably had the
best description for Big Daddy. He called him 'the playful but lone-
some giant.' Lipscomb wasn't as great a pass rusher as he was a
lateral mover. I don't know why, but for some reason he didn't care
about rushing the passer. A little like Donovan but a lot like [Don]

Joyce, he concentrated on holding his own ground. They weren't as good at getting rid of their blockers as Marchetti was—Gino flew right by his man—but you couldn't move Joyce, Donovan, or Big Daddy. And I'll tell you, Lipscomb could pursue a play better than any big man I ever saw. He looked like a building sliding down the line. And he was a sure tackler. When Big Daddy tackled you, you stayed tackled. In nineteen fifty-seven—was it fifty-seven?—he led our club in tackles, which is usually linebacker territory. That may be why Pellington made so much fun of him all the time; like, yanking his notebook away and showing everybody that the pages were all blank. I'm surprised those two didn't kill each other. Mostly I saw the sweet side of Big Daddy, the funny side, the way he was with kids. We had a forced landing one time at Friendship Airport in Baltimore. Big Daddy came bouncing down the steps of the airplane and shouted into the first TV camera he saw, 'Only way to travel!' He could make the whole team laugh. But I knew about the other side. Big Daddy told me once that he had been scared all his life. 'You wouldn't know it to look at me,' he said, 'but it's true.' "

Quoting Plunkett, a sometime roommate of Lipscomb's downtown, Parker said, "Daddy would push chairs and dressers up against the door at night, so no one could break in on them. He kept a gun under his pillow. Sherman had a big dog, too, and Daddy would tie its leash to the end of his bed. In a way, I could almost understand. I wouldn't want to meet the burglar, either, who had the nerve to break into a room where Sherman Plunkett [six foot four, 310 pounds] and Big Daddy Lipscomb [six foot six, 288 pounds] were sleeping. Not that Daddy slept too much."

Lipscomb and Parker were confederates in many late-night escapes from training camp at Westminster. "Daddy never snuck out himself," Parker said. "He'd stay awake in the dormitories all night long, pacing the floors. But he helped me get away almost every night. You won't believe this, but in eleven years, I think I only slept there about a week. I couldn't sleep in that bed. Every night at one o'clock, Big Daddy would go get my car from its hiding place behind the cafeteria, and I'd take off and drive forty minutes home to Baltimore. In all that time, there were only two slipups. Once, I got a flat tire and didn't have a jack. I waved a fellow down on Reisterstown Road at one-thirty in the morning, and when I told him who I was, he loaned me his jack. He said, 'I'm going to stay ten yards behind you and put this light on you. Don't come near my car.' He was scared to death. I would have been, too. The second incident didn't end so good. Weeb caught us red-handed heading for the door. 'What are you guys doing up?' he said. I told him Daddy had been sleepwalking and I was following him around to make sure he didn't fall down an elevator shaft. Weeb fined both of us, but me a little bit extra, for telling that terrible story."

(It wasn't all rollicking fun and sweet sadness with Moobie-Foobie. Shortly after Lenny Lyles joined the Colts in 1958, John's old Louisville teammate found himself at a party that included Mr. and Mrs. Lipscomb. One of the Mrs. Lipscombs, that is; there were two. "I watched him put a cigarette out on his wife's leg," Lyles said. "He was too big for me to go up and fight him. I froze. I just sat there, ashamed.")

●

When a team is 3–0 and leading its fourth game by twenty-four points in the third quarter, it sounds ridiculous to say that everything then turned around on one play. But at Detroit it did. To be sure, the game turned around on three Colt fumbles in the last five minutes. But the season turned around on just one of them. Moore, who had already caught two touchdown passes, one for seventy-two yards, fumbled a pitchout from John that seemed so certain to bounce harmlessly out of bounds that the Colts who were chasing it abruptly pulled up and just stood there, staring at the accident. In a slow-motion catastrophe, the football took a final hop on its nose and, defying several laws of physics, bounced first straight up in the air and then backward into play. The Lions' Yale Lary recovered. The '57 Colts never did. Their 27–3 lead dissolved into a 31–27 loss to a team they had held to twenty-three yards rushing on opening day (the one, incidentally, that would go on to win the NFL title).

"As great as he was, Lenny Moore had not reached a place in his career," Berry said, "where he was a disciplined athlete. He knew it. We all knew it. He fumbled later at a critical time in what amounted to the deciding game at Kezar Stadium in San Francisco. As I told Lenny, I'd been there myself. I had an experience with fumbling in college. 'Every time you handle the football,' I said, 'tuck it away. If you catch fifty balls at practice, tuck every one of them away. Carry a ball around with you wherever you go. Keep tucking it away.'" Berry once fumbled as a pro. In thirteen seasons, catching a record 631 passes for 9,275 yards and 68 touchdowns, Raymond lost the ball exactly one time. "All that being said," Berry continued, "no play or player was the reason we didn't win in nineteen fifty-seven. We had the best team, we really did. We could have won—*easily.* But we still lacked one thing: the *belief* that we could win. We just didn't realize we could."

Before their heads cleared, the Colts were three and three. "Weeb's job was on the line again," said Ordell Braase, the right defensive end. "He figured he had to win that seventh game. So, he got up in front of the team, just before we took the field in Washington, and said, 'We've lost to Pittsburgh, we've lost to Green Bay, teams we should never lose to, and we absolutely have to have this game today. Before I came up here, Gino said he wanted to address the team.' Gino was way in the back, where he always was, prowling like a nervous cat. I could see in his face that this 'address' was news to him. 'Okay,' Weeb said, 'I want everybody out but the players and the coaches. Equipment men, out. Medical men, out. Gino has something to say.' So Gino came striding to the front. I could see him thinking, What in the hell am I going to say? He looked around. There was a long silence. Finally he said, 'Does everybody know that the party after the game is at my house tonight?' Yeah, we knew. 'Does anybody need directions on how to get there?' No, we're fine. 'Well, then let's go out and win the game so we don't ruin the fuckin' party.' Sure enough, when I grabbed the *Sun* the next morning—I don't know whether it was Cameron Snyder or who it was—but there was the headline in bold type: 'Colts Spurred on by Inspirational Talk from Marchetti.'"

Throwing 108 passes, only one of them for an interception, Unitas strung four November and December victories, over the Redskins (that was the day John and Raymond pulled the wings off Don Shula), the Bears, the 49ers, and the Rams. Though the Colts wouldn't be mathematically eliminated until the final Sunday, their realistic chance came in the second-to-last game, a rematch against Y. A. Tittle, Hugh McElhenny, Leo Nomellini, and Joe Perry in San Francisco. Thanks to an eighty-nine-yard touchdown pass from Unitas to Moore, but no thanks to Lenny's fumble at the end of another great run, or to field goal attempts by Bert Rechichar (long) and Steve Myhra (short) that were both blocked by Nomellini, the Colts had a 13–10 lead at the two-minute warning. Approaching the end of their first winning season, they were actually in sight of the conference championship.

Yelberton Abraham Tittle was already balding and wore the unlikely number 63—unlikely for a quarterback—when he broke into professional football with the original Baltimore Colts in 1948. In Cameron Snyder's advance story of the big game in San Francisco, Snyder referred to the 49er quarterback as an "old acquaintance" who may be remembered. Starting the last drive at his own thirty-eight-yard line, Tittle tossed a stream of short passes to Perry and Billy Wilson that brought the 49ers into Colt territory. After Marchetti flung him back to his own forty-two, Y.A. hit McElhenny at about the thirty-yard line, and Hugh maneuvered his way to the fifteen. "He ain't called the King for nothin'," Unitas said afterward. In the process of overthrowing Perry in the end zone, Tittle was injured and had to leave the game with forty-six seconds left.

A young quarterback named John Brodie came on, and though his first pass was slapped down by Don Shinnick, the next was caught by McElhenny for a touchdown. If, as the Colts always swore, Hugh pushed off to get open, the officials didn't see it. Unitas had time for only two desperation flings. When the second was intercepted, the 49ers were the winners, 17–13.

"As the impact of losing soaked in during the off-season," Berry said, "we all suddenly realized something: we were there. We had reached the top." Buzz Nutter said, "If we had had a punter [no offense, Cotton Davidson] and some luck, we'd have won in fifty-seven." Marchetti said, "That team was probably as good as any we ever had. There were so many close games that turned around on just one play. Against Detroit, I can still see Lenny dropping the ball and Yale Lary falling on it. Then everything came down to a single pass in San Francisco, all or nothing. I'll tell you, we couldn't wait for nineteen fifty-eight. That was our rallying call to each other. We didn't just have an idea of what was coming. We knew it in our hearts."

Though Bobby Layne had quarterbacked the Lions to a third NFL title in six years, it was Unitas who was summoned to New York City to collect the Jim Thorpe Memorial Trophy signifying the best player in the league. In his first full season as a starter, John had completed 51.7 percent of his passes (172 of 301) for 2,550 yards and twenty-four touchdowns. "This is my second trip to New York," he told John Steadman on the train. "When Louisville played in the NIT basketball tournament three years ago, a few of us made the drive and went in together on the tiniest hotel room you've ever seen. I slept on the floor, and there was hardly enough room for that. One guy slept in the bathtub. We didn't have any money. So we just walked around the town and looked at the skyscrapers." Steadman laughed and said, "John, your days of strolling cities anonymously are numbered."

Both a decade and an era were winding down; the NFL was turning over again. Paul Brown and Otto Graham were through in

Cleveland; Buddy Parker and Layne had had their day in Detroit. George Wilson coached the Lions to that last championship, as Coach Parker moved over to Pittsburgh, soon to be joined by Bobby. Having broken a leg against Cleveland late in the '57 season, Layne was on crutches when backup quarterback Tobin Rote finished off the Browns in the title game. Weeb Ewbank and Johnny Unitas were up.

Though Layne and John had only a nodding acquaintance, Bobby must have figured the situation called for a handoff, and he wouldn't wait for the fifties to run out. "In the fifty-nine Pro Bowl," said Jimmy Orr, who represented the Steelers and the Eastern Conference in that all-star game, "it was Norm Van Brocklin and Layne for us against Unitas and somebody else [Tittle] for the Western Conference. [Franchise shifts had made a mockery of geography.] Van Brocklin got sick or something, so Layne had to go the whole way. Of course, that didn't keep Bobby from staying out all night Saturday." Layne was the Lancelot of the thirsty quarterbacks, too alive to observe a curfew and too tough to wear a face mask. Once, at the bottom of a pile of players, he recognized Marchetti and said in his raspy drawl, "Gino, get the boys together later. We're having a party at the Romney Plaza after the game." Among Layne's teammates, the mantra was always "When Bobby said block, you blocked; when Bobby said drink, you drank."

"He called Unitas at about three o'clock on the morning of the game," Orr said. "John's telling the story: 'Layne woke me up with a shout. *Unitas!* Yeah, Bobby. I recognized his voice. *I got something I want to tell you.* Shoot. *Pass when they think you're gonna run, and run when they think you're gonna pass.* And then he hung up.'"

◆

"In my dreams, I still play football," Jim Parker said. "I dream of 'thirty-four traps' and 'thirty-eight sweeps,' when it's the pulling guard's job to hit anything with the other color shirt on. In my dreams, I'm lined up across from all of my old opponents, like Henry Jordan of the Packers. Leo 'the Lion' Nomellini played for the San Francisco 49ers. His face was so ugly, I only dream of Nomellini from the neck down. Doug Atkins of the Chicago Bears. Now, he was tough. He was tall. He was a real competitor. Others, too. Alex Karras. A whole lot of them. I told Johnny U in the huddle, 'That fuckin' [So-and-So] just called me a nigger.' Unitas said, 'We can't have that. Let him through this time.' John hit him right in the forehead with a bullet pass. He fell like a fuckin' tree."

Parker was sitting in a wheelchair between his bed and the window in a semiprivate room of the Lorien Nursing Home in Columbia, Maryland. "Go see Parker," Lenny Moore had said, "and if he's not himself, go back the next day, and the next. Eventually, he'll be Jim." "For a while there, I was lost," said Parker, who was seventy. "I didn't know where I was at. They say I'm losing my mind, but I don't think so. I have to admit, though, that there are days when I look out this window and I can't remember whether it's Columbia, Maryland, or Columbus, Ohio." Without prompting, he repeated a few of his stories more than once. More than twice. The "I'll take your ass out" story he told six different times, including twice in a row, word for word. But they were good stories.

Thinking of Columbus wound him up again. "Remember when Woody hit that boy on the sidelines and lost his job? I saw it on the news and called him up. Ann said, 'He doesn't want to talk to anybody.' 'Tell him it's me. He'll *run* to the phone.' She said, 'Jim Parker's on the line.' I could hear Woody in the background saying, 'I don't care if it's the president of the United States on the line! I don't want to talk to any-goddamn-body!' Two days later, he called me back. 'I don't want to talk to you on the telephone,' he said. 'Come on down Friday and stay till Sunday. We'll talk about this.' He gave me a million reasons why he did it. He always thought he was right. 'But you shouldn't hit anybody else's child, Woody,' I said. 'The school asked you for an apology, and you wouldn't give it. So they ran your ass out of there.' 'Goddamn it,' he said, 'you don't say ass to me!' We looked at each other and started to laugh. We couldn't stop laughing. We hugged. I kissed him on the cheek."

Gazing out the window, Parker said, "Guess who came to visit me here three times? He sat right where you're sitting now. Roosevelt Brown. Did you know, I beat Rosey to the Hall of Fame by two years? That's a crying shame. Rosey should have gone in first. He was a hell of a ballplayer." (Parker went into the Hall in a three-man class that included Raymond Berry and the disappearing linebacker, Joe Schmidt. Rosey went in with Lenny Moore. At the end, Jim and Rosey graced the same offensive line, for the NFL's seventy-fifth-anniversary team. They were, of course, protecting Unitas.) A twenty-seventh-round draft choice, the 321st player taken in 1953, Brown has the highest draft number of all the saints in Canton, Ohio.

"I returned to Canton a few years ago," Parker said. "I hadn't been back, but they invited me to come back for an autograph signing. It was for two thousand dollars, but they put five hundred extra in the envelope for me. I told them they didn't have to do that, but they did. One guy in line gave me an old Ohio State Buckeyes photograph to sign. When I finished signing it, I looked up and said, 'I know you.' 'No you don't,' he said—'What's my name?' 'Let me ask you something first, smart-ass. Years and years ago, did you room with a big ugly boy, a big ugly black-ass boy?' 'Yep,' he said. 'And his name was Jim Parker, wasn't it?' 'Yep.' 'And your name is Don Clark, isn't it?' Lord, I remembered. He jumped right up on top of the table.

"I took all of my kids to Canton—I have twelve kids—in a parade of cars. No, wait a minute, there were only ten of them along, I think. On our way home, we stopped at a Howard Johnson's just a few miles down the turnpike. Taking a head count, I realized little Sheri was missing. She was about ten years old then. As quick as I could go, I made a U-turn on the pike and hurried back to Canton.

There she was sitting in the office, talking to the director. I was so happy to see her, I didn't even spank her. She said, 'I'm sorry, Daddy, I went to say good-bye to Rosey.' She meant his bust in the Hall of Fame. I got to thinking of that when he was sitting here, dozing in the chair. 'There's something wrong with Rosey,' I told Lenny Moore. 'He's sick.' I was right, too. He died in June, two months ago." Jim went back to looking out the window.

Did Unitas keep his promise always to be on Parker's side?

"Oh, yes. In everything. One time I remember specifically, in the sixties I think, I was sitting in the locker room, reading the newspaper, and saw that Jack Nicklaus was in town to play golf. 'I believe I'll drive up to Towson and see my old buddy,' I said. 'I haven't seen him in ages.' 'Who are you talking about?' [offensive tackle] Bob Vogel asked. 'I'm talking about Jack Nicklaus.' 'Bullshit!' somebody else said. 'You don't know Jack Nicklaus, you lying son-of-a-bitch!' Now, the wallets came out. 'How much money you got?' There were bills all over the floor. I couldn't cover it all. Johnny U stepped up and said, 'I'm covering whatever Jim can't. My money's on the Perfessor.'"

During Parker's playing days in Columbus, he often had the use of Woody's car. "Woody had two cars," Jim said, "a Buick with power brakes, automatic steering, and everything on it, and a raggedy-ass old Chevy with no windshield wipers or heat. Because it was my job to pick up recruits at the airport and train station and show them around campus and buy them a T-shirt and a cap, he always wanted me to take the good car. I felt bad, leaving him with the wreck. I said, 'If they don't want to ride in the Chevy, they can walk.' But he told me, 'No, take the Buick.' Jack Nicklaus's father was a druggist in town. Jack couldn't play golf then. He was just learning. He'd go out to the golf course every day and work on his two iron, his three iron, his four iron. I'd give him a lift sometimes. His father wanted to pay me, but I said, 'You don't have to pay me.' So he gave me all of the shaving stuff and underarm deodorant I could use. 'Take anything you want,' he said."

Two carloads of Colts headed to Towson to find out if Nicklaus knew Parker. "You needed a sticker to park at the golf tournament," Jim said, "unless your car was filled with Baltimore Colts.
Then you could park any damn where you wanted to. So, we went
out to the first hole . . . second hole . . . no, first hole, and there he
was, walking along. 'Hey Jackie,' I said from off to the side, 'it's
Jim Parker.' Nicklaus stopped and looked around, and then he ran
across the golf course and grabbed me. 'What are you doing here,
Jim?' 'You know I'm playing here now,' I said. We talked for just a
second, because he was in the middle of a tournament. 'It's really
great to see you,' he said, and then he went back to his ball. I
looked around at the boys. 'Money, money, money,' I said. They
about had a shit fit."

Leaning forward in his wheelchair, speaking in a low voice
that could break a heart, Parker said, "I'm pretty sure that happened."

It did. "I don't remember the rides in Woody's car or the
shaving stuff from my dad," Nicklaus told the sportswriter, "but I
remember Jim Parker. I even remember his number: seventy-
seven. That was probably an exhibition in Towson, rather than a
tournament. It might have been at Pine Ridge. But it happened, all
right. I'm sure of it."

On the way out, the sportswriter encountered a doctor in the
elevator, a young woman with long brown hair. After the door
closed, he turned to her and said, "That's the greatest offensive
lineman who ever lived." He probably would have said it even if no
one else had been on the elevator. "Jim? That's what he tells me,"
she replied with a musical laugh. They rode down two floors to the
lobby. "May I ask you something?" she said as they arrived.
"Sure." "Who's Gino Marchetti?"

SEVEN

1957

"To him, I never stopped being a kid."

Something Inside Gino

Gino was born in West Virginia, in a town that no longer exists, near Smithers and Gauley Bridge, just south of Charleston. His father and mother, Ernest and Maria, had been starving in Italy. But, deciding a coal-mining life wasn't much of a gain, they scraped together a second stake and moved on to Antioch, California. Next door to San Francisco, legalized poker games were under way. Setting up two or three tables in the back room of a saloon, Ernest was in business.

Unlike Maria, he had some English. She interacted mostly with her children and a few Italian-speaking families of ship chandlers and restaurateurs. Only Ernest officially became an American citizen. When he was sworn in, Maria also held up her right hand. As the new citizens sang "The Star-Spangled Banner," she tried to sing along. But Maria never filled out her papers. So, when the United States entered the war in Europe, she was the only one in the family who was (at first) assigned to an internment camp, and then, even more humiliating, drummed out of Antioch entirely. "She cried," Gino said. "Imagine this little Italian lady, five foot one, five foot two, who spoke only broken English, being told that she had to get out of town and stay out because she was a threat to our national security. Her oldest son was already in the army, and I was about to enlist. What the hell danger could she have been to anybody? Try to picture Antioch: four thousand people, one factory—paper products." All the same, they packed up and moved, just three or four miles outside the city limits. "But I could still go into town," Marchetti said, "my four brothers could, my sister could, my father could. Only my mother couldn't. She wasn't permitted to go to the store. She didn't blame anybody, though. She loved America. Like a lot of people who came from the old country, she and my father appreciated the U.S. probably more than you and I do. Whatever the law said, they were going to abide by it." She cried because of the shame and the inconvenience she felt she was bringing on the others.

Young Gino had less reverence for the law. "I wasn't real, real bad," he said, "but I was a little wild." Following "a certain difficulty" with one of his high school teachers, Gino preempted the possibility of expulsion by joining the army. "I figured I could either face the Germans or I could face my father. Plus," he said, "any senior who signed up for the service was automatically handed a diploma. I was seventeen." A few days after his next birthday, Marchetti landed in London. "We stayed there two or three weeks and then moved up." His division was the 273rd Unit of the Sixty-ninth Infantry, the first U.S. regiment that would make contact with the Russians. "Everybody always says I was in the Battle of the Bulge," Gino said, "but I arrived there right about the time it was getting over with. The war wasn't over, just the Battle of the Bulge." The cannonade has never stopped thundering in his ears. "It changed my whole life around," he said.

"We were on the Siegfried Line, the first time I was under fire. I'll never forget it. We had moved up the night before. It was cold. Me and my buddy, a guy named McKinney, who was from Pittsburgh, were protecting the north end of our company, manning a machine gun section. We heard these shells and we were kind of having fun at first. 'That one's ours,' we'd say. 'Here comes one of theirs.' You could tell by the *wsshhhhooooo*. Two guys came up, offering to relieve us, and we told them, 'Nah, we're okay.' Then, just a few minutes later, there came the damnedest whistle I ever heard in my life. *Pssssssooooooo*. God, I looked at McKinney, and he looked at me. We both dived down as deep as we could go. Shells were landing all around us. The closest one might have been ten yards. The funny part is, from the time I heard the whistle to the time the shell exploded—it couldn't have been more than a second or two—do you know what went through my head? Everything I ever did that hurt my mother. Once I made her so mad that, as I was walking out the door, she threw a coffee cup. It missed me and hit the refrigerator, putting a nick in it. Her brand new refrigerator. The only new thing she had. How proud she was of it. I swore that if I lived through this, I was going to go home and fix that damned refrigerator, and I was going to be a different kind of guy."

Home for a year and a half (having long since repaired the ding in the icebox), Gino took a job as a bartender. His hair was as long as a lion's and he roared around Antioch on a Harley-Davidson motorcycle that could drown out a panzer division. He wore "engineer boots" with quarter-inch plates on the heels that banged like a hammer on an anvil when he walked, and sometimes gave off sparklers. At six foot five *without* heels, Marchetti was an imposing sight. "I was cool," he said. Topping off his ensemble, of course, was the black leather jacket of legend and lore, eight full years before Marlon Brando. "Seventeen zippers," Gino said mock smugly.

How Marchetti got back to football was complete happenstance. "People say they have goals, but I never did. I just kept putting one [noisy] foot after another. A few of us felt like we wanted to play a little football, so we organized a semipro team called the Antioch Hornets. You know, we went around to local businessmen and got fifty bucks for uniforms. One day I was driving with some of the guys along Tenth Street—we had a game later in San Rafael—and, passing by my block, I don't know why, I just happened to glance down the lane and saw a red Chevrolet parked in front of our house. 'Let's go see who it is,' I said. Two coaches from Modesto Junior College were there, trying to talk my brother Angelo and a pal of ours named Nick into going out for football at Modesto, about forty-five minutes away. I pulled up a chair and listened quietly. Angelo was a hell of a football player, a hell of an athlete, and Nick was a good receiver. Both agreed to a tryout. Meanwhile, not a word was spoken to me until, as they were walking away, one of the coaches turned and said, 'Say, you look like you're big enough to play, too. Why don't you tag along?' Those were his exact words. So I tagged along. Angelo and Nick were there three weeks and quit. I stuck it out. They were first-string right away. I had to work for it. A year later, Brad Lynn, the freshman coach at the University of San Francisco, came into the joint where I was tending bar and asked me if I'd like to play football at USF. I dropped my cigarette on the floor, stepped on it, and said, 'Sure.'"

The University of San Francisco Dons were coached by a former Notre Dame All-America, Joe Kuharich, who was born in South Bend and grew up folded into the archangel wing of Knute Rockne. As a small boy, Kuharich regularly crawled under a broken plank into old Cartier Field until, one Saturday, he wriggled through the fence to find Rockne standing with crossed arms on the other side. From then on, Joe met the coach every game day by the main gate at precisely 11 A.M. and triumphantly marched in with Rock. Blooming into a manic lineman, Kuharich put in three high-strung seasons with the Irish and played on the 1938 College All-Star team that beat Sammy Baugh and the Washington Redskins, 28–16. Though drafted by the Steelers, Kuharich set out instead to be a coach, like Rockne. In fact, he would become a coach associated mainly with losing. At Notre Dame and in Chicago (the Cardinals) and Washington—and especially in Philadelphia—"Joe Must Go" banners fluttered from every upper deck. He was the original Lombardi, the one who didn't win. In 1954, when Vince was just settling in as an assistant with the New York Giants, Kuharich stood up at his first "Welcome Home, Redskins" luncheon as the new Washington head coach, and told the assembly, "Winning isn't everything; it's the only thing." Nobody except Morrie Siegel of the *Evening Star* ever associated that line with Joe. At the 1958 Senior Bowl in Mobile, Alabama, Kuharich coached the North team against Paul Brown and the South. "In our first meeting," said Alex Hawkins of the University of South Carolina, "Brown told us, 'Everybody on the winning team gets five hundred dollars. Everybody on the losing team gets three hundred dollars. You can start spending the five hundred now, because I could beat Joe Kuharich with a team of trained monkeys.'"

Once, however, in San Francisco, Joe presided over something sublime.

●

In 1951—when Frank Gifford and Dick Kazmaier were running wild at the University of Southern California and Princeton; when the West Point Cadets were decimated by a cheating scandal that implicated coach Earl "Red" Blaik's own son; and when Johnny Unitas was a freshman at the University of Louisville—Marchetti, Ollie Matson, Burl Toler, Ed Brown, Merrill Peacock, Red Stephens, Ralph Thomas, and Mike Mergen were all seniors at the University of San Francisco. Bob St. Clair and Scooter Scudero were juniors. To begin to know what kind of a team they had (single platoon), consider that all ten of these men went on to the NFL. Three of them—Marchetti, Matson, and St. Clair—made it to the Pro Football Hall of Fame (four, if you want to count Pete Rozelle, USF '50, the boy publicist destined to become the boy commissioner). No other college team has ever sent three players to Canton. Marchetti and Matson were inducted on the same afternoon, a great day for both justice and poetry. In the team photograph of the final edition of the San Francisco Dons (unbeaten, untied, and, most famously, "uninvited"), Marchetti is seated in the second row, smack in the middle of thirty-eight smiling players. Matson is on his immediate right, Toler on his immediate left. Ollie's and Burl's are the only black faces in the picture.

It was the final edition because the Jesuits were out of money and the January payoff that they had counted on to save the program never materialized. Muttering something about the weakness of the Dons' schedule, the Sun Bowl officials in El Paso invited Lilliputian quarterback Eddie LeBaron and his College of the Pacific team (record: six victories and four defeats), which lost at home late in the season, 47–14, to the Dons. After a Pacific fumble at the one-yard line, both caused and recovered by Marchetti, Matson bulled into the end zone for a 20–0 halftime lead. At the start of the fourth quarter, "All the Way" Ollie ran sixty-eight yards for another score, and Pacific Memorial Stadium began emptying to a chorus of the San Francisco theme song: "Goodnight, Irene. Goodnight, Irene. I'll see you in my dreams." In just nine games, Matson led the nation's rushers with 1,566 yards and twenty-one touchdowns, only four yards and one TD short of the all-time collegiate marks. Per game, Marchetti, St. Clair, and the rest of the defense allowed an average of 51.6 yards on the ground.

"The Orange Bowl, the Cotton Bowl, the Gator Bowl—they all wanted us," Kuharich later told Jack Kiser of the *Philadelphia Daily News*, "on one condition. That Ollie and Burl be left home." Speaking to Dave Anderson of the *New York Times*, Matson recalled, "Joe went around and asked the guys if they'd go to a bowl game without Burl or me, but Gino Marchetti said, 'No, we ain't gonna go without Burl and Ollie.'" The implication has always been that Gino said no for everyone. Reportedly, Kuharich put the proposition to the entire team in a Pasadena locker room after the final 20–2 victory over Loyola. "We can play in a big Southern bowl game," he told them, "or stay home. It's up to you." And Marchetti replied, "Fuck the big Southern bowl games."

"It wasn't anywhere near that dramatic," Gino told the sportswriter. "It was just one word. 'No.' That was it. And it didn't come from me alone. It came from every one of us. Through the years, people have asked me, 'Were there guys in one corner saying we should go, and guys in another corner saying we shouldn't?' No. God be my judge, I swear to you—you can take my wife, my children, my home, everything I have—I never heard one player say, 'We should go' or, later, 'We could have gone.' Not one, ever. Hell, we didn't *want* to go without them. We all felt exactly the same. On every successful team, you always hear, 'We were close.' Well, we *were* close. We're still close."

In his opinion, of all the greats on that team, the greatest was Toler. "Burl was not only our best player," Marchetti said, "he was also our nicest guy. Four of us went to the College All-Star game to play the Los Angeles Rams [and barely lose to them, 10–7]. Burl was a linebacker. In scrimmages leading up to the game, he was outhitting all of those big-name linebackers. But at the time, blacks weren't usually thought of as linebackers. So, figuring that they ought to start Burl somewhere, the coaches put him in at defensive right end. About the second or third play of the game, the Rams ran a sweep, and Burl went under, taking everybody down with him. He tore up a knee. The Browns had already drafted him after his junior year, but he was finished." Not exactly finished. Toler returned to school to acquire a teaching credential and later a master's degree. He ended up an inner-city high school principal. Not exactly "ended up." In 1965, he became the first black referee in the NFL, or any other professional sport. During twenty-six seasons, Toler officiated in over five hundred games, including playoffs and championships. He was the head linesman in Super Bowl I.

How could the unpolished Marchetti have been so enlightened in 1951? "Maybe because of my mother," he said. "I remember one time, after a game, I walked into a bar with Toler, our quarterback Ed Brown, and the left halfback Scooter Scudero. Because of Burl, they wouldn't serve us. I felt so goddamned bad. Right there, I told Burl how my mother had been kicked out of town. For a minute I considered roughing up that bar a little. But

Brown said he'd just as soon not have Father Giambastiani know that we went in there in the first place." Brown, incidentally, would represent the Chicago Bears in two Pro Bowls and win a comeback award in Pittsburgh. But most interesting of all, on the last day of his pro career, under a very unusual circumstance, Brown would quarterback the only game he played for the Baltimore Colts, a game they had to win and did.

"You have to know," Alex Hawkins said, "not just what regular life was like in the fifties, but what *football* life was like in the fifties. I grew up in South Charleston, West Virginia, where the public schools weren't integrated, of course. We didn't have very many blacks in the state of West Virginia to begin with. In Saint Albans, I saw a few black families living under a bridge, and in Charleston there were a few more black families that also lived under a bridge—I'm talking about, like, four or five. I swear to God, I grew up thinking that black people were people who lived under bridges. The worst team we played in high school was Charleston Catholic, who had one black player. A teammate of mine, Ronnie Steele, based on nothing, said, 'Let's one or two of us hit that nigger every time,' and we did that. Ronnie was the linebacker on one side, I was the linebacker on the other. Here are two boys with no knowledge at all of black people beating up on this unsuspecting kid just because he's different and it's the fifties." Proving God has a sense of humor, Steele wound up getting a football scholarship to West Virginia State College, where he was the only white player on an all-black team.

"We're talking about nineteen fifty-one," Marchetti said. "But in nineteen fifty-nine or sixty, when Alan Ameche opened his restaurant in Baltimore, Jim Parker came in to eat and Alan had to go to him and say, 'Jim, I can't serve you.' Jim, being the kind of guy he is, said, 'I understand. Don't feel bad.' And he drove off. Do you think that wasn't tough?" "I wasn't going to cry about it," Parker said, "but I believe Alan did. I don't think he ever stopped feeling bad about that. Ask Lenny [Moore]. After he retired, Alan went around to every one of us and said he was sorry." "It was at the Valley Country Club," Moore said, "Donovan's place, some kind of Colt reunion. The Horse and I were just standing there. I could tell he wanted to say something, but it took him a while to get it out. 'Lenny,' he said finally, 'the black players on our team were treated very unfairly in the glory years. I want you to know it bothered me then, more than anything in my career, and it has bothered me ever since. And what bothers me the most is, I never did a thing about it.' He said, 'I don't know what it was that held us together, that allowed us to do all those great things on the field.'"

"I don't know either," Moore told the sportswriter, "but I think it was something inside Gino Marchetti."

●

Drafted in the second round by the New York Yanks, Marchetti, like Artie Donovan and Buddy Young, made his way to Baltimore through Dallas. "When Carl Taseff and I were in the service," Don Shula said, "we went to see Dunny and Marchetti play for the Texans in the Cotton Bowl. Jimmy Phelan was the coach. Their crowds were so small that Phelan said, 'Never mind the pregame introductions, we'll just go up into the stands and introduce ourselves individually.'" Four games into the season, the owner gave up the ghost, and the rest of the year was an endless road trip. "We were horseshit," Donovan said. "Phelan was the only coach I ever knew who hated practice more than the players did. He would say, 'Aw, the hell with it, let's go to the racetrack.'"

They could hardly hear the quarterback's signals for the sound of all the records breaking around them. "'There's a new record!' 'That's a new record!' 'Hugh McElhenny has just set another all-time record!'—it was depressing," Marchetti said. "After the team declared bankruptcy, and we went out on the road for eight straight weeks, the older guys started quitting. They didn't try anymore. We were playing a game in Los Angeles, and Dan Edwards, a good tight end from Georgia, got hurt. 'Who can play tight end?' Phelan yelled out on the sideline. 'We need somebody in there right now!' I ran into the huddle and, just teasing, said, 'Hit me for six!' Probably that was the first Hail Mary pass in the history of the game. I caught it, believe it or not, and scored my first touchdown. I remember feeling great until I heard the announcer say, 'L.A. forty-two, Dallas six.' Shit."

Marchetti came to value the experience of losing big at least once in your life. In Ameche's first season of football, his high school team lost every game, scoring only one touchdown along the way. But in his last year, the team was undefeated. "From anyone else," Marchetti said, "I'd figure that for a slight exaggeration. But not from Alan. One of his proudest accomplishments was that every football team he ever played for, including Wisconsin, was dead last at one point and went all the way to the championship. That's the satisfaction we were beginning to feel in nineteen fifty-seven. You're at the absolute bottom, getting the shit kicked out of you, and slowly you start to rise, and you keep climbing, a little higher, a little higher, until you've come so far that you're almost there. In a way, that's my earliest memory of Unitas. I've thought about this a lot. I honestly don't have one specific first memory of John. Hell, I hardly remember him being in training camp in fifty-six. I don't think *anybody* really noticed him until Shaw got hurt. I can't say exactly when it was, but one of the first conscious thoughts I had about John, studying him from across the room, was, Here's a guy who's done some bad losing and has had enough of it."

To his brother, Leonard, Unitas spoke incessantly, uncharacteristically (incredibly uncharacteristically) about Marchetti. "I know everything there is to know about Gino Marchetti," Leonard said with a laugh. "Any day that Gino happened to find himself in a white shirt, he went out on the town that night, because he didn't want to waste it. You can guess who usually went with him. John didn't look up to too many people, but he looked up to Gino." John told Ed Fitzgerald of *Sport* magazine, "I think Gino was the only football player I ever came across who loved to play even more than I did, who loved the camaraderie even more than the game. Gino always called me 'kid.' To Gino, I never stopped being a kid."

"What really impressed me about Unitas," Marchetti said, "was that, when he threw an interception, he didn't wave his arms all around or anything like that. You know, like quarterbacks do to signal to the crowd that it wasn't really their fault? John didn't give a damn about things like that. He'd quietly go up to the intended receiver and say, 'You weren't where you were supposed to be on that play. If you don't start studying and knowing your plays, I'll never throw to you again.' Then, when the newspaper guys came into the locker room, John would say, 'My fault. Overthrew him.' His throwing hand is blown up to twice its size, and Cameron Snyder or somebody puts it to him, 'John, I guess you didn't have a very good day because of your hand.' And he says, 'My hand didn't bother me at all. I just had a terrible day.' If John wanted to, he could have held up that hand and said, 'Take a picture of this, why don't you?' What do you think would have been the lead story? But that wasn't him. He took the bad with the good. No rah-rah stuff. No bullshit. Dead honest with himself. Dead honest with you, if he trusted you. The better I got to know Unitas's character, the more excited I became about our chances."

Raymond Berry said, "We had a variety of personalities and backgrounds, but we were all alike in one way. We were serious about football. Both Unitas and Marchetti had a certain blend of humility and self-confidence that was unusual, to say the least. When you can find one guy like that, you have a leader. When there are two of them—and one's on offense and the other's on defense—you have a football team." Often, after practice, half of the team could be found in a bar called Andy's, washing out their wounds with National Bohemian beer, hobnobbing with the fans. "Some fifty-five or sixty thousand people came to our games on Sundays," Marchetti said. "I honestly believe, at some time or other,

I shook hands with every one of them." On the brink of success, Marchetti and Unitas were suddenly summoned to the team offices on North Charles Street. "We wondered what the hell it was," Gino said. "We knew it wasn't a raise. [By 1957, Unitas's salary had risen to $12,500.] John and I walked in, and there stood [owner Carroll] Rosenbloom, [general manager Don] Kellett, Weeb, and two special agents from the FBI. I thought, Holy shit. Evidently, one of the customers in Andy's, Nick Somebody—Padello or Padrino, something like that—was a big-time gambler, a mafioso. While we'd be sipping our beers, he'd be asking us about somebody's sprained ankle. 'Oh, he's fine,' we'd say. 'He's going to play.' We were stupid. The newspapers often referred to Unitas as a 'riverboat gambler,' but John didn't even know you could bet on football games. The next time we were in Andy's, Nick came in and sat down next to John and me. 'Hey, Nick,' I said, 'we just got called in on the carpet because of you.' 'Say no more,' he said and walked out the door. We never saw him again."

After the breakthrough season of 1957, Marchetti and Unitas went together to the Pro Bowl in Los Angeles, John's first. "Who else was with us?" Gino tried to remember. (Donovan, Ameche, Mutscheller, and Rechichar. In fact, Forty-four was named the back of the game, Pittsburgh defensive tackle Ernie Stautner the lineman.) "John and I roomed together out there," Marchetti said. "One morning, the phone rang, and I picked it up. It was somebody from Regis Philbin's office. They were hoping Unitas would come on a television talk show, but John didn't want to do it. So they asked me if I was available. 'Nah,' I said. 'Thanks anyway.' 'Well, if you can think of somebody for us, we'll pay him three hundred and sixty-five dollars.' I said, 'I think I can find the time.' John was laughing. I took a taxi; it cost me twenty-five bucks. When I got to the studio, I had to sign a union card. Then, after the show was over, I spent another twenty-five cabbing back to the hotel. Up in the room, I looked at the check. It was for three dollars and one cent. The rest went to union dues. So, I spent fifty dollars to earn three dollars and a penny. I didn't think John was ever going to stop laughing."

Ernest Marchetti never saw his son play football for either Modesto Junior College or the University of San Francisco. Although Kezar Stadium was only a thirty-five-mile drive from Antioch, he avoided even the thought of football, filled with dread that Gino might be injured. Until almost the last day of Marchetti's pro career, his father never saw him play for the Colts either—not in person, anyway, just once on TV, when pretty much the whole country was watching (and Ernest's fear was realized; Gino broke an ankle). "Whenever we played the 49ers," Marchetti said, "I would shoot by home. As I was heading back, my father always told me the same thing: 'Whatever you do, Gino, stay out of their way.'" Before a day of appreciation for Marchetti in Baltimore, the Colts sounded him out on a gift. What about a new car? No, thanks. "What I wanted more than anything," Gino said, "was for my father to see me play football." At first Ernest resisted the Colts' invitation. But his daughter, Frieda, informed him, "If you don't go see Gino play, I'll never set foot in this house again." Of course, Ernest couldn't risk that. So, the team flew him to Baltimore, hid him out for a day at the home of former linebacker Joe Campanella, and then sprung him on Gino in *This Is Your Life* fashion. That Sunday, the Colts beat the Redskins, 45–17. "He sat with the players on the bench," Gino said. As the clock was winding down, Ernest turned to his son and quietly said he was proud of him. "'I still think your brother Angelo was a better football player,' he told me and everybody else later. And he *was*. Dad was just telling the truth." In a rolling tide of Colts, Ernest was swept off the field, down a dark dugout, up a windy ramp, into a brilliantly lit locker room. Gino said, "I went into the bathroom for a minute, and somebody told me, 'You better go see to your dad.' He was standing like this in the corner." Jumping up from his chair, Marchetti went to a corner of his living room and leaned into it like a penitent child. "Do you know why? Because players were walking around naked, and he was embarrassed. He could never bear even to look at my sister in shorts. God, I loved that man."

The Colts opened the 1958 season against Detroit in Baltimore. It was during a Lions game, years earlier, that Marchetti had his other Siegfried Line moment and made a second resolution to change. After tackling Doak Walker, Gino gratuitously rammed the heel of his hand into Walker's nose. "I was waiting for him to hit me back, but he didn't. He just looked up at me with disgust. Worse than disgust, disappointment. Did you ever know Doak Walker? You should have. The pro game was a tough game, but it didn't have to be ugly."

It could be beautiful.

EIGHT

1958

"There was a big game before *'the Big Game.'"*

4 TDs

he season that would change football, sports, television, and the rhythms of American life began inauspiciously for the Colts. In six exhibition games, they beat only one team, the New York Giants—twice. Within eight days, as the preseason wound down, they took the Giants first in Baltimore, 27–21, and then in Louisville, 42–21. Two years earlier, seeing a number 19 lope disjointedly onto Braves Field in Boston, New York quarterback Charlie Conerly turned to halfback Frank Gifford and said, "Look at that goofy son-of-a-bitch." But John was growing on them.

Come the real games of 1958, two Unitas-to-Berry touchdown passes beat the defending champion Lions, 28–15, and by an average margin of twenty-four points, Baltimore quickly added five more victories. The Bears were overrun, 51–38 (and later shut out, 17–0—George Halas's first zero in 149 games). The Packers were shut out worse, 56–0. *Probably in every sport, but definitely in football, it starts with defense.* However, in that sixth game, the forgotten man, George Shaw, had to play most of the second half at quarterback. "Early in the third quarter," Artie Donovan said, "John was already down when this jerk, [Johnny] Symank, a defensive back for Green Bay, landed on Unitas's chest with both knees, breaking three ribs and—though nobody knew it at the time—puncturing a lung. Rat bastard." At Baltimore's Union Memorial Hospital, practically next door to the stadium, the first X-rays showed only the cracks. John returned to the bench in the fourth quarter, not to play, just to watch, in the rain. "When I left, we were leading, twenty-something to nothing," he said. "When I got back, it was forty-something, and Bert Rechichar was playing right defensive end. I had to laugh, even though it hurt like hell to laugh." By this time, Forty-four was mostly just a placekicker, and only the longer kicks at that. "But in moments of confusion," Unitas said, "he liked to put himself in somewhere or other for at least a play or two, until Weeb would catch sight of him and yell, 'Get that son-of-a-bitch Rechichar off the field!'"

The team physician was Dr. Edmond McDonnell. The head and assistant trainers were Eddie Block and Bill Neill. Six months of the year, Block worked for Neill at an orthopedic hospital, the Kernan Hospital, that specialized in treating crippled children. The other six months, Neill worked for Block on the Colts' sidelines. "John went home that Sunday night," Neill said, "with his brother, Leonard, who happened to be visiting from Pittsburgh. Whatever they were watching on television, it must have been hilarious ['It was *The Steve Allen Show,*' Leonard said. 'You know, Don Knotts, Tom Poston, and Louie Nye, man-in-the-street interviews?'] because, despite himself, John got to laughing so hard that for a moment he couldn't breathe. He barely made it upstairs to bed." The next morning, Dr. McDonnell called up with alarm bells sounding in his voice. "I told John, 'Get your ass to the hospital right this minute.'" Unitas spent Monday afternoon blowing on a water pipe, trying to move the liquid from one beaker to another, to reinflate his left lung. But too much blood was choking it shut. They had to operate. He was still in the hospital, watching on TV, when the Colts took their perfect record to New York to play the Giants in

Yankee Stadium. A crowd of 71,164 gathered that Sunday. At least in part because of a newspaper strike, only 64,185 would return seven weeks later, to see the Colts and Giants play again. Though it was Shaw's first start since the 1956 knee injury, George played more than passably well, throwing for 238 yards and three touchdowns. But rookie Lenny Lyles dropped a ball in the end zone, and the Giants won, 24–21.

"We outgutted them," Conerly "wrote" in a newspaper column the following morning. That didn't sound like Charlie. The phrase may have come from Dave Eisenberg, his *Journal-American* ghostwriter. Inevitably, the insult reached Baltimore, and when it did, Conerly was given full credit. Weeb Ewbank took particular note. But as far as Weeb was concerned, the Colts' wives were to blame for the season's first defeat. In a weak moment, as a reward for the 6–0 start, he had invited them along to New York City, where he billeted the team at a midtown Sheraton amid the brightest lights of Manhattan. Though there was no hard evidence, the coach suspected that his Tuesday Rule had been flagrantly violated. On the return trip, three days after Christmas, the players would be spouseless, and their quarters would be the dimly lit Concourse Plaza Hotel in the Bronx.

The team's first loss devastated Shaw. On the train ride home, George sat alone, brooding, until the Philadelphia stop, when John Steadman moved up a few rows to join him. Staring out the window, the former star of the team told the man from the *News-Post,* "The last couple of years sitting on the bench haven't been easy. You watch the rest of the players wanting so much to win. You sit there and hope that if your chance does come, you'll be able to make a contribution. If my efforts could have helped us win today, I would have been happy. That's all I wanted—just to make a contribution to a victory."

Shaw lived with his young family near Memorial Stadium in a row house off Loch Raven Boulevard. When George got home Sunday night, his wife, Patti, handed him an envelope. "It came in a taxi," she said. Inside was a note written on hospital stationery, unsigned. "Great game," it read.

"After that," Donovan said, "they put some kind of a steel cast halfway around John's body, and of course that weasel bastard Weeb didn't inform the league. John was some kind of tough. That's how he led, really. Norm Van Brocklin had been an underwater demolitions guy in the navy. Bobby Layne was a merchant marine gunner. But without having gone to war, John was a tougher quarterback than either of them, and a better leader. Most of the players had been in the service. You were used to being told what to do, and you did it. But to do it well, you had to respect the guy who was giving the orders. We respected Unitas most of all for his toughness."

Also, he told a good joke. "When I first met him," Donovan said, "John was kind of a naïve guy. I'd be telling him stories about the old league, and naturally I might improve the truth just a little bit, and he'd be going, 'Honest to God? Really? Honest to God?' We told John our dirtiest jokes, and he liked dirty jokes. At first he was no good at telling them back, but he was always great at listening to them. Then, in front of just a few of us one day in the locker room—come to think of it, we might have been in a cab—I think it was a Jimmy's Cab—Christ, what a memory I've got!—John went through this whole comedy routine. It was really filthy, and really funny. He had us in stitches. You see, he figured out how to communicate with each of us individually, on our own terms. He didn't even have to communicate with the defensive players, but he did it anyway. He figured out how to communicate with Lenny Moore, he figured out how to communicate with Jim Parker, he figured out how to communicate with Weeb Ewbank. He learned everybody's language, and they were all different. Man, he was a quarterback."

Where did Unitas come up with a comedy routine? "On an airplane," his sister Shirley said. "He was sitting near Minnie Pearl; you know, the country comedienne? The lady with the price tag hanging off her bonnet, who goes, 'Howdy!' John asked her if

she had any salty material that he could use to warm up some football players, and she put together a string of jokes for him. John
told me she had their section of the plane rolling in the aisles."

According to Bill Neill, Donovan's "steel cast" was actually con-
structed of aluminum and foam rubber. To test it out, Unitas threw
himself on the ground a few times. It worked. "Just a customized
orthopedic brace," Neill said, "made from a plaster image of his left
side. It hooked to his shoulder pads and hip pads. Two weeks after
the injury, John dressed in Wrigley Field, but we knew he wasn't
going to play. [That was the 17–0 game.] Weeb had John throw
longer and longer passes throughout the pregame warm-ups, just
to drive George Halas crazy." But it was Shaw's time to make a contribution to a victory, on the very field where he had lost his job.
He was impeccable. The following Sunday, Unitas started against
the Rams and immediately threw a fifty-eight-yard touchdown pass
to Moore. That was the twenty-second game in a row for a Unitas
TD pass, tying Cecil Isbell's record. After Los Angeles was beaten,
34–7, the Colts were 8–1 and pretty much back to speed.

Lyles received no notes of encouragement from John. For
some reason, the quarterback never tried to learn *his* language.
When they greeted each other on the first day of training camp,
Unitas shook Lyles's hand and inquired about his mother back in
Louisville. But that was it. As the third number one draft choice in
a line with Moore and Parker, Lyles was expected to have a similar
impact. Though he failed to dislodge L. G. Dupre from the starting
backfield, Lyles had his moments. In the second game of the season, against the Bears, he returned a kickoff 103 yards. Two weeks
later, he brought back a Redskin kick 101 yards. Until then, two
hundred-plus returns had never been put together by any pro
player in any year. Lyles had done it in less than half of his first
season. But he would score only two other touchdowns in 1958,

one rushing and one receiving, and the rank and file reacted coolly toward him because John did.

"Nobody embraced me except my roommate, Johnny Sample," Lyles said. A fleet defensive back from Maryland State on the eastern shore, Sample was selected sight unseen, six rounds after Lyles, on Buddy Young's recommendation. Eventually Sample would start at right safety, but in 1958 he was used mostly on the special teams. "He was a strange guy," Lenny said, "but a good person at heart. He was good to me. Once, when we were shopping together in a downtown department store, I saw him stuff a suit of clothes into his bag. *'Don't do that,'* I whispered. But Johnny had to have that suit. I ran away and left him. I couldn't stay there. I don't know what it was with Johnny, but as I said, he was the only Colt who ever sent any warmth my way. None of them looked at me and said, 'This guy can really run. Let's teach him some things. Let's build up his confidence. Let's help him.' Pro football wasn't that type of a business. I kept thinking, Do they want me here? What kind of place is this? I glanced over at Unitas, who sat just a few lockers away, and thought, He crashed, too. He crashed the party. They had George Shaw. How did he manage to win these guys over? If I had to go through all this stuff, what in the world did he have to go through?"

Lyles would have been willing to return punts as well as kickoffs, but Carl Taseff was charged ("trusted" is a better word) with that responsibility. Though not half the athlete Lyles was, Taseff was twice the football player. (The players called Taseff "Gaucho"; he was even more bowlegged than Unitas.) "Gaucho could almost do everything," Donovan said. A starter at cornerback, Taseff spent most of the practices assaulting running backs who had the gall to go out for passes. "Taseff knocked the living fool out of me every single day," Lyles said. He wasn't the only one. "Donovan, who was, like, the original Colt, would keep chasing me even after I was out of bounds. Man, here he'd come. Six three, two hundred and eighty pounds. No matter how far out I went, he'd just keep coming. It was, like, until *I* got hit, the play wasn't really over. My goodness, I kept saying to myself. What kind of place is this? Where did these people come from? I really wanted to be a Colt. God, I really wanted that."

The following season, Lyles would be shipped off to San Francisco, where the coaching staff would move him over to the defensive side. Then, after a couple of years, Lenny was sent back to Baltimore, a much different player, a much different man. "I returned with zeal and passion," he said. "Mean as a dog. Didn't care about nobody. Right away, I had a fight with Bill Pellington at practice. I figured I might as well start at the top. 'Okay, you're tough, you're tough' he said, 'whoever you are.'" Then, on the other end of the spectrum, Lyles jammed Raymond Berry as he came off the line. "Leonard started cheap-shotting me," Berry said. "I don't know what he was going through there. Someone had put a burr up his butt, whatever it was. I went after him." Lyles said, "I hit Raymond, kicked him, climbed all over him. You know, Berry could look at your shoes and tell exactly where you were going. He could *read* a defensive back. He was a genius. 'Stop it,' I said; 'stop trying to trick me'—and I knocked him on his ass. Raymond jumped to his feet and started swinging, shouting, 'I'm tired of this!' Right there, I managed to do something no one else had ever done. I got Raymond Berry to come up punching. Gino Marchetti told me later, 'We had you all wrong, Lenny. I'm glad you're back with us.' Gary Glick [the old Pittsburgh bonus pick] was one of the starting corners then. Man, I thought, this guy can't beat me. How old is he? Forty? Charlie Taylor was eating him up one day in Washington, so I put myself in at right corner, and stayed there seven years. You know, I used to think the Colt veterans were scum. Building relationships with people you thought were scum does something for you. I still wondered about the backgrounds of some of them, but I came to sort of love them. And standing out there in the secondary, looking around at all the horseshoe helmets, I thought, Well, you're one of them finally, and I laughed."

—

Donovan's background was right out of a dime novel. His grandfather Mike Donovan was a fourteen-year-old Civil War soldier who marched to the sea with Sherman. Later he drove cattle with Wyatt Earp. On March 10, 1881, boxing under the name Professor Mike Donovan, he beat up George Rooke in New York's Terrace Garden to become the middleweight champion of the world. Abandoning the title for the more lucrative position of barnstorming against heavyweights (including John L. Sullivan in Boston), Donovan came out of "retirement" in 1888 to fight middleweight champion Jack Dempsey (the original Jack Dempsey, "the Nonpareil") to a draw. Mike eventually settled down as a boxing instructor at the New York Athletic Club, where one of his pupils was police commissioner Teddy Roosevelt.

Of Mike Donovan's fourteen children, the son most like him was Arthur Donovan Sr., who fought in the Mexican border war with Black Jack Pershing, in the French trenches of World War I, and on Okinawa in World War II. In a noncombat position with the navy, refereeing a boxing match sponsored by the USO, Arthur Sr. bumped into Arthur Jr. on Guam, where Artie was a marine loader of antiaircraft guns aimed at Japanese dive-bombers. "I guess you could say we were a fighting family," Artie said. "I was born at my grandmother's house in the Bronx, in the same bed where about a dozen of my first cousins were born. I weighed sixteen pounds and change. My poor mother couldn't walk for three weeks. Born big, I stayed that way."

In 1946, a grand jury declined to indict Arthur Sr., charged in the death of his best friend after punches were exchanged in a drunken argument on the street. "My dad was a mild-mannered guy," Artie said, "unless he got a couple of Manhattans in him.

Then it was Dr. Jekyll and Mr. Hyde. The curse of the Irish." The old man's celebrity may have kept him out of jail. "Everyone in New York knew who my father was," Artie said. "He refereed all of the big New York fights during the Depression, including three world championships one time in the same week. His first big fight that I remember [twenty-four days after Artie's eighth birthday] was Primo Carnera against Jack Sharkey in the Garden Bowl. They called Carnera the Ambling Alp, and everybody thought he was a big stiff. But he beat the shit out of Sharkey. My father was in with Carnera and Max Baer when Baer dropped Carnera about a hundred times and took the title away. In a light-heavyweight title fight, Dad pulled Baer off Max Schmeling before Baer killed him. Nobody remembers that one." With a black bow tie tucked under his collar and a handkerchief hanging out the back pocket of his gray flannel trousers, Dunny's father shared prize rings with Willie Pep, Barney Ross, Henry Armstrong, Fritzie Zivic, Jimmy Braddock—all of them.

"When Zivic took the welterweight title away from Armstrong, it was my dad who stopped the fight in the twelfth round. Schmeling's corner tried to throw in the towel during the second Joe Louis fight, but Dad flung it right back at them. It snagged on the ropes. You see, stopping a fight, or letting it go on—that was *his* job, not theirs." Arthur Donovan worked nineteen of Louis's title bouts, and some of the nontitle ones, too, many of the big shows and just about all of the "bums of the month." "The sportswriters used to refer to my dad as Joe's personal referee," Artie said, "but the funny thing is, they didn't even know each other."

In 1951, when Artie was long finished at Notre Dame and Boston College, working as a defensive tackle for the New York Yanks, he sat down with his father in a Bronx apartment and watched on television as the graying Louis was clubbed through the ropes by Rocky Marciano. "My father wasn't a man who showed his emotions," Artie said. "There weren't any tears, I don't think, even when my mother died. But watching Joe taking that beating, Dad started to cry. He had a lot of reason to cry in his life, and he finally did."

—

The tenth game of the twelve-game season was against San Francisco in Baltimore. To the Colts, it meant everything at the time, and it still does. "You have to understand," Donovan said, "we always finished the year on the West Coast against the Rams and 49ers. It was a tradition. We'd fly out there, stay for ten days, have a hell of a good time, and lose both fuckin' games." This was a minor exaggeration. While it was true that the Colts were swept on the West Coast in 1953, 1955, 1956, and 1957, they split the games in 1954, beating the Rams, 22–21, for their only win in California. "Anyway," Donovan said, "we could all but clinch the Western Division at home against the 49ers, and we figured we better do it. They had ruined our season out there the year before. If we won this one, and the Bears happened to lose to Bobby Layne at Pittsburgh that same afternoon, it was all over. We were champs."

On the telephone with Cameron Snyder of the *Sun,* Y. A. Tittle "guaranteed" a San Francisco victory, thereby beating Joe Namath to the punch by more than a decade. For a half, Y.A. looked as prescient as Joe Perry appeared inspired. Behind Tittle's sure passes and Perry's end runs, the 49ers opened with a seventeen-play, nine-minute, eighty-yard march to a touchdown. Though Unitas scored on a four-yard keeper to tie the game, 7–7, another extended San Francisco drive followed, and still another. Near the end of the half, a Unitas pass was tipped into the arms of Matt Hazeltine, who ran thirteen yards for a fourth 49er score. Defensive end Ordell Braase's block of one of the extra points earned him a new Dobson hat from Ewbank, Weeb's standard bounty for blocked kicks, and limited the damage to twenty points, 27–7. "That was my third hat of the year," Braase said proudly.

"In the locker room at the half," Marchetti recalled, "Weeb went straight to the blackboard, but not to write out any X's and O's. All he put up there was 'four TDs.' 'We have to score four touchdowns,' he said, 'and we have to hold them to nothing. That's the deal.'" Lenny Moore said, "J.U. was having one of his worst passing days ever [five for seventeen at the half]. Because of the tight coverage, he had to run the ball quite a bit himself. I'll bet he had almost as many carries as I did [five to eight]. Other than what he said there at the blackboard, Weeb didn't even talk to any of us. But he yelled at John. That's the only time I ever saw him do that. John got terribly quiet and flushed. He didn't say anything to me, but he said something to [offensive tackle] George Preas. They talked for about five minutes." The defense sat all together in a row, looking like paratroopers on a static line steeling themselves for a jump. "Donovan didn't even eat his hot dogs," Buzz Nutter said—an unprecedented situation. "Gino smoked about a half a pack of Luckies."

Lyles fielded the second-half kickoff at the five-yard line and brought the ball to the thirty-eight, where Unitas began a thirteen-play series that led to a one-yard touchdown run by Alan Ameche. The score was 27–14. On the next offensive series, Unitas fumbled at his own twenty-four-yard line, the exact error they had no margin for. But testing the ground on first and second down, San Francisco couldn't make an inch, and Tittle's third-and-ten pass was intercepted by safety Ray Brown. Spacing out his throws to Berry, Moore, and Jim Mutscheller, Unitas took just six plays to advance seventy-seven yards, to the 49ers' three. Then, right before the third period ran out, the public-address man interrupted his play-by-play to announce that Bobby Layne and the Steelers had defeated the Bears, 24–10. Commissioner Bert Bell had already coined a phrase that was soon to become a slogan: "On any given Sunday, any team in the NFL can beat any other." But in fourteen games over twenty-four years, this was the first time Pittsburgh had ever beaten the Bears. "*That,*" Tittle said afterward, "was not a good omen." Marchetti said, "After the game, we sent Bobby a couple of cases of champagne. He didn't waste them."

A minute and eleven seconds into the final quarter, Ameche broke through the middle to score his second touchdown, and the Colts were within six points, 27–21. One exceptional carry did the rest. After Taseff fair-caught a punt at the Colt twenty-seven-yard line, John called for a sweep left and handed the ball to Moore. "Art Spinney pulled and I followed him," Lenny said, "for what at first looked like an average gain. But then Raymond threw a sensational block, and a lane opened up wide—like a highway—straight down the sideline. I heard somebody yell, 'Run, Lenny, run!' It was *me.* Every time a tackler hit me and I started to go down, another one hit me from the opposite direction and stood me back up again. I kept going. Around the twenty-yard line, when I was sure they had me stopped, here came George Preas, fifty yards down the field, to knock two guys away. I thought, Oh, so *that's* what John and George were talking about.'" Lenny was so thoroughly turned around by then that he ran the last ten yards into the end zone backward.

The extra point was good, and Baltimore led, 28–27. After Tittle's next pass was intercepted by Taseff, Unitas played catch with Berry and Mutscheller until the Colts were again in scoring territory, fourth and one at the nineteen. Calling time-out, John went to the bench to confer with Weeb. *Should Steve Myhra try a field goal? Should Rechichar? Or should they go for the first down?* "What do you think, Weeb?" John asked. But Ewbank couldn't think. He started to walk away, with John right behind him. Then he turned around and walked back again, with Unitas still at his heels. Finally, the whistle blew and the quarterback hurried back onto the field. "Weeb had great strengths," Berry said. "Unitas complemented his weaknesses." Moore said, "John ran back into the huddle, laughing, which was always a good sign. He called an off-tackle play for Ameche, but he checked off to me at the line, and I caught a quick pass for the first down. There was just something magical about that whole second half. I think we could have done anything. From there, Raymond took us in. We were the Western Conference champions." Unitas's last, seven-yard pass to Berry, the fourth TD on Weeb's blackboard, was the one that broke Cecil Isbell's record of twenty-two games in a row with a touchdown pass.

Donovan said, "Back when we were lining up for the go-ahead point—of course I was in there with the fat-ass team—I looked across at Leo Nomellini and asked as politely as I could, 'Are you coming, Leo?' He said, 'You're goddamned right I am!' But Myhra's kick was good anyway. After we scored the final touchdown, the fat-asses returned to the field, and I said to Nomellini, 'Are you still coming, Leo?' But this time, he said, 'No, I guess not, Arthur. It's all over.'"

Berry, who caught nine passes for 114 yards, said, "That's the best single football game I ever played. All that year, I had been making a study of 'a hundred percent effort.' You know, people who say they're giving a hundred percent—they usually say 'a hundred and ten percent'—don't know what they're talking about. They don't realize how difficult it is to overcome human weakness. Even while doing dramatic things, your concentration can stray. I used to pore over the game films afterward. Did I do my assignment, or not? I graded myself on each play as ruthlessly as I could. In that San Francisco game, I got an eighty-seven. The rest of my career, I never even approached that number again." In the Giant game to come, Berry would stir the country, break Dante Lavelli's eight-year-old record for receptions in a title game, smash Wayne Millner's twenty-one-year-old standard for yards gained, and privately mark himself down for a fifty-seven. "Against San Francisco," he said, "I was a wild man. It was a bitterly cold, sub-twenty-degree day. Yet I lost eight pounds. I went in at one eighty-three and came out at one seventy-five. It was a game we had to have, and it literally took every ounce. I think that was the real 'greatest game' any of us ever played."

"It was the best game I ever played," Donovan said. Marchetti said, "It's the best game I was ever in." As Monday morning's *Sun* went for the record in exclamation points, Big Daddy Lipscomb contributed the simplest sentence to Cameron Snyder's game story. "This is my happiest day," he said. They would soon play a game widely hailed as the greatest ever, but all of them knew that it was really only the most important. "There was a big game *before* 'the Big Game,'" Unitas said many years later, "that, only to us, meant even more." He dined out forever on the tale of Weeb going walk-about on the sideline (although, to the sportswriter, Ewbank hotly disputed it). In the right company, especially if beer was involved, John could be talked into doing his two impressions: Humphrey Bogart in *Casablanca* and Weeb Ewbank elephant-walking his way up and down the sideline, to the accompaniment of John's whistle, in the great San Francisco comeback. "But let's not forget," Unitas said, "who wrote the 'four TDs' on the chalkboard, who allowed me to check off to Sput at the end; and for that matter, who taught me how to check off in the first place."

Before every game, Ewbank gave Unitas three or four plays to start. "Sometimes I changed them," John said, "but most of the first-down calls in the opening series were his, and if you go back and check, more than a few of them went for big gains. Weeb liked to take a deep shot right away, and so did I. 'If nothing else,' he figured, 'it'll get them thinking.' He wanted me to begin the Giants game with a bomb to Moore. But I went with that sweep again, and this time it lost yardage. I didn't try Weeb's play until maybe the third or fourth series. By that time, I had already fumbled and had a ball intercepted. And do you know what? Weeb's play went for sixty yards."

◆

"So," Donovan said, "we finished up the regular season on the West Coast against the Rams and 49ers. We flew out there, stayed

CLOCKWISE FROM TOP LEFT:

Baby John in the arms of mother Helen, 1933.

Johnny in grade school.

John as quarterback at St. Justin's High School, around 1949, with sister Shirley. When John tried out for the St. Justin's team, the coach told him he was too light to play football. Undeterred, Unitas soon became the team's starting quarterback.

All courtesy Shirley Green

Unitas and University of Louisville coach
Frank Camp, "the silent man."
Courtesy University of Louisville

Colt rookie Johnny Unitas.
Courtesy Frank Gitschier

This grainy photo is one of the few remaining
images of Unitas's time on the Bloomfield Rams,
the semipro team he joined after being cut by the
Pittsburgh Steelers in 1955. Johnny U played for
the Rams at both defensive back and quarterback;
here, wearing number 45, he helps make a tackle
on defense. *Courtesy Chuck "Bear" Rogers*

Jim Parker, the Hall of Fame pass
blocker, had a habit of making linebackers disappear.

ABOVE LEFT: Free-wheeling Bert Rechichar owned the field goal record, but never a checkbook.

ABOVE RIGHT: Defensive tackle Eugene "Big Daddy" Lipscomb joined the Colts in 1956, after being waived by the Los Angeles Rams. Unitas said of him, "'Lipscomb could pursue a play better than any big man I ever saw. He looked like a building sliding down the line . . . [and] when Big Daddy tackled you, you stayed tackled." *NFL/WireImage.com*

Early in Unitas's career, a victory was celebrated by *(from left)* L. G. Dupre, Royce Womble, trainer Ed Block, Unitas, Gino Marchetti, and Alex Sandusky.
Courtesy The Ed Block Courage Award Foundation

ABOVE LEFT: The Colts drafted defensive back Johnny Sample sight unseen in 1958, on the recommendation of running back Buddy Young. Sample's career—and later life—were marked by great controversy.

ABOVE RIGHT: Tight end Jim Mutscheller was one yard shy of being the hero of the 1958 championship game against the Giants, catching an overtime pass from Unitas and stepping out of bounds at the one-yard line. It would fall to Alan Ameche to punch the ball into the end zone on the next play, winning the game. *NFL/WireImage.com*

The 1960 Baltimore Colts' starting backfield consisted of Alex Hawkins, Alan Ameche, John Unitas, and Lenny Moore. *Courtesy Alex Hawkins*

TOP: Airplane flights in the '60s often involved a card game with *(left to right)* Bill Saul, George Preas, Unitas, Alex Hawkins, and Gino Marchetti. *Courtesy Alex Hawkins*

CENTER: John Mackey became the second tight end elected to the Pro Football Hall of Fame. His long-distance, open-field runs were the stuff of legends. *Courtesy The Ed Block Courage Award Foundation*

BOTTOM: Tom Matte joined the Colts in 1961 and shared running back duties with Lenny Moore until taking over the starting role in 1967. In the memorable final game of the 1965 season, Matte filled in for an injured Unitas at quarterback and helped propel the Colts to a 20–17 win over the Rams. *NFL/WireImage.com*

The Colts claimed the Super Bowl after the 1970 season and Unitas accepted the Lombardi Trophy in Memorial Stadium along with Coach Don McCafferty and fellow co-captains Ray May and Fred Miller (76). *Photo © Hugh B. McNally Jr.*

In his last appearance as a Baltimore Colt, Unitas took off his jacket when he got the call to replace Marty Domres. *Photo © Hugh B. McNally Jr.*

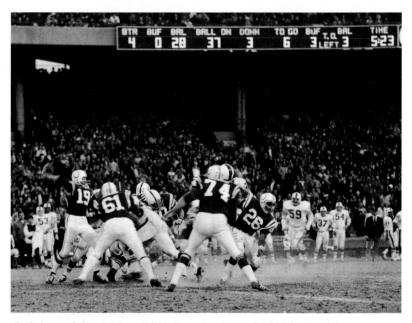

The light was fading in Memorial Stadium when Unitas fired his last touchdown pass as a Baltimore Colt. *Photo © Hugh B. McNally Jr.*

LEFT: John and wife Sandy, circa 2000.

BELOW: John with *(from left to right)* his three youngest kids: Joe, Paige, and Chad.

Both courtesy Sandra Unitas

Earl Morrall, a disappointment in one Super Bowl, a hero in another, was part of the "Hump and Rump" duo with John Unitas. The two became close both on and off the field. *Courtesy Larry Harris*

Two of the greatest met at an awards banquet in Baltimore. Weeb Ewbank *(left)* was the winning coach in the two most important games in NFL history. Don Shula succeeded Ewbank as Colts coach and went on to become the winningest coach in league history.
Courtesy The Ed Block Courage Award Foundation

One of the last photos taken of Unitas was at a special luncheon honoring the quarterback and Babe Ruth's daughter, Julia Ruth Stevens.
Courtesy Sports Legends Museum at Camden Yards

The Baltimore Ravens' color guard still sports a tribute to number 19 at every game.
Courtesy John W. Ziemann and J. Patrick Kelly

for ten days, had a hell of a good time, and lost both fuckin' games. It was a tradition.

"Incidentally," he said, "when Weeb put us up at the Concourse Plaza in the Bronx, he didn't know that the Concourse was one of my old haunts. As a teenager, I used to swipe beer from them, whenever the American Legion put on a mixer. After we checked into the hotel, Don Joyce and I took a walk to Yankee Stadium. Everybody was out and about, riding their bikes and pushing their baby carriages. It was a sunny day, not too cold—a typical, beautiful, New York Saturday. 'Hey, Donovan,' somebody on the street yelled, 'the Giants are going to kick your fat ass!' I looked at Joyce and said, 'These are my people.'"

The apartment house where Donovan grew up sat directly on top of a subway line, four miles north of Yankee Stadium. Sleeping in Artie's room was like sleeping in a Pullman car. "My aunt—the last aunt who died—was the oldest parishioner in our church," he said. "She came over from Ireland to help build it. Because I was a famous football player, the neighborhood never stopped claiming me as being one of them. So, in a way, I never really left home. Of course, I'd have to be a hundred and fifty-three years old to have had a drink with everybody who has said I had a drink with them." As Donovan was speaking, he was, in fact, seventy-nine. He was sitting in the stainless steel kitchen of the Valley Country Club, his country club without a golf course, in Baltimore. He and his wife, Dottie, had hosted wedding receptions and bar mitzvahs there since the sixties. "Come on," she said to her husband, "we have an appointment to get you a flu shot." On the ride to the doctor's office, with his wife at the wheel and the sportswriter in the backseat, Artie said, "I had a dream about the Bronx just last night. I dreamed that I went back up there and didn't know anybody. I kept looking around for Joe Brady, but I couldn't find him."

Brady was Donovan's New York cop. Every neighborhood kid who managed to stay out of jail seemed to have his own personal cop. "He was my knight in shining armor," Artie said, "the one who got me playing football in the school yard. He was in charge of all the cops at Yankee Stadium." On December 28, 1958, Captain Joe took Sunday off to attend the National Football League title game with Arthur Sr. "I put them on our bench," Artie said. "I didn't know where else to put them." He watched as his father took a long look around the stadium. "Dad could remember when ninety thousand people were there for Louis and Schmeling. This was just a little football game, the NFL championship. I was having a terrible time trying to keep the two of them quiet, and especially trying to keep Joe from sharing his flask with my dad—Jesus, Mary, and Joseph! Brady was already lit by game time, and I could see Weeb wasn't too thrilled. Just before kickoff, he buttonholed two uniformed cops and, pointing to Joe, said, 'Get that bum off the bench!' 'Coach,' one of the cops said, 'you go before he does.'"

NINE

1958

"Nothing against Myhra; I had more confidence in me."

Colts 23, Giants 17

The *New York Times,* the *Herald Tribune,* the *Daily News,* the *Mirror,* the *Journal-American,* the *World-Telegram and Sun,* the *Post,* the *Long Island Daily Press,* and the *Long Island Star-Journal* were in the twenty-first (and, as it turned out, final) day of a delivery workers' strike that had left the city without newspapers since December 12, ruining Christmas for both Macy's and Gimbel's. Sportswriters like Dave Anderson of the *Journal-American* were on a busman's holiday. Only the syndicated columnists, like Red Smith and Bob Considine, would definitely be writing for Monday. Sports columnists of the day, the fedora set, wholeheartedly embraced only four games: baseball, boxing, horse racing, and *college* football. That was another thing that would change forever on December 28, 1958. In his pregame "plugger," to be subbed in a later edition, Smith seemed to be missing the racetrack when, describing Baltimore's blue-Stetsoned cheerleaders, he wrote, "Fillies of provocative design paraded wearing the letters COLTS across bosoms that pointedly contradicted that label."

Some 45 million people across the country, the largest television audience in the history of the NFL, sat down to view the game over NBC on approximately 11 million TV sets, many of them freshly delivered. This included nobody in New York City. At prices of $10, $7.50, and $4, only 64,185 customers were counted on a mild day in Yankee Stadium, 6,979 fewer than had paid to see the same two teams in November. So commissioner Bert Bell insisted on a seventy-five-mile blackout of the telecast, telling syndicated columnist Milton Gross, "If we ever start valuing the TV audience more than the paying public, we'll be in trouble."

Several hours before the game, Weeb Ewbank was papering the locker room with "We outgutted them" signs, recalling New York quarterback Charlie Conerly's slur. At the same time, Raymond Berry walked the field alone. "Over by the Giants bench," he said, "there was a slippery spot. When the tarp had been removed, a little water was dumped. It was the only place on the field that wasn't dry and hard." He decided to wear the special shoes that equipment man Fred Schubach had devised for him, with the two regular cleats in the front, the two regular cleats in the heel, and the two mud cleats—just a little longer than the others—over the balls of the feet. "I didn't like wearing those shoes; they were uncomfortable," Raymond said, "but I had a feeling."

"I was in the head," Artie Donovan said, still speaking like a marine. "The only guy in there with me was Bert Rechichar, who was working on his own game plan. 'Weeb thinks I'm only kicking off,' he said, 'but some damned way or other, I'm going to get into this fuckin' game.'"

For all of Weeb's attention to Conerly's insult, Charlie wasn't even in the starting lineup. Giant coach Jim Lee Howell liked to use backup Don Heinrich for the first series or two, the "feeling-out" phase, so that Howell, Conerly, and offensive coach Vince Lombardi could form their own huddle on the sideline, look over the defense, and then begin.

◆

At midfield, referee Ron Gibbs introduces cocaptains Kyle Rote and Bill Svoboda of the Giants to captain Gino Marchetti of the Colts. New York wins the coin flip and elects to receive. Rechichar kicks off to rookie Don Maynard (who would make his name years later with the New York Jets). Maynard downs the ball in the end zone.

First Quarter

GIANTS

1-10-G20	Quarterback Don Heinrich passes incomplete
2-10-G20	Heinrich passes to halfback Alex Webster for seven
	Official time-out. Baltimore left linebacker Leo Sanford is helped off the field with a leg injury

"Nobody knew it," Berry said, "but that was a big moment in the game. Our field-goal kicker, Steve Myhra, was Sanford's backup. Steve had to play the whole game for Leo, and pretty much played the game of his life. But most importantly, I think, Myhra didn't have to stand around on the sidelines waiting for the big kick. He wasn't the greatest field-goal kicker in the world, you know. He couldn't think about that now. He was too busy playing football."

3-3-G27	Heinrich passes incomplete
4-3-G27	Don Chandler's punt is fair caught by Carl Taseff at the Colt thirty

COLTS

1-10-C30	Halfback Lenny Moore sweeps for loss of three
2-13-C27	Fullback Alan Ameche runs for seven
3-6-C34	Quarterback Johnny Unitas fumbles at the Colt thirty-seven, recovered by Giant defensive back Jim Patton

GIANTS

1-10-C37	Webster runs for loss of one
2-11-C38	Heinrich fumbles at the Colt forty-five, recovered by Marchetti

COLTS

1-10-C45	Unitas passes to L. G. Dupre for four
2-6-C49	Dupre runs for one
3-5-C50	Unitas pass intercepted by Giant defensive back Lindon Crow at the New York forty-five

GIANTS

1-10-G45	Halfback Frank Gifford runs for loss of one
1-11-G44	Fullback Mel Triplett runs for zero
3-11-G44	Heinrich passes to Triplett for six
4-5-G50	Chandler punts to Taseff at the Colt fifteen

COLTS

1-10-C15	Unitas passes to Moore for sixty
1-10-G25	Ameche runs for five
2-5-G20	Dupre runs for loss of one
3-6-G21	Five-yard Colt penalty, delay of game
3-11-G26	Moore runs for two
4-9-G24	Steve Myhra misses thirty-one-yard field goal, but Giants are offside
4-4-G19	*Myhra's twenty-six-yard field goal attempt is blocked by Giant linebacker Sam Huff*

"In our huddle," Huff said, "the linebackers were Sarah, Wanda, and Meg. The strong-side linebacker was Sarah. The weak-side linebacker was Wanda. The middle linebacker was Meg. I was Meg. That came from [defensive coach] Tom Landry. He believed that when you say a woman's name in the huddle, you get the players' attention. You do, too."

GIANTS

1-10-G22	Webster runs for zero
2-10-G22	Quarterback Charlie Conerly passes to Triplett for nine
3-1-G31	Gifford runs for thirty-eight
1-10-C31	Triplett runs for two
2-8-C29	Conerly passes incomplete
3-8-C29	Conerly passes incomplete
4-8-C29	*Pat Summerall kicks thirty-six-yard field goal (2:02)*

Huff said, "If Summerall doesn't make a fifty- or fifty-five-yarder two weeks before—to this day, because of all the snow on the field, nobody really knows how long that kick was—the championship game would have been in Cleveland. It wouldn't have been the same, would it? New York is New York. If you're going to play a revolutionary game, you might as well play it in New York."

GIANTS 3, COLTS 0

Chandler kicks off to Lenny Lyles, who runs for nineteen

COLTS

1-10-C21	Unitas passes to Moore for five
2-5-C26	Dupre runs for three
3-2-C29	Unitas passes incomplete
4-2-C29	Ray Brown punts to Crow, who runs for a loss of ten (0:00)

Second Quarter

GIANTS

1-10-G18	Conerly passes to Gifford for two; Gifford's fumble is recovered by Colt tackle Ray Krouse

COLTS

1-10-G20	Moore runs for four
2-6-G16	Ameche runs for five
3-1-G11	Ameche runs for one
1-10-G10	Moore runs for eight
2-2-G2	Ameche runs for two and the touchdown; Myhra kicks the extra point (12:34)

COLTS 7, GIANTS 3

Rechichar kicks off to Giant tackle Rosey Brown, who laterals to Triplett, who runs for twenty-one

"When I wasn't on the field," Jim Parker said, "I watched Rosey. I was so nervous that I kept telling Johnny U, 'Don't talk to me, I'm too nervous.' My man was Andy Robustelli. Ro-bus-telli. Just the name scared me. It sounded like a freight train. *Ro-bus-telli, Ro-bus-telli.* Pickin' up speed. Headin' my way."

Huff said, "Andy couldn't get around Parker; he couldn't come under him; he couldn't go over him. [He could only applaud.] The immovable object, that's what Jim Parker was."

Robustelli said, "I used to think there wasn't a big tackle I couldn't outmaneuver. But Parker was too strong. Too smart. Too good."

GIANTS

1-10-G33	Triplett runs for one
2-9-G34	Conerly passes to flanker Kyle Rote for fourteen
1-10-G48	Conerly sacked for loss of nine
2-19-G39	Conerly hands off to Gifford, who hands off to a reversing Webster, who runs for four
3-15-G43	Conerly passes incomplete
4-15-G43	Chandler punts to Jackie Simpson; Simpson's fumble is recovered by Giant guard Melwood Guy

| 1-10-C10 | Gifford's fumble is recovered by the Colt defensive end Don Joyce |

COLTS

1-10-C14	Unitas passes incomplete
2-10-C14	Unitas passes to end Raymond Berry for five
3-5-C19	Unitas passes to Ameche for ten
1-10-C29	Moore sweeps for ten
1-10-C39	Ameche runs for six
2-4-C45	Moore runs for three
3-1-C48	Ameche runs for three
1-10-G49	Unitas passes incomplete
2-10-G49	Dupre runs for three
3-7-G46	Unitas scrambles for sixteen
1-10-G30	Moore runs for one
2-9-G29	Five-yard Colt penalty, illegal motion
2-14-G34	Unitas passes to Berry for thirteen
3-1-G21	Ameche runs for six
1-10-G15	Unitas passes to Berry for fifteen and the touchdown; Myhra kicks the extra point (1:20)

COLTS 14, GIANTS 3

"You couldn't outthink Unitas," Huff said. "When you thought run, he passed. When you thought pass, he ran. When you thought conventional, he was unconventional. When you thought unconventional, he was conventional. When you tried thinking in reverse, he double-reversed. It made me dizzy. It bothered me. We were one of the greatest defensive teams ever put together. We were so much a defensive team that sometimes we wouldn't allow the offense in the locker room at training camp. We put up a sign on the door: DEFENSE ONLY! But we didn't have a defense for Unitas."

Rechichar kicks off through the end zone

GIANTS

1-10-C20	Fullback Phil King runs for loss of one
2-11-G19	Conerly sacked for loss of eight
3-19-G11	Webster runs for nine (0:00)

Third Quarter

Chandler kicks off to Lyles, who runs for nineteen

COLTS

1-10-C19	Moore runs for five
2-5-C24	Unitas passes to tight end Jim Mutscheller
1-10-C32	Moore runs reverse for loss of seven
2-17-C25	*Unitas passes to Berry for fifteen*

"That's when Weeb Ewbank punched me!" Huff said. "Right there in front of the Colts bench! He thought I hit Berry late on that sideline pattern. At the end of his route, Raymond is only about a millimeter in bounds. It's hard not to hit him a *little* late. Weeb threw a left hook that got me right in the face mask. 'What the hell's wrong with you, Weeb?' I said. 'Are you losing it?'"

3-2-C40	Five-yard Colt penalty, offside
3-7-C35	Unitas passes to Dupre for three
4-4-C38	Brown punts to Maynard, who runs for nine

GIANTS

1-10-G21	Gifford runs for zero
2-10-G21	Conerly passes to Gifford for loss of three
3-13-G18	Conerly sacked for loss of five

4-18-G13	Chandler's punt is fair-caught by Moore on the Colt forty-one

COLTS

1-10-C41	*Unitas passes to Mutscheller for thirty-two*

As Mutscheller was catching his breath on the sideline, Unitas called a sweep for Long Gone Dupre. Just before John broke the huddle, he said to the new tight end, "I see you made it, Bert." "For Christ's sake, hurry up," Forty-four said, "before Weeb sees me!"

1-10-G27	Dupre runs for one
2-9-G26	Unitas passes incomplete
3-9-G26	Unitas passes to Berry for eleven
1-10-G15	Unitas passes to Moore for twelve
1-G-G3	Ameche runs for two
2-G-G1	Unitas sneaks for zero
3-G-G1	Ameche runs for zero
4-G-G1	*Ameche sweeps for loss of four*

This was the play that could have changed the game entirely, better for the Colts, worse for history. Unitas wanted a "428," a right halfback pass, the least likely play in the book. Moore was split out, making Ameche the right halfback. "I hand off to Ameche," John said, "and he starts on an outside run. But then he stops and flips the ball to Mutscheller in the end zone. At least that's the way we drew it up." But Ameche heard only the "28." He missed the "4," the passing part.

"We hadn't run the thing for years," Ameche said. "I thought it was just a straight pitchout. Mutscheller didn't block Cliff Livingston at all, so he had me before I took two steps. I blew it. Jim was wide open in the end zone."

"I'm standing there by myself," Mutscheller said. "Alan couldn't throw at all, you know; he threw like a girl. But even Alan could have completed that one."

GIANTS

1-10-G5	Gifford runs for five
2-5-G10	Webster runs for three
3-2-G13	Conerly passes to Rote for sixty-two; Rote's fumble is picked up by teammate Webster and advanced another twenty-four—eighty-six yards in all
1-G-C1	Webster runs for zero
2-G-C1	Triplett runs for one and the touchdown
	Summerall kicks the extra point (3:46)

COLTS 14, GIANTS 10

Chandler kicks off to Simpson, who runs for twenty-three

COLTS

1-10-C25	Dupre runs for two
2-8-C27	Unitas sacked for loss of seven
3-15-C20	Unitas scrambles for nine
4-6-C29	Brown punts to Maynard, who runs for four

GIANTS

1-10-G19	Webster runs for three
2-7-G22	Conerly passes to end Bob Schnelker for seventeen (0:00)

Fourth Quarter

1-10-G39	Conerly passes to Schnelker for forty-six
1-10-C15	Conerly passes to Gifford for fifteen and the touchdown
	Summerall kicks the extra point (14:07)

GIANTS 17, COLTS 14

Chandler kicks off to Simpson in the end zone

COLTS

1-10-C20	Unitas passes to Moore for eleven
1-10-C31	Unitas passes to Berry for thirteen
1-10-C44	Unitas passes incomplete
2-10-C44	Unitas scrambles for one
3-9-C45	Crow interferes with Mutscheller at Giant thirty-eight
1-10-G38	Ameche runs for loss of one
2-11-G39	Unitas passes incomplete
3-11-G39	Unitas passes incomplete
4-11-G39	Rechichar's forty-six-yard field goal attempt is short

GIANTS

1-10-G20	King runs for four
2-6-G24	Conerly passes to tight end Ken MacAfee for fifteen
1-10-G39	Gifford runs for two (Giants offside; penalty declined)
2-12-G37	Triplett runs for seven
3-5-G44	Gifford sweeps for ten
1-10-C46	Gifford runs for four
2-6-C42	King fumbles; Krouse recovers for the Colts at the Giant forty-two

COLTS

1-10-G42	*Unitas passes incomplete*

"I caught that pass just out of bounds at the goal line," Moore said. "I thought I was in, most definitely. But you always think you're in. That was our first long strike since the early going, when I rolled over on the ball and thought I broke a rib. I came to Weeb at the

sideline and said, 'I can't turn. I can't bend. I can hardly breathe.'
He said, 'Don't say anything. Don't tell anybody. Does John know?'
'Hell, Weeb,' I said. 'John knows everything.' 'Well, tell him he's
going to have to use you as a decoy.' 'He knows that.'"

2-10-G42	Unitas passes incomplete
3-10-G42	Unitas passes to Berry for eleven
1-10-G31	Dupre runs for four
2-6-G27	Unitas sacked for loss of eleven
3-17-G38	Unitas sacked for loss of nine
4-26-G47	Brown punts to Patton, who runs for fourteen

GIANTS

1-10-G19	Webster runs for five
2-5-G24	Gifford sweeps for zero
3-5-G24	Conerly passes to Webster for ten
1-10-G34	Webster runs for one
2-9-G35	Gifford sweeps for five
3-4-G40	*Gifford runs for three and two-thirds*

"I was able to slip my blocker and get out into the flow," Marchetti said. "Gifford ran right and I tackled him. To make sure Frank didn't go any further, Big Daddy hit the whole pile. He just wasn't going to let anybody or anything get to the forty-four-yard line. Daddy, not Gifford, was the one who broke my ankle."

"A runner knows when he makes a first down," Gifford said. "It was close, but there's never been any doubt in my mind that I made that one. In all the confusion around Gino's injury, the refs blew the spot. Then, even though we only had about a foot to go for the first down, I think the decision to punt was the right one."

Carried off on an old-fashioned, wheel-less stretcher, with assistant trainer Bill Neill at his side, Marchetti told the six men it took to carry him, "Put me down here," and they did, just two yards beyond the chalk line of the field. "What the hell," he said.

"After all those years when we were so bad, I wanted at least to see the finish."

4-1-G43	Chandler's punt is fair caught by Taseff on the Colt fourteen (2:20)

COLTS

1-10-C14	Unitas passes incomplete
2-10-C14	Unitas passes incomplete
3-10-C14	Unitas passes to Moore for eleven
1-10-C25	Unitas passes incomplete
2-10-C25	*Unitas passes to Berry for twenty-five (1:04)*

From the day they met, Unitas and Berry regularly stayed after practice to pass and catch. "When Weeb saw what we were doing," Berry said, "he told me kind of quietly, 'Keep working with this Unitas.' Looking back, I wonder if Weeb didn't already know." In one of their earliest sessions, Berry was running "little L-patterns," square-ins, and John asked him, "What if a linebacker got right up on top of you?" "It hasn't happened," Berry said. "What if Joe Schmidt is standing right there? What would you do?" "I guess I'd give him an outside fake like this, try to make him come after me, then jump underneath him like this." John nodded. Neither of them mentioned or thought of it again for more than two years, not until Berry crouched down in his stance on the left side of the line with a minute and a few seconds to go in a game the Colts were losing, 17–14. Raymond looked up and there stood the linebacker. But it wasn't Joe Schmidt of the Lions. It was Harland Svare of the New York Giants. Berry glanced over at Unitas, who smiled.

"John had called a ten-yard square-in for me," Berry said. "I went to the line and there was Svare. I'll never forget the look

John gave me, the look that we gave each other. I made that fake I had described to Unitas two years earlier, and Svare came right after me. I jumped underneath him and John zipped it on a perfect line about seven yards down the field. I ran for the rest of the first down. Working the middle, because they were expecting sideline passes that would stop the clock, he hit me with another one."

1-10-C50   **Unitas passes to Berry for fifteen**

"Unitas threw that ball right by my ear," Huff said. "I was in the right place but I couldn't get my arm up in time. It *whooshed* past the ear hole of my helmet."

". . . And another one," Berry said.

1-10-G35   **Unitas passes to Berry for twenty-two**

"'Unitas to Berry,' 'Unitas to Berry,' 'Unitas to Berry,'" Huff said, mimicking PA announcer Bob Sheppard. "His voice echoed in my head."

"There was just enough time," Berry said, "for the kicking team to come on and tie it. Years later—decades later—I asked John, 'Why, all of a sudden, did you come to me three times in a row?' Good grief, three times in a row! He smiled and said, 'Because I figured you'd catch them, Raymond.' John wasn't overly analytical. He was instinctive. You know, when something like that is going on around you, you miss a lot of it, you don't grasp it all. Because we didn't have time to huddle, the Giants were also operating without perfect communication. So all of us were in a different rhythm. The game had kind of moved inside our heads. That's the two-minute drill in spades. Maybe the whole deal came down just to how well John and I knew each other."

1-10-G13   **Myhra kicks twenty-yard field goal (0:07)**

"Don't drop the ball, don't drop the ball," holder George Shaw kept repeating to himself. "It felt like a hunk of ice," he said to the reporters after the game. Years later, Shaw told John Steadman, "I've woken up since then in the middle of the night, thinking, Don't drop the ball."

GIANTS 17, COLTS 17

Rechichar kicks off to Maynard, who runs for eighteen

GIANTS

1-10-G18   Conerly sneaks for zero

"The police made me move inside then," Marchetti said. "They didn't want to, but they had to. 'It could end any second now,' they said. 'If the stands empty, you'll be trampled.'" "He was getting a little shocky, too," Bill Neill said. "It had turned really cold." "In the locker room," Gino said, "it was as quiet as it is sitting here. We were underground and the crowd noise was muffled. There was no radio. It was terrible."

How much did his leg hurt?

"I'd have cried," he said, "if I wasn't Gino Marchetti."

Overtime

In Marchetti's place, Unitas walks alone to midfield to meet referee Ron Gibbs and the Giant cocaptains. The mild day has turned raw. Rote and Svoboda are wearing two of the hooded capes that have bloomed on both benches. In the dingy light, they put Dave Anderson of the *Journal-American* in mind of medieval cloaks. Gibbs flips a coin. Being the visiting captain, Unitas has the call. "Tails," he says before the coin hits the ground. Heads it is. The Giants will receive, of course. Pivoting, Unitas turns his back to the goal that Baltimore prefers to defend, and in a flash of temper, he kicks the ground just the way Joe DiMaggio once did on the base paths. Rechichar kicks off to Maynard, who fumbles, recovers, and runs for ten.

GIANTS

1-10-G20	Gifford runs for four
2-6-G24	Conerly passes incomplete
3-6-G24	Conerly keeps for five
4-1-G29	Chandler punts to Taseff, who runs for one

"I had a feeling of inevitability," Summerall said. Rookie defensive back Johnny Sample said, "Milt Davis was injured at the end of regulation, and I had to go in at cornerback for the overtime. Those were the three longest plays of my life."

"John told us," Ameche said, "'We're going to go right down the field and score.' No doubt about it. You could just feel the confidence."

COLTS

1-10-C20	Dupre runs for eleven
1-10-C31	Unitas passes incomplete
2-10-C31	Dupre runs for two
3-8-C33	*Unitas passes to Ameche for eight*

"Ameche lined up in the backfield," Berry said. "I was split out. His route was a wide flair. I was running a hook pattern and Svare was trying to help Karilivacz with me, instead of covering Ameche. Unitas dropped back. To catch the pass that John threw Alan, you couldn't have just ordinary hands. Ameche made the first down by less than a yard."

1-10-C41	Dupre runs for four
2-6-C45	Unitas sacked for loss of eight
3-14-C37	*Unitas passes to Berry for twenty-one*

"Third and fourteen," Raymond said. "Here's where attention to detail paid off. John scrambled left and I ran a route we called 'come open late.' I was the third choice on this play. I cut a stutter-step pattern straight into that muddy spot that I had found before the game. Behind me Karilivacz slipped and fell right on his butt. I didn't see him go down—I was already turned toward John—or we would have had a touchdown. Unitas flapped that big left hand at me, signaling, 'Take off!' But I didn't react quickly enough. So he just drilled me in the hands. First down in Giants territory. Now, those two mud cleats weren't bothering me a bit."

1-10-G42   *Ameche runs for twenty-three*

Fifteen Sucker wouldn't break again for about three years, not until Unitas called it as an audible on the Giants' forty-two-yard line in overtime at Yankee Stadium. "I was tired," Berry said ruefully. He had just caught a pass for twenty-one yards, his eleventh (second-to-last) reception of the game. "What's that old saying? 'Fatigue makes cowards of us all.'" Ameche gained twenty-three yards on the play, but if Berry had done his job, the game could have ended right there. Nobody in the stadium knew it except Raymond and John. "He didn't say a word as we hud-dled up," Berry said. "He just looked at me as if to ask, 'Where were you?' But then he smiled as if to say, 'Don't worry about it.' Johnny U."

"Our audible system consisted of colors," Raymond said. "Red was the live color. So, when Unitas came to the line of scrim-mage, he'd go, 'Blue eighty-one! Blue eighty-one! Set! Hut!' But this was a red call, a two-hole trap. Sam Huff had started cheating to the left, trying to help out on all these quick passes."

Unitas said, "Sam kept dropping back a little more, a little more. Also, Modzelewski had just sacked me two plays before. I figured he'd be pumped up, and trappable. If Art Spinney could trap Modzelewski, and Buzz Nutter could cut back on Spinney's man—was that Roosevelt Grier? [no, Frank Youso; Grier had gone out with an injured knee]—then all George Preas had to do was shield Huff a little—he didn't even have to block him—and Ameche could shoot through. There wasn't anything magical about it. I didn't pull it out of a hat. The defense told me what to do. It's what you worked on all year, when you practiced the two-minute drill."

1-10-G19	Dupre runs for zero
2-10-G19	*Unitas passes to Berry for eleven*

Just as Berry caught the ball, TV screens all across the country went to snow. The stomping crowd had dislodged a cable. Though the power was out for about two and a half minutes, only the finish of the Berry play and the start of a short Ameche run were missed. A drunken fan loose on the field, rather well dressed for a drunken fan, bought the repairmen some time. Subsequently, broadcaster Lindsey Nelson told Summerall that the trespasser was an NBC employee. In years to come, the legend would be given a name: Stan Rotkiewicz of the business department. But Unitas never believed it. "Nobody is that good an actor," he told the sportswriter. "As the cops were dragging him off, he was shouting, 'Don't grab me, god-dog it! Get that god-dog number nineteen! He's the son-of-a-god-dog-bitch who's killing us!'" Soon after the picture blinked on again, the Colts would be lined up at the seven-yard line, second-and-goal.

1-G-G8	*Ameche runs for one*

"John came over to the bench," Ewbank said, "to see what I had in mind. And I said, 'Well, Ameche's a fine ball carrier.' Then he came up with that pass. I almost fainted on that one." Weeb would tell an Ohio neighbor, the baseball manager Walter Alston,

"Unitas didn't say a word when I mentioned Ameche. He just stood there staring at me, like he couldn't quite remember who I was."

2-G-G7   *Unitas passes to Mutscheller for six*

"The play was called for Alan," Mutscheller said. "But when John checked off, I didn't think a thing of it. He was always pulling out plays we hadn't run since training camp. If he thought this would work, so did I. You could tell from his confidence that he was going to make it work. Everyone in the huddle got confidence from him."

Unitas said, "The strong-side linebacker ['Sarah'] took an inside position on Mutscheller, which surprised me. That was Cliff Livingston. You'd expect him to play Jimmy straight up, if not a little on the outside. The defensive back, Lindon Crow, was well into the end zone. And I knew Crow had to worry about Lenny Moore coming out of the backfield. Really, they were the only two defenders in the picture. Where was Emlen Tunnell? [In the middle of the end zone, also fairly deep.] So, Jimmy was open on a diagonal from the very first step he took. People said it was a gamble, but they couldn't see what I was seeing. If Jimmy had been able to keep his footing on the icy sideline—his momentum basically slid him out of bounds—he would have walked into the end zone instead of out at the one. I actually overthrew him a little. It was my fault that it wasn't a touchdown."

Mutscheller said, "John never stopped telling me, 'Geez, Jim, I tried to make you the hero.' But then, if I had scored that touchdown, Ameche wouldn't have been able to sell all those hamburgers."

3-G-G1   *Ameche runs for one and the touchdown* ("Blue twenty-five! Blue twenty-five! Hut! Hut!")
The extra point is forgotten (6:45)

COLTS 23, GIANTS 17

Without the slightest show of emotion, Unitas turned and walked off the field. "You weren't going to see him jump up and down," said the Colt safety Andy Nelson. "He didn't have to do that. It was one of the best things about him."

"He has every gift a great quarterback needs," Vince Lombardi said, "in abundance."

"He was like a great conductor," Bob Considine wrote in his column, "bulling a discordant orchestra together and moving it to a crescendo. Ameche was that crescendo."

"The play was 'sixteen power,'" Mutscheller said, pulling an old wire photo out of his desk in Baltimore. "I blocked down on Cliff Livingston. Lenny blocked out on Emlen Tunnell. George Preas hit Jim Katcavage. Wait a minute, 'sixteen slant,' it must have been. What was in John's head is that, earlier, we had been going straight up the middle and not making it. He wanted the fullback to slant into the six slot, right tackle. It was a pretty big hole."

"All game long, my man was Dick Modzelewski," Alex Sandusky said. "To this day, my dominant memory is how exhausted I felt when it was over."

"We heard cleat sounds on the ramp outside," Neill said, "*click-click-clicking* up to the locker room door."

"It burst open," Marchetti said, "and there was Buzz Nutter with the football, saying, 'We're world champions.'"

They gave the ball to Gino.

●

"Twelve players from that game went on to the Pro Football Hall of Fame," said Huff, who was one of them. "Twelve players plus Lombardi, Landry, and Ewbank. Fifteen Hall of Famers on the same field. And one master. Unitas was the master. From last year's

Super Bowl, can you name fifteen players? Today you don't know who is playing for who."

"Year after year after year," Berry said, "we stayed together, when there wasn't so much player movement, and the fans didn't have so many of us to learn."

"Today they root for the uniform," Marchetti said, "that's all."

"In nineteen sixty-six," Sam said, "Unitas, Willie Davis [the Green Bay defensive end], Gifford, and I went to Vietnam for the USO. Holy Christ! We were basically in the middle of a war with no guns. General Westmoreland asked, 'Is there anything I can do for you guys?' Willie Davis said, 'Yeah, get us a gun.' At one point on that trip, Unitas turned to me and said, 'Sam, this is the most exciting thing I've ever done.' I looked at him and said, 'On top of everything else, I have to listen to that shit?' John was hobbled with a sore knee at the time. 'If we come under attack,' I told him, 'I'm leaving your ass behind.'"

●

Dave Anderson, who would move over to the *Times* from the *Journal-American,* said, "I was the one who asked Unitas in the locker room, 'What about that pass to Mutscheller? Weren't you taking a chance on an interception?' He looked at me with those wonderful, cold eyes, and said, 'When you know what you're doing, you don't get intercepted.'" Therefore, Unitas must not have known what he was doing when he was intercepted in the first quarter. "I made pretty much that same crack to John once," Cameron Snyder said, sitting at his dining room table in Baltimore. "John just laughed. 'Hell,' he said, 'if Mutscheller wasn't open, I'd have thrown it away. Once you've figured out what's the right thing to do, all you need then is the nerve to do it. I've always liked touchdowns better than field goals, Cameron. Nothing against Myhra, but I had more confidence in me.'"

Immediately after the game, a representative of *The Ed Sulli-van Show* offered Unitas $500 to appear on that evening's telecast. John declined, saying he wanted to fly home with the team. (Only one player rode the train, the Inebriated Special, back to Baltimore with the fans: Bert Rechichar.) When the offer was sweetened to $700, Unitas said, "Give it to Ameche." In a suit and tie (and for the original $500), the Horse was introduced onstage by Sullivan: "This is Alan Ameche of the Baltimore Colts, who today, in the first sudden-death playoff in professional football, went across the goal line with the winning touchdown. So let's have a tremendous hand for Alan Ameche!"

Each of the winning players received $4,718.77, a significant bonus to men whose annual salaries ranged from $17,550 (Unitas) to $11,250 (Marchetti) to $9,000 (Huff) to $8,000 (Myhra) and below. The losers drew $3,111.33 a man. Voting partial shares to a number of players who had come and gone during the season, the Colts sliced their pie into forty-two and a half pieces. By the same formula, they quietly split another $50,000: $25,000 from their TV-radio sponsor, the National Brewing Company, and $25,000 from an unnamed "friend of the team," who everybody knew was owner Carroll Rosenbloom's gambling pal Lou Chesler. The Colts had been three-and-a-half-point favorites. John Stead-man wrote, "When the reporters asked Unitas why he went for the touchdown instead of the field goal, he made a joke about having placed a bet. Later, he told me, 'I didn't even know what the points were! I didn't even know how the points worked!' Though Unitas said Bert Bell read him the riot act [that was Steadman's phrase; John's was, "I got my ass handed to me"], Bell closed their conversation by telling him, 'You're the best advertisement we ever had.'"

"I remember seeing Commissioner Bell standing in the back of our locker room after the game," Berry said. "He was crying. I think he knew what we didn't—yet. That this was a watershed for the NFL." Don Shula, who by then was a twenty-eight-year-old assistant coach at the University of Virginia, said, "That's the game that changed professional football. The popularity of it started right there." Pro football had finally staged a championship game that could hold its own with a World Series. This wasn't the best team the Giants ever had, only the most compelling. Their high-wire act of five straight must-win victories, including a conference playoff against the Browns, had done more than just deliver them to the title game. It had brought them into the wider conversations of New York City, where the sponsors, the advertisers, and the media happened to live. Cue television; then, bring on a hero, a perfectly ordinary guy in white. The radio game, baseball, didn't step aside that Sunday night. But the process had definitely begun. Nobody knows the precise moment when baseball did shove over, but the impression is that Jerry Kramer and Fuzzy Thurston were pulling out of the Green Bay line to lead a Packer sweep. Fuzzy's young face, incidentally, can be found in the space between Ameche and Preas in the third row of the team photograph of the '58 champions.

With 349 yards passing, John broke Sammy Baugh's title game record from 1937. But more than all of the numbers, good and bad, the two late drives engineered by Unitas were what "changed Sundays," in the pretty phrase of Bell's successor, Pete Rozelle. These grizzled football players and part-time stonemasons and ironworkers on the Tappan Zee and at Bethlehem Steel laid a cornerstone in Yankee Stadium and started to build a bridge to the Super Bowl.

◆

"I had given John a lift to the airport in Baltimore," Andy Nelson said. "We couldn't believe the scene when we got back. All those screaming people. But we finally made it to my car."

As the two of them drove home, did they talk about the game?

"I think we listened to the radio."

What did John say when Andy dropped him off?

"See you tomorrow."

Within days, Unitas returned to New York to appear on *The Pat Boone–Chevy Showroom,* where *Sport* magazine presented him a red-and-white Chevrolet Corvette as the Most Valuable Player of the championship game. John's brush-cut hair, the companion piece to his high-top shoes, made Boone look almost shaggy. Unitas wore a dark suit and a checkerboard tie, Pat a tennis sweater and his trademark white bucks. Their exchanges couldn't have been more scripted and wooden. For the first time in years, Unitas actually seemed his age, twenty-five.

Normally a fast talker, John said haltingly, "This-Corvette-is-really-going-to-look-nice-sitting-in-my-garage. You-know, we-already-have-a-Chev-ro-let."

"No kidding?" Boone said. "Well, this makes a set."

Unitas's older sister, Millie, and her husband, Lou, were along with John and Dorothy on the trip. At lunch, Johnny Mathis came over to say hello, and sang a few bars of "Chances Are." During dinner at the fabled Harwyn Club, the headwaiter pointed out the corner table where Elizabeth Taylor and Eddie Fisher rendezvoused the night before Fisher asked Debbie Reynolds for a divorce. Jackie Gleason invited them all to Toots Shor's for a drink before the theater. In Yankee Stadium, Toots had sat next to Frank Gifford's father, watching his son play as a pro for the first time. The Unitas party had tickets to *My Fair Lady.* At Shor's, the Washington lawyer Edward Bennett Williams told John he had seen the musical two years earlier, courtesy of Mafia boss Frank Costello, who was in jail at the time. Frank had sent someone over with the tickets: Albert Anastasia, who was later gunned down in a barber chair at the Park Sheraton Hotel. John's world was spinning pretty fast now, but he kept his balance.

Julie Andrews and Rex Harrison had recently transferred to the London production of *My Fair Lady*, but it made no difference to Unitas, who had never heard of either of them. "I don't think it was halfway through," Millie said, "when I looked over and saw that both John and Lou were sound asleep."

The Corvette was traded in for a station wagon.

TEN

1959

"He's a teammate; let's try to save him."

Trouble, and Another Title

Bert Bell died on October 11, 1959, at Franklin Field in Philadelphia while watching one team he founded, the Eagles, play
another team he briefly coowned, the Pittsburgh Steelers, when
they were the wartime Steagles. For two months and twenty days,
the league treasurer, a former FBI agent named (perfectly) Austin
Gunsel, served as interim commissioner of the National Football
League. On January 1, 1960, Gunsel yielded to thirty-three-year-
old public relations whiz Pete Rozelle, who would define the word
"commissioner" for nearly thirty years before handing the job off
to attorney Paul Tagliabue.

In 1958 and 1959, Tagliabue was a freshman basketball
player at Georgetown University in Washington. "Growing up in
Jersey City, as close as I was to the Giants, and going to college at
Georgetown, as close as that was to Baltimore, the sudden-death
game of nineteen fifty-eight was probably the biggest game of all
for me personally," Tagliabue said. "As far as Unitas was concerned, you couldn't find three cities that were more similar in
terms of the school yards, the playgrounds, and the hardscrabble
football fields than Jersey City, Pittsburgh, and Baltimore. So there

was a real identification there when I was a young, impressionable seventeen-, eighteen-, nineteen-year-old athlete. To me, Unitas and his team and that game are inseparable from what I would call the blending of the European ethnic football players with the African-American guys."

Tagliabue's mother came from Brooklyn, and many of his relatives lived there, all Dodger fans, of course. "I had a cousin who used to go sit on the stoop of Gil Hodges's house to greet him when he came home from Ebbets Field, to get his autograph for the hundredth time and throw flowers at him. The Dodgers, of course, represented the interaction between the Pee Wee Reeses from the South and the Carl Furillos, with the Italian surnames— he was a huge hero to everyone in my Italian-American family— and the Jackie Robinsons and the Don Newcombes and the Roy Campanellas. In Unitas's Colts, you got the same thing, the Ameches and Marchettis, the Jim Parkers and Lenny Moores. They were tremendously gifted athletes, courageous beyond the imagination, amazing under pressure. I think of the fifty-eight game as a link-age, the end of a thread that ran through the fifties, tying these kinds of players, who grew up in the ethnic neighborhoods of working-class communities, to the integration of American sports. It all came down to the drama of that game, and the drama of that place, and the two teams that were pitted against each other, and Unitas."

For Tagliabue, the sudden-death game was not the first great televised sports event. "For me, the first big television event was the forty-nine World Series, the opening game of the Series, when Allie Reynolds pitched against Don Newcombe, and Tommy Hen-rich hit a home run in the last of the ninth to win it for the Yankees, one–zip. That's the first sporting event I can ever remember watching on television. We didn't even have a television set at the time. I was eight years old." Everyone on Tagliabue's Jersey City street gathered at the house of a fortunate neighbor who had just unpacked a TV. Half of the people in the room were screaming for

the Yankees. Half were hollering for the Dodgers. Tagliabue wondered, "Can you ever forget something like that?" Yogi Berra was
on deck when the game ended. Joe DiMaggio was in the hole. He
was Italian, of course. But to Tagliabue, he was "the enemy." Years
later, when they shared a dais at an Italian-American Foundation
dinner, Paul told Joe about his first memory of televised sports.
"I was the most relieved guy in the stadium," DiMaggio said. "I
couldn't touch Newcombe that day. I couldn't get the ball out of the
infield."

    "A lot of the TV in the fifties was *college* football," Tagliabue
said. "You know, it was Ohio State and Vic Janowicz and those
guys. College football was big in the fifties, bigger than the NFL."
Because the Browns regularly practiced at Georgetown before they
played the Redskins in Washington, Tagliabue shared locker room
space with the Cleveland players and, as a result, had a sense of
this young industry when he was still a young man. He rubbed
elbows with Jim Brown and Mike McCormack, and sometimes
exchanged elbows with them, in pickup basketball games. The
drinking age in the District of Columbia, for beer anyway, was
eighteen. At pizza bars on Wisconsin Avenue, pubs like Maggie's
and the Devonshire, the Browns were usually buying, twenty-five
cents a goblet. "Later, when I was a young attorney for the league,"
Tagliabue said, "Pete Rozelle told me, 'If you ever need to talk with
a player, I'll have Gino Marchetti come and see you.' They were
together, you know, at the University of San Francisco." Sometimes
it seems that the fixed point around which the whole solar system
spun was Gino.

Some money was missing.
    Returning to work in 1959, the champion Colts beat the Col-
lege All-Stars in a suspenseless 29–0 game at Soldier Field in Chicago. After that, they easily handled the Giants, Redskins, and

Steelers. The biggest drama of the training camp (or the season, as far as that goes) was in the clubhouse. Jim Parker said, "Freddie Schubach, our equipment man, always told us to put our valuables in a suitcase at Westminster. But I never did. Most of the guys didn't. Who's gonna steal from the Baltimore Colts? I'd been missing a few dollars here, a few dollars there, but I thought I was just mistaken. Then I looked in my wallet one day and two hundred was gone. I went to practice the next morning and said, 'Fred, some son-of-a-bitch took my money, and I don't like it.' He went, 'Shh, I know where your money is.' 'Well, give it to me then.' 'Shh, we know who took it.' 'Well, you better start speaking now,' I said, 'before I go off.' He said, 'It's Johnny Sample.'"

A few days earlier, Weeb Ewbank had reached into his pocket to pay for a haircut, and found only $5 where $30 had been. Other players had registered complaints with Schubach. Nobody lost his whole poke, the majority of them just $10 or $20. "Finally," Jim Mutscheller said, "Freddie hid his assistant, Dick Silver, up in an air-conditioning vent in the ceiling of the shower room next to the lockers. Little Jewish guy, nice sort of elderly guy, who lived around the stadium somewhere. Only a really small person could crawl around up there in the ceiling." Marchetti said, "*I* set that up. Schubach and I set it up. Too many guys had been saying, 'Geez, I thought I had more money.' So, this old guy, Silver, he's hiding up there in the ceiling and he sees Sample sitting by himself next to a locker and then casually slipping his hand inside. I told Weeb and he told Unitas. All hell broke loose."

Owner Carroll Rosenbloom was summoned, and a kind of court-martial was convened, Marchetti and Unitas presiding. "Rosenbloom asked me what I thought," Gino said, "and I told him, 'Carroll, if he's my own brother, and he goes through my clothes and steals my money, I don't have any fucking use for him.' Rosenbloom looked at me and said, 'What do you think we should do?' I said, 'I think we should get rid of him. He shouldn't be here disturbing what we've got.'" Parker said, "Sample came in, crying, asking for another chance. We had a few heavy words. I told him, 'How can a teammate do a teammate this way?' I'd never heard of anything like it in my whole life." Raymond Berry had. "In college, we ran a similar sting to catch a guy," Raymond said. "It's pretty depressing stuff." "We all voted," Parker said, "and every one of us voted that motherfucker out, except Unitas. 'He's a teammate, he's got a family,' Unitas said. 'It's a chickenshit thing for him to do, but let's try to save him.' 'Fuck him,' I said."

The final tribunal consisted of Marchetti, Unitas, Ewbank, and Rosenbloom. For some reason the owner was reluctant to act. Maybe Weeb had told him what a terrific training camp Sample was having. Maybe Unitas influenced Carroll. But eventually Rosenbloom said, "Okay, I'll cut him." Then he turned to Marchetti and added, "But I expect you to take full responsibility." "'What do you mean, Carroll?' I said. 'It's *your* team.' I looked over at Weeb for help, but he just turned away. 'I'm washing my hands,' Rosenbloom said. 'If we release him on your say-so, and something goes wrong, you're responsible.' 'You mean if we lose a game, Carroll, or if we lose the championship?' 'Exactly.' 'No. I'm the captain of the team. I'm telling you what I think. But you're the owner. It's *your* responsibility.'" So, Sample stayed.

"After the meeting broke up," Marchetti said, "Big Daddy came strolling into the locker room—late. 'We found out who's been taking the money,' I told him. He didn't ask who it was. He just said, 'Black or white?' Big Daddy was a racist. [Marchetti said this in the same dispassionate voice that he had used earlier to say Lipscomb belonged in the Hall of Fame.] 'Black,' I said. 'Johnny Sample.' He nodded and started unbuttoning his shirt. There was so much commotion about this that we got the shit kicked out of us in the last two exhibition games. Nobody could concentrate on football for a while. But we were okay by the time the opener rolled around. Sample started at Ray Brown's old spot, right safety, and played real well."

Inevitably Cameron Snyder and his colleagues got wind of the story, but they had the good taste to leave it out of the papers, resisting an almost irresistible quote from Brown. "First he took my money," Ray said. "Then he took my job." While none of them reported the story, Bill Tanton of the *Evening Sun* at least confirmed it. "The Colts were working out at Loyola College," Tanton said, "and all of the buzz among the writers was this thing with Sample. When practice ended, I went up to Bert Rechichar and whispered, 'Hey, Bert, is it true that Johnny Sample is a kleptomaniac?' 'Kleptomaniac, hell!' he shouted. 'He's a fuckin' thief!'"

●

"They said I stole some stamps out of one of the lockers," Sample told the sportswriter. "I didn't do it."

The only child of a barber and a secretary in Cape Charles, Virginia, Sample was the smilingest kid in the neighborhood, which earned him the nickname Happy. The school he played for, Maryland State College, is now called University of Maryland Eastern Shore. In 1958, even among all-black schools, it was obscure. "Buddy Young told the Colts to draft me, and they did, seventh," Sample said. "I came up from Princess Anne on a Saturday to work out for Weeb at Clifton Park. Unitas was there, helping. They had already drafted me, but they still hadn't seen me, which is pretty funny. There were eight or nine guys running sprints, and I was killing everybody by five, six, seven yards. I heard Weeb say, 'Who is that?' At the end of the workout he pulled me aside to tell me, 'We want to get you into camp early. We're going to take a good look at you at defensive back.' I said, 'Well, I can't come early, I've been invited to play in the College All-Star Game.' I was the first player from an all-black school to be asked. 'Oh yeah,' he said, 'you're *that* guy. I heard about you.'"

The coach of the College All-Stars was the former Cleveland quarterback Otto Graham. By the time Sample reached the practice ground in Evanston, Illinois, Graham had already penciled him in as one of the running backs. Sample said, "I asked him to let me play defensive back—I had played both ways at Maryland State, of course—and he said to me, 'Aren't you a team player? Don't you want to help the team?' I repeated what Weeb had said and told him, 'If you play me on offense, it'll hurt my chances of making the Colts. This All-Star game is only a three-week deal. I have hopes of being in Baltimore for ten years.' 'Well,' he said, 'go ahead and practice with the defense then. It really doesn't matter anymore, because I'm not going to play you anyway.' So, I got into the game for just a minute at the end, and I came out of it with a reputation for not being a team player." At the following All-Star game, playing for Baltimore, Sample dumped two poor kids at Graham's feet, saying both times, "I wish it was you."

As preposterous as it sounds that the Colts had never seen Sample, consider that Sample had never seen Unitas. "I know," he said, "it's weird. John had been the sensation of the league for two years, and I was just across the Bay Bridge from Baltimore. But I'd only heard of him, I'd never seen him, even on television. Here he was, in those black high-top shoes, and I thought, *This* is him? The quarterbacks we had in college could run. John couldn't run a lick. I mean, he would stick his head up in there and get hit—he wouldn't duck anybody, he'd try to run over them—but, you know what I'm saying, he had absolutely no speed at all. They say he played defense in college. Can you imagine him trying to cover anybody?"

However, with the first pass he received from Unitas, Sample understood. "The football spun in your hands," he said. "You had a feeling that if you squeezed it too tightly, the ball would stop spinning in your hands and you would start spinning around the ball. Unitas had a distinct way of throwing. It always reminded me of a basketball player who, at the height of his release, kind of flips his shooting hand over. You know what I mean? In a pose. As if to say, *Swish!* It was really different, but kind of beautiful. I always loved to watch Unitas passing, and even more, I loved to watch him running the show. Sure, he had great players around him, but he made them all better. That's what the greatest player does."

At different times in 1958, Sample understudied Milt Davis, Andy Nelson, Carl Taseff, and Ray Brown. But his steady job was with the "suicide" squads. "I was eased into professional football," he said, "which was all right by me. That's how they did it then. Lenny Lyles and I would stand aside and just watch. Everybody had to learn the business. It was a funny little business." Among all the illustrations of how quaint the NFL was in that era, Sample probably had the best anecdote. "In nineteen fifty-eight the league office was here in Philadelphia," he said. "It was on City Line Avenue. I was here then because my parents had separated and my mother had just moved to Philly. I was in the process of buying a house, but I needed my championship money, and the league hadn't sent out the checks yet. So I decided to call Bert Bell. He had always told us to call him, anytime. So I dialed the NFL office and the commissioner answered the phone. Bert Bell, himself, answered the phone! 'Mr. Bell,' I said, 'I'm trying to buy a home, and I need X amount of dollars for a down payment, but I haven't received my check.' He said, 'Well, that's no problem, Johnny. Come on down here and I'll give you your money.' I drove down to City Line Avenue and he handed me an envelope with four thousand seven hundred and some dollars in it, and seventy-seven cents change. Can you imagine? You call the NFL office and the commissioner answers? How long do you think it would take the two of us right now to get Paul Tagliabue on the phone?"

●

Winning four of their first five games in 1959, the Colts subsequently lost to Cleveland at home (38–31) and to the Redskins in Washington (27–24) to slip to 4–3 and plunge Baltimore into a citywide depression. By this time, the mood of the town fluctuated entirely according to the fortunes of the team. Manager Ned Hanlon's old Baltimore Orioles copped the last of their three straight National League gonfalons in 1896. So, from then until Unitas, the area knew only losing, which may have played a part in *Sun* critic H. L. Mencken's famous declaration "I hate all sports as rabidly as a person who likes sports hates common sense." Mencken died in January of 1956, just missing Unitas. During twelve years in office, from 1947 to 1959, Mayor Tommy D'Alesandro (Big Tommy, Nancy Pelosi's dad) championed the old Colts, the stadium, and the new Colts, first needling the business community into action ("Pittsburgh has the Mellons; we only have watermelons"), later leading the entire citizenry in cheers. "Johnny Unitas is Horatio Alger," Mayor D'Alesandro told the local press. "He's Frank Merriwell. He's Francis Scott Key. And he's ours."

"When we got to four-and-three," Ewbank said to the sportswriter in Oxford, "I gave the team a good talking-to. I knew what was wrong. Because of their tremendous faith in John, they didn't worry anymore about falling behind in ball games. They figured John would always bring them back. For the moment, I snapped them out of it, but that problem would crop up every now and then." The Colts didn't lose again in 1959, sweeping the last six games, even the two on the ten-day West Coast trip at the close of the regular season. They followed up a 34–14 victory over the 49ers, their first success ever in San Francisco, by scoring twenty-one points in about four minutes of the fourth quarter to overtake and overwhelm the Rams, 45–26. That set up a rematch against the 10–2 Giants, with essentially the same rosters as the previous December (although George Shaw was backing up Charlie Conerly now), this time in Baltimore.

Unitas was collecting records by the bushel. With thirty-two touchdown passes in 1959, he became the first quarterback in NFL history to log more than thirty in a twelve-game season—and the only one, as it turned out, because the Dallas Cowboys and the Minnesota Vikings were about to be born, and the fourteen-game schedule was just around the corner. In 1960, the last chance for everybody, John would become the only quarterback ever to pass for three thousand yards in a twelve-game season, and Raymond Berry would collaborate on 1,298 of them.

In the NFL Championship Game of 1959, the sold-out Baltimore crowd of 57,545 had just settled in at Memorial Stadium when Unitas threw a fifty-nine-yard touchdown pass to Lenny Moore. Managing only a Pat Summerall field goal in each of the first three quarters, the Giants couldn't keep the Colts from taking a mere 7–6 halftime lead and rolling it into a 31–9 rout. With thirty-two seconds to go, New York scored its only touchdown, making the final score 31–16. Unitas was named MVP again, earning another Corvette he didn't keep, but the star of the game was the Baltimore defense. And the star of the defense was Johnny Sample. Intercepting two passes, he returned one of them forty-two yards for a touchdown. "I never felt so good," he said, "or so sad." At a Sunday Mass, not that day, but that season, Sample had dropped a dollar or two into the collection basket, and Artie Donovan had yelled out, "Gino, he's giving our money to the church!"

"We handled their running game," Sam Huff said, "but Unitas clobbered us with quickie look-ins and slants. I don't care what you say, there's no way of stopping that."

"On one third-down play," Giant coach Jim Lee Howell said, "Unitas needed seventeen yards and threw for twenty-nine. Another time he needed twenty-one and threw for thirty-one. Those are the things that break your spirit."

In the *Journal-American,* columnist Jimmy Cannon wrote,

> They chased Conerly to the frontier of panic. Even when
> he had loose receivers, he seemed to feel the Colts press-
> ing him. Meanwhile, like a pacifist ignoring a gang rum-
> ble, Johnny U stood there, insolent in his deliberation. If

he were about to introduce a long pass, he would fake
with an elaborate deceit, turning in rapid body feints. The
passes for distance were meant for Lenny Moore, who fled
as if he knew a secret shortcut through the forest of the
Giants' pass defense patterns. The short flips, Johnny U
jerked with a wrist-flicked quickness to either Raymond
Berry or Jim Mutscheller. Unitas suggested a man trying
to complete a dart game before the bartender put out the
lights.

●

In 1972, three years after Sample retired from football, a federal
court convicted him of check fraud. Johnny served one year and a
day at the Allenwood Federal Prison in Pennsylvania, just south of
Williamsport, on the Susquehanna River. "They said I was fencing
federal checks," he told the sportswriter. "I didn't do it. I was bro-
kering theater tickets, circus tickets, stadium tickets, Spectrum
tickets, legitimately. Johnny Sample's Ticket Agency. But someone
who looked like me was buying federal checks and cashing them at
my bank. The government handwriting expert testified on my behalf, saying it definitely wasn't my signature. But I was convicted
anyway. The sentence was probation. Then the probation got violated. Two Secret Servicemen came to my house, handcuffed me,
and dragged me back to the same judge, not for a new trial, just for
a hearing. A guy was there to testify against me, a guy I knew. He
lied and told the judge that I'd bought some checks from him. This
time I got three years. I only stopped off at the penitentiary in Dan-
bury [Connecticut], thank God. Then I went to Allenwood to join
Jeb Magruder and all of that Watergate bunch, for three hundred
and sixty-six days."

Though the food was "rancid enough for a prison," Allenwood seemed "more like a summer camp" to Sample. "I didn't
have a job. There wasn't anything I had to do. So I played tennis

every day from about noon to four. My roommate in college had been a tennis player, but this was my first full-scale attempt at the game. I played until my knees throbbed, and then I played some more. I loved it." Upon his release, Sample got into the tennis community in Philadelphia; and before long, he was a tennis official, a linesman, even a chair umpire, at bigger and bigger events. "I was back in the game," he said, this time on the side of the rules. "I needed to be connected somehow to sports. I had thought of coaching football, but the only letter I could ever bring myself to write wasn't answered. I won't tell you who." (Unitas?) More than his stretch in the pen, among Mainline Philadelphians, the biggest thing Sample had to live down was the title of his 1970 memoir, *Confessions of a Dirty Football Player*. "I was far from the dirtiest player in the league," Sample said, "but my philosophy was that the receiver sitting over there on the bench can't be anywhere near as good as the receiver you're about to hit in the small of his back. So if you knock this guy out of the game, it's all to the good, isn't it? For the team?" (And Otto Graham said he wasn't a team player.) "Next to Bill Pellington," Johnny said, "I was Little Red Riding Hood."

In one of the comebacks of the century, Sample came to officiate at Wimbledon, the U.S. Open, the French Open, and the Australian Open, in matches involving Jimmy Connors, John McEnroe, Chris Evert, Martina Navratilova, and most of the celebrated players of the day. He had photographs to prove it. They're hitting shots in the foreground; he's judging lines in the background. "You might remember a match at the U.S. Open," Sample said, "when Connors played Aaron Krickstein [1991]. Connors came back from five–two down in the fifth set to win in a tie-break. He turned thirty-nine years old that day. At a high point in the action, knowing where the TV mikes were, Connors shouted into one of them, 'This is what they came for! This is what they want!' Remember? I was sitting right there on that line."

During tennis matches, perhaps at the changeovers, did he ever flash back to a football field? "No, I felt too much intensity," he said, "to think of anything except the call. I mean, that was always there subconsciously, in the sense that I remembered how upset I used to get with officials who threw a flag on me that I didn't deserve. But now I was absolutely desperate not to deprive any of these players of a point that might be crucial, something for which they had worked their whole lives."

Sample's final season in Baltimore was 1960. For two years there, he was a pariah. "Don't let anybody ever kid you," he said, "that the Colts were the closest team in the world. The blacks didn't hang out with, or have dinner with, or go to a club with, or go to a party with, the whites. We knew at the start of every season that an even number of us would make the team. Why? Because you had to have a roommate. Big Daddy Lipscomb was my best friend on the team. He was the sweetest guy. He was the jolliest guy. He'd walk down the street in Baltimore and just stop a stranger and start talking. If you look at any of the old films from fifty-nine and sixty, you'll see me coming off the field with Daddy, always with Daddy. I wasn't sorry to move on to Pittsburgh, where I played for a couple of seasons. Then I went over to Washington, which was no good at all. That was too close to Baltimore. All of the old stories followed me there. It was really bad with the Redskins. It just never stopped."

Though Sample left Baltimore in '60, he and the Colts weren't through with each other yet. Nearly a decade later, they would meet again, on January 12, 1969, for a game in Miami. "That was my final NFL game," he said. Technically this was true. It was his final real game. But he lasted into the following preseason, just long enough to appear for the NFL champion in one more College All-Star Game and have a sideline shoving match with Otto Graham.

People often refer to the game in Miami as "the Joe Namath game," but it ought to be called "the revenge of Johnny Sample."

Unitas entered the game late—too late. "John was always good to me," Sample said. "Here in Philly, he'd come on my radio show every year, whenever I asked him. We'd talk and we'd laugh." Jogging onto the field that Sunday in Miami, Unitas passed right by Sample, who said in a stage whisper, "Not today, John. Not this time, big fella."

Coolly, Unitas responded, "Do you still have my watch?"

"So long, Weeb. I love you."

Shula Returns

Winning six of their first eight games, the two-time-champion Colts seemed on schedule for a third title. In a 38–24 victory over Green Bay, John threw the hundredth touchdown pass of his pro career. But a bloody 24–20 gang fight in Chicago, won by Baltimore on a late throw from Unitas to Lenny Moore, took out both teams. "We lost our last four games," Gino Marchetti said. So did the Bears. "That was the game that put the scars on the bridge of John's nose. His nose was bleeding like a running faucet. Our trainer, Eddie Block, wanted to get him out of there. John said, 'If you take me out of this game, I'll kill you.'" "I couldn't even look at John's face," Jim Parker said. "I kept staring at the ground, he looked so horrible." "Tommy Bell was the head ref," Buzz Nutter said. "He whispered to Unitas, 'Take all the time you want, John.' John said, 'Blow your whistle, Tommy. I'm ready to go.' 'You sure you're all right?' Bell said. 'Get off the ball!' John shouted. Then he threw that touchdown pass to Lenny."

In the second-to-last game of 1960, a 10–3 loss in Los Angeles, Unitas failed to throw a touchdown pass for the first time in four years, two days, and forty-eight games. "I dropped a pass in

the end zone," said Alex Hawkins, who had succeeded L. G. Dupre
at halfback. "It was a little behind me, but it was definitely catchable. John never said a word about the record. I don't even think
he knew. There was an airport delay that night, and six or eight of
us went to Chasen's or some other real nice restaurant in the city—
I think it was Chasen's. Louella Parsons, the gossip columnist,
came over to our table, cane and all. 'Oh, Mr. Unitas,' she twittered
like a bird, 'I'm Louella Parsons, and I'd love to have a word with
you.' John leaned straight back to see her and, not being disre-
spectful, just being himself, said, 'Sure, Louella, sit your ass down
and let's have a beer.' She dropped her cane and ran."

Unitas and the straw-haired Hawkins, whom John called
Whitey, were near enough in numbers, 19 and 25, to be locker
room neighbors. "One day," Hawkins said, "John was reading a
letter at his locker, and shaking his head. 'What's the matter?'
I asked, and he handed it to me. It was from a Catholic priest telling John he was going to go to hell because he didn't go to Notre
Dame. 'Oh, Whitey,' John said. 'If he only knew.'"

In 1961, both Raymond Berry and Jim Mutscheller were injured (Mutscheller would retire after the season), and as Nutter
said, "Big Daddy Lipscomb and I were traded to Pittsburgh for
Jimmy Orr and three other warm bodies." The cast of characters
was changing. Bob Harrison had replaced Johnny Sample. Palmer
Pyle would soon go in for Alex Sandusky. Both Dupre and Alan
Ameche were done. A snapped Achilles tendon put the Horse out
to pasture at the unkind age of twenty-eight. Hawkins and old
pro Joe Perry from San Francisco represented the new backfield.
R. C. Owens, known for the "Alley Oop" passes he caught in full
leap from Y. A. Tittle, followed Perry to Baltimore. Against Redskin
kicker Bob Khayat, Owens performed the singular feat of jumping
up at the crossbar and blocking a forty-yard field goal.

During the final exhibition game of 1962, Moore cracked a
kneecap. (Lenny would recover to have his greatest season in '64.)
Artie Donovan was forcibly retired. He might have taken the hint

the year before when Baltimore's number one draft choice, Tom Matte of Ohio State, shook his hand and said in all sincerity, "It's nice to meet you, Mr. Donovan. I'm looking forward to playing with your son." ("I wasn't trying to be funny," Matte said. "He looked older than my father.") Dunny was thirty-six. Because the 1962 season was the third straight without a title, Weeb Ewbank was fired.

"Weeb was too nice a guy," Marchetti said. "I warned him. The moment the nice guy slips, he's gone." (Like Sample, Ewbank wasn't finished with the Colts. Weeb's next team would be the Jets.) Years after that, following a Gridiron Club dinner in Washington, Ewbank, Orr, and Unitas walked out together. "As we were saying good night," Orr told the sportswriter, "John said something to Weeb that stunned me. You know John, he didn't express many personal feelings. 'See you guys later,' Weeb said. 'See you, Weeb,' I said. 'So long, Weeb,' John said. 'I love you.' I damn near fell over."

◆

"On May the tenth, nineteen sixty-three, a Friday morning," Lenny Moore said, *"Big Daddy and I were supposed to go to New York. We had been trying to figure out whose car we were going to take—his or mine. We were going to go listen to some jazz. When we got back, he would decide whether to go straight to Pittsburgh to sign his new contract—he had just been the MVP of the Pro Bowl, you know—or go to Detroit and see his grandmother first. Seven o'clock that morning, I hear on the radio: 'Big Daddy Lipscomb is dead.' I couldn't believe it.*

"I called Sherman Plunkett. The phone was busy. I called Buddy Young's house. No answer. Buddy was at the hospital. Big man's gone. He was playing softball Thursday evening. Coming back across town, he stopped at one of the bars on Eastside.

Then he ended up over at Monroe and Edmondson Avenue, a bar there. They found the body about three blocks down around that corner, Brice Street. What the hell was he doing on Brice Street? We all knew that was drug-infested. We figured a woman, or women. Maybe he went there to take care of business, which wasn't out of line with the way he operated.

"We come to find out he was with this guy [Timothy Black], who's dead now, too. [Black] tried to tell us Big Daddy had sent him out for some beer. We knew that was a lie. Big Daddy never drank beer. All he drank was Seagram's VO. That was his drink. Hard liquor. So nobody knew whether he was hit with the needle or what happened. How did he end up with the crew he ended up with? People that Sherman didn't know, that Daddy didn't know, that I didn't know. You can ask anybody on that Colt team and they would tell you. Not only that he wouldn't stick a needle in himself. But ain't nobody else ever going to stick a needle in him either. Not even for a booster shot. The coroner told me there were three puncture marks in his arm. Aside from the heroin shot—enough heroin to kill five men—they hit him with two saline solution shots. Somebody murdered Big Daddy, all right."

"Three days before he died," Johnny Sample said, "he was here in Philly, at my house. We went to the Penn Relays. Partying, having fun, drinking VO. I couldn't believe it."

"Plunkett called me," Jim Parker said. "He was screaming like a dog. I said, 'What the hell's wrong, Sherman?' He said, 'Big Daddy's dead.' I just felt like everything inside of me died, too. Carroll Rosenbloom gave me ten thousand dollars in an envelope to give to Daddy's wife. But which wife should I give it to? Ophelia out in California, or Ceci in Baltimore? Ceci used to come by my package goods store on Garrison Boulevard. She was nothing but a drunk. Ophelia had two small kids, so I gave her the money. I flew out there in Rosenbloom's private plane. It seated ten or twelve people, but it was just me. I did what I was

told. Daddy wasn't even with the Colts then. Riding back in that
plane, I looked around at the empty seats and started counting
up all of the players who had come and gone."

●

As pro football changed from black-and-white to color, both the
Colts and Unitas continued to have big moments. In 1964 and
1968, Baltimore fielded teams that, until the last day of those seasons, were thought to be among the best of all time. Of course, they
weren't. In '64 and '67, John collected two more Player of the Year
trophies. "In his whole life, I don't know if he ever threw the ball
better than he did in sixty-seven," Orr said. But it probably is fair
to say that the real glory days of both the Colts and Unitas weren't
the ones in Technicolor. Paul Brown and Otto Graham had handed
off to Buddy Parker and Bobby Layne. Parker and Layne had
handed off to Weeb Ewbank and Johnny Unitas. It was Ewbank's
and Unitas's turn to hand off to Vince Lombardi and Bart Starr. For
much of the sixties, including another overtime game of some significance, the Colts would be the Packers' main foil.

Before Alex Hawkins reached Baltimore in 1959, he paused
in Green Bay, where the league's last-place team had made him the
first pick of the second round of the draft, the thirteenth selection
overall. Being an iconoclast, Alex hadn't completely charmed
Coach Brown at the Senior Bowl ("Hawkins, you're a dog," Paul
said), and Alex didn't figure to be Lombardi's cup of tea either. "In
the exhibition season," Hawkins said, "the Packer starters would
play the whole first half unless they did something bad wrong. If
Vince yanked you before halftime, you might consider getting up
Monday morning and checking the waiver wire. We were playing
an exhibition in Winston-Salem, North Carolina, and Bart Starr,
Jim Taylor, Paul Hornung, and I were the starting backfield. It
didn't go great for me, or Bart. And before the first quarter ended,
we were both on the bench. I heard this sniffling off to my left.

I looked over, and Bart was sitting there, crying. Can you imagine John Unitas crying?"

A year younger than John, Starr also came to the NFL in 1956, just as unheralded. He was born in Montgomery, Alabama, and played quarterback at the University of Alabama in the woeful pre–Bear Bryant era that, from Huntsville to Mobile, is a repressed memory today. Bart's college coaches were Red Drew and Ears Whitworth, neither of them Hall of Famers. During Starr's junior season, 1954, the Crimson Tide won just two games. In his senior year, they were 0–10, shut out by Rice, TCU, Tennessee, and Auburn (averting a fifth zero only by a two-point safety against Georgia Tech). Starr, who spent more of that horrid season on the bench than on the field, was selected for Montgomery's Blue-Gray game only as a favorite son, and hardly played. He cried that day, too. The lowly Packers drafted him in the seventeenth round.

In high school, Starr dreamed the same dreams as Unitas. Though Bart wasn't from western Pennsylvania, and he just missed Bryant, he had a general sense of both of them, courtesy of Babe Parilli. Starr told the sportswriter, "Our high school coach, Bill Moseley, played for Bryant at the University of Kentucky. Prior to my senior year in high school, Coach Moseley asked me if I'd like to go to Lexington and train with the Kentucky quarterback Parilli. Oh, man. Babe was generous with his time, and he was a great teacher. He taught me more about the position than I had ever learned before from anyone else. I had his pictures all over the mirror in my room." The same day that Lombardi dealt Hawkins to Baltimore, Vince released Parilli, who thought his five-year pro career had ended. But he was salvaged by the Oakland Raiders of the new American Football League, and after a Hall of Fame turn in Boston, wound up with Ewbank and Sample on that Miami Sunday, holding Joe Namath's coat at Super Bowl III.

It took Starr a few years to stop crying and stand up to Lombardi. When he did, the NFL changed. "Unitas became a star with the Colts," Bart said, "years before I was even a starter with the

Packers. I studied John closely, for a long, long time. I admired his play, his technique, but especially his leadership—the way he conducted himself. I enjoyed watching him run an offense." Before almost anyone else, perhaps everyone except Lombardi, Unitas saw something in Starr, too. "When I had finally worked my way up to the level of being invited," Bart said, "we were together at Pro Bowls. We became friends." Sometimes, quietly, they compared notes, not on the game, but on the NFL. Throughout the sixties, curious teammates who inquired about John's contracts got a stock reply from Unitas. "The only player I ever talk money with," he said, "is Bart Starr, because we're in the same business. I respect him, and I think he should know what I make."

Reminded of their conspiracy, Starr laughed. "Yeah, we chatted at times about those kinds of things," he said. "I was honored that he was comfortable sharing his thoughts with me, and I certainly shared mine with him. I had immense respect for him." Starr called the sudden-death game of '58 "a special moment in the league's history, the start of the increased public attention," and he referred to Unitas's forty-seven-game streak as "one of pro football's most amazing records. [With runs of thirty-six and thirty, Brett Favre and Dan Marino stand a distant two and three.] But John would tell you that football is a team game, and the real accomplishment is taking all of the individual pieces and building them into a cohesive group. John never cared at all about records, but he cared a great deal about his teammates."

In retirement, Starr telephoned Unitas once to ask if he would come to Birmingham for a United Way event. "He said, 'Sure.' When he got here, I took him for lunch at a barbecue place about a mile down the road. He enjoyed it so much that every year at Christmas, I would send him a big Styrofoam box of barbecue—sauce, buns, cole slaw, everything. Take it out, heat it up, and it's ready. He started sending me crab cakes from Baltimore. I called him and said, 'John, I'm getting the best of this deal. Crab cakes cost more than barbecue.' He just laughed. We played golf together one time, in Annapolis, me and Bart Jr., John and John Jr. That was a great day, one of my most cherished memories. It's thrilling just to be in the company of special people. You're with a guy who's your hero—and he was—a guy you competed against very, very hard but respected and admired. During the games, we were competitors. Before and after them, we were friends."

◆

"Gino was the one who got me the job," Don Shula said. "Carroll Rosenbloom loved Gino. Carroll told him, 'I'm letting Weeb go. Who should I hire?' 'There's only one guy,' Gino said. 'Who's that?' 'Shula.' *You mean that guy who used to play defensive back here?'* Carroll called me up to say, 'You've been recommended.'"

Working for George Wilson in Detroit, coordinating the Lion defense for three seasons, Shula had a hand in a couple of narrow victories over the Colts, and Marchetti recognized his fingerprints. Shula said, "That's what helped me get credibility in the eyes of these guys I used to play with, who were much better players than I was. All of a sudden I'm going back there to coach them, and I'm just thirty-three years old." Immediately he named Marchetti and Bill Pellington playing assistants. In Pellington's case, it was like pinning a badge on a Wanted poster.

Though "a screamer" (as John would say) and a taskmaster, Shula was still at heart the teammate who had colluded with Pellington and Carl Taseff to "borrow" the taxicab in Green Bay. Like a lot of football disciplinarians, Lombardi included, Shula was a sucker for the bad boys, as long as they did their work. "Jimmy Orr was not a very physical player," he said. "In fact, Jimmy probably looked less like a pro football player than anybody I ever coached. Of course, he was a tough clutch receiver. But I was trying to get Orr to block downfield. So, in front of the whole squad one day, I decided to embarrass him. I slowed the film down and then stopped it. 'Jimmy' I said, 'if you had made that block right there, we would have had a chance to go all the way. You know, Ray Renfro has always thrown that block for Jim Brown. You're down there and you're not hitting anybody. You've got to hit somebody! You've got to be physical!' He said, 'Can I say something?' I said, 'What?' He said, 'You can't ask a Thoroughbred to do a mule's work.' It brought me to my knees. Everybody broke up."

Hawkins was another exasperating character Shula couldn't resist. He wore Don's old number, 25. A much better running back and receiver than he ever let on, Alex acted dumb with the writers but played smart in the games. He had everything but speed. And to bolster his case for long-term employment, he made a specialty of the special teams. Appointing Alex their captain, Shula sent him out with Unitas of the offense and Marchetti of the defense for the pregame coin flips. "Gentlemen, this is Captain Unitas, this is Captain Marchetti, this is Captain . . . who?" Captain Who became a legend. "I fined Captain Who one time," Shula said, "for staying out after curfew. I called him into the office and told him, 'You missed bed check last night. What the hell time did you get in?' He said, 'I don't want to hear any of this bullshit. Just tell me what the fine is, and I'll pay it.'" It was all Shula could do to keep a stone face. The fine was $100.

Another time, Hawkins arrived at practice wearing sunglasses. Lifting them up to reveal an eleven-stitch seam under one eyebrow, Shula demanded to know what happened. (Alex had "acquired" his wound the previous evening in a bar; a woman was involved.) "It's like this, Coach," Hawkins said. "I had an early breakfast this morning at a pancake house, and the guy sitting beside me at the counter wouldn't stop saying, 'Ewbank was a hell of a lot better coach than Shula.'" That fine was $200. In his most celebrated scrape, Hawkins got pinched by the Baltimore County police in a 4:45 A.M. Halloween night raid on a poker game in the back room of a barbershop that the cops had been staking out for two months. Posting a $55 bond, Hawkins told the magistrate, "I just came in for a haircut." Shula said, "I can forgive your being out at five in the morning, with the Packers due here Sunday. What I can't forgive is your consorting with lowlifes and undesirables. One of those guys had thirty-three arrests on his rap sheet!" "Coach," Hawkins said, "it's hard enough finding a card game at five in the morning, without screening the applicants, too." Again, Shula surrendered. Don couldn't help himself.

He reveled in the head job when it wasn't breaking his heart. "The first guy I had to tell he didn't fit into my plans was Joe Perry," Shula told the sportswriter. "I'm a thirty-three-year-old head coach and I'm sitting opposite *Joe Perry*, who was a great player and a great, great guy, and I'm telling him, 'Joe, we're going in a different direction.' I just felt so humble when I did it, but it had to be done." Eventually he would have to do it to Parker. Eventually he would have to do it to Moore. "People today don't know how good Lenny was," Shula said. "Lenny at his best could play now and be as great as anybody. Just like Paul Warfield, who I had later in Miami. Those two could play anytime, anywhere."

The hardest case of all for Shula to crack was Unitas.

"If you were going to spend any time with Unitas, the first thing you had to know," Buzz Nutter said, "was never to say anything nice about Shula in front of him." Dr. Edmond McDonnell said, "There was an enmity there that never ended. I'd whisper, 'For God's sakes, John, throw him a bone.' But John wouldn't. He didn't believe in diplomacy. 'If that's what you want,' he'd tell Shula, 'that's what you'll get.' John doesn't let up. He'd say to the writers, 'Don't ask me, ask Shula. It's his team.'"

"That was a hot-button item," Raymond Berry said. "You didn't want to push that button. As soon as you got on the subject, it was going to flow. There's a New Testament line, one of Paul's letters, that goes, 'To get respect, give respect that's due.'" Each seemed to think the other withheld it. Maybe both were right. Maybe both were wrong. Maybe one was right and the other wrong. "But there's no question," Raymond said, "John hated him." "With a passion," Orr said.

Fred Miller, an All-Pro defensive tackle who arrived with Shula in 1963, said, "I'll tell you just exactly what John told me. This was years later now, when Shula had that opening of his Baltimore restaurant in a downtown hotel. I went to it. Most of the guys who were still in the area showed up. About a week later I saw John somewhere, and I asked him, 'How come you didn't go to Shula's grand opening?' He looked at me and said, 'If that son-of-a-bitch was across the street and his guts were on fire, I wouldn't walk over and piss in his mouth.' That's the first time I really knew how John felt about Shula."

●

"Early on," Marchetti said, "it was fourth down and a half yard to go, and Shula sent in the field-goal team. John waved it off and got the first down. After the game, Shula summoned John to the coaches' room. I was a player-coach then, so I was there, too. We were the only three in the room. You have to know, Shula was a screamer, but he wasn't screaming now. He was very calm, quiet. 'Listen, John,' he said. 'If you're going to show me up like that, I can't be the coach of this team. From now on, when I send the field-goal or the punting team in, you come off. It has to be my decision whether we kick or not.' I turned to Unitas and said, 'John, he's right.'"

"It was John's personality," Shula said. "It was my personality. It was his confidence in his own ability. It was my belief in how things should be done. I'm not a guy who *finesses* things, and John was never a finesse guy either. You always knew where John stood, just like you always knew what I was thinking. It's not like we didn't listen to him while making up the game plans. We wanted to know everything he thought. You're not going to ignore that kind of experience. Don McCafferty, the backfield coach, was responsible for charting the plays, and John would pretty much call them. We always made sure the things we were doing were the things he liked to do, the things he was most comfortable with. We never ignored his opinions. We incorporated them. A big part of coaching is always putting your guy in a position where he can get the most out of his abilities. Not to use Unitas's strengths would be counterproductive. But there were times in the game when we wanted to help him."

Jim Parker said, "At the exact moment that John had been setting up and pointing to all game long, a play would come in from Shula. In the huddle John would say, 'We're not running that play. We're running this play. Don't let me down.' *Don't let him down?* Fuck! I could hardly breathe!"

"You know, there were times in Miami," Shula said, "when I sent in a play to Marino that didn't work, and he'd come off the field glaring at me. That's kind of the way it is. John and I had some conflicts. But there was nothing but respect from my side of it, for what he was as a competitor. We did have some disagreements. Those things did happen. By the same token, we coexisted. And it wasn't always a conflict, believe me. We had some great times together, too."

For a remarkable stretch that almost no one remembers—starting on December 18, 1966, and ending on January 12, 1969—Shula's Colts played a total of thirty football games and lost two. In the fourteen-game season of 1967, when Unitas completed 255 of 436 passes (58.5 percent), for 3,428 yards and twenty touchdowns, Baltimore was undefeated for its first thirteen games, lost the fourteenth, and missed the play-offs. That season, the Colts led the NFL with over five thousand yards gained. They allowed fewer than two hundred points, a club record. In the defining moment, down 10–0 to the Packers with two minutes to go, Unitas pulled the game out with touchdown passes to Hawkins and Willie Richardson sandwiched around the recovery of an on-side kick. Still, with an 11–1–2 record, the Colts went nowhere. "What has happened to us," offensive tackle Sam Ball told John Steadman, "shouldn't happen to a cur dog."

Because the date of Super Bowl II (still going by the NFL-AFL World Championship Game) was set in granite, with no leeway for any extra play-offs, the owners agreed before the season that if two teams tied at the top of a division, the point totals between them would settle it. The Colts and Rams tied atop the Coastal Division. At Baltimore in October, Los Angeles managed a 24–24 standoff when Bruce Gossett banked a forty-seven-yard field goal off an upright. In the last regular season game, at Los Angeles, the Rams thrashed the Colts, 34–10.

Flying home on the team charter from L.A., Larry Harris of the *Evening Sun* was tapping out his story on a portable typewriter when something made him glance to the left side of the plane, one row back, where Unitas was sitting by himself in a window seat. "Just as I turned my head," Harris said, "a single tear fell out of John's eye and rolled down his cheek. [To answer Alex Hawkins's question—yes, one can imagine Unitas crying.] John asked me, 'What the fuck are you looking at?' 'Nothing,' I said." Of course, Larry left the teardrop out of his story.

In those days, the beat writers were free to critique the players, the coaches, and the games. But they weren't entitled to undress the principals in public, or to be mean. (That was the columnists' job.) Cameron Snyder of the morning *Sun,* N. P. Clark of the *News-American,* and Harris of the *Evening Sun* worked slightly different street corners. Snyder concentrated on the plays, Clark on the numbers, Harris on the people. But they all traded in trust, and John liked and respected all three. Among them, Cameron was the bona fide character. The first time Joe Unitas—John's cousin and former Louisville teammate—visited the Colt locker room, he had no idea who Snyder was. A gaggle of writers was already encircling John when Cameron approached. Being Cameron, he sounded off in a booming voice, "All right, Unitas, when are you going to start throwing the ball to your own team instead of to the *De*-troit Lions?" Who is this son of a bitch? Joe thought, and waded straight into him with fists flying. Cameron, who wouldn't have been afraid to fight

Sonny Liston, started returning lefts and rights. John shouted, "Joe! Joe!" while helping to break them up. "For Christ's sake, Joe! He's a friend of mine! He's all right!"

One sunny afternoon, a day or two before a Pro Bowl in Los Angeles, Unitas and Harris were walking back to the hotel when Larry stopped to buy flowers from a vendor. "What do you want with those?" John asked. Harris, a romantic (with four wives to prove it), said, "I'm going to give them to the first pretty girl we meet." When two young women came along, Harris bowed to the prettier one, saying, "It's a beautiful day and you're a beautiful girl, and I want you to have these." She burst into tears. As it happened, she had just left a doctor's office, where she'd received a bad diagnosis. Harris felt terrible when she told him. "Let's all get a cup of coffee," Unitas said.

As Larry chatted with the friend, John spoke with the stricken girl. "I couldn't hear what they were saying," Harris told the sportswriter. "He had his hand over hers. Their foreheads were almost touching. Eventually she smiled. Then she laughed. We said goodbye and left."

Of course, Harris didn't include this scene in any of his dispatches, or ever mention it again to John. And although all of the beat men were fully aware of the vinegar between Unitas and Shula, none of them wrote it.

●

To Unitas, Shula may just have represented the changing game. Others would revel in football's increasing complications, but not Unitas (or Berry, either). They would miss its simplicity. "Inflation was setting in," Raymond said perfectly. "More and more plays. More and more formations. Longer and longer practices. No way in the world was there time to rehearse everything in our playbook." Situation substitutions were just up ahead. Radio receivers in the quarterbacks' helmets were on the drawing board. Paul

Brown would have piped Muzak through them if it would have kept the quarterbacks from thinking for themselves.

Two of the last blasts from the past—a short gust of intoxicatingly fresh air, and then a longer one—were emitted in 1965. Jimmy Orr figured in the first. The second involved Tom Matte.

"We were playing Philadelphia at home," Orr said, "and I caught a long pass down the right sideline in the opening quarter. The defensive back and I flipped over on the ground, separating my shoulder ever so slightly." Returning to the locker room, Orr changed back into his civvies and went to Union Memorial Hospital. "There were seventeen people in a line outside the X-ray room," he said. "I counted them. I was seventeen. Two guys were on stretchers. Three radios had the Colts game on."

The sixteenth person in line said, "You're Jimmy Orr. Go ahead of me." Orr said, "No, stay there, you're fine." But one by one, despite his protestations, they passed him to the front. "Even the two guys on the stretchers," he said, "who had been in a car wreck." With his shirt off and his shoulder pressed against the machine, it was oily warm in the X-ray room. Jimmy started to feel much better. Not waiting for the results, he rushed back to Memorial Stadium ("Hitchhiked back," Shula said). "I threw my uniform on, not bothering to put on my jock. Of course, my ankles weren't taped. I looked outside. It was late in the fourth quarter. Time had been called. I came out of the first base dugout and ran through the end zone under the goalposts. You can't believe the sound I heard. When I first came to Baltimore in sixty-one, I'd get right up in the tunnel when the defense was introduced before the game. The band would be playing the Colt fight song and Gino would run out first. It was like breaking the sound barrier. I had always wondered what he heard. Now I knew."

Shula said, "Orr came out of the dugout and I saw him running under the goalposts. I waved to him like this, and instead of coming to the bench, he went right down the middle of the field into the huddle. You talk about the emotions and the fans."

"Where have you been?" Unitas asked.

"I was kind of embarrassed about all this," Jimmy said. "I told John, 'Let me run a corner pattern, will you?' 'Sure,' he said, 'on two.'" John threw a pass into a section of the end zone that was mostly cinders, the area of Memorial Stadium that had come to be known as Orrsville. "Probably eighty percent of the touchdown passes I caught in Baltimore were in that corner," Orr said. "It was a little downhill there, you know. At practice once, I laid down at about the twenty-five-yard line, and the field was so concave, I could only see the top railing of the front row of the box seats. I knew that little patch of cinders pretty well." "Jimmy caught a touchdown pass right there in Orrsville," Shula said, "and we won the game. Is that any good?"

This was Baltimore's ninth victory against just one loss (to Green Bay). But two weeks later, wrestling with the old Bears, Unitas shredded the ligaments in a knee, underwent surgery Monday afternoon, and was on crutches the rest of the season. The following week, against the Packers again, backup quarterback Gary Cuozzo unhinged his throwing shoulder and was through for the year as well. Pro football players weren't finished drawing up the damn plays on the damn ground in the damn dirt after all.

◆

Tom Matte was a running back. His father, Roland Joseph Matte (pronounced "Mat" by the French Canadians), had been an eighteen-year-old pro for the Detroit Red Wings of the National Hockey League in its storied six-team era. Roland's father had been the champion decathlete of all Canada, and Roland was considered one of the fastest men on skates. Shifting to the Chicago Blackhawks, he came to be known as Joe Matty. Later on, in the American Hockey League, you might say Joe had all of the moves: to the Saint Louis Flyers, to the Pittsburgh Hornets, to the Cleveland Barons, to the

Akron All-Stars—ultimately coming to a full stop in Ohio. "He played seventeen seasons," said his son Tom, who most Colt fans never even knew was a Canuck. "He was the toughest, meanest, dirtiest— he had absolutely no teeth at all. He took a slap shot in the forehead once and was blind for a month. Football just never seemed that scary a game to me, until nineteen sixty-five."

Shula said, "With Unitas and Cuozzo out, I looked down the roster and saw that four years earlier, Matte had played quarter- back at Ohio State. So I called Woody Hayes and said, 'Tell me about Matte as a quarterback.' He said, 'Great kid, wonderful young man—' 'Yeah, yeah, Woody,' I interrupted him, 'but we're trying to beat Lombardi and the Packers here! Were there any negatives you can remember? It might help me prepare.' I'll never forget his answer. 'Well,' he said, 'he had a little trouble taking the snap from center.' Oh, God."

One game was left in the regular season, an away game against the Los Angeles Rams. By rule, because a quarterback had gone down, the Colts could add a quarterback for the final game. But not being on the roster by a specified date, he wouldn't be eli- gible for any postseason play. "We picked up Ed Brown," Shula said, "Gino's old teammate at the University of San Francisco. We had one day to get him ready." In the last game of his pro career, Brown threw five passes against the Rams and completed three of them, including a sixty-eight-yard touchdown pass to tight end John Mackey. Meanwhile, Matte ran sixteen times from the quar- terback position, gaining ninety-nine yards. He also threw seven passes, completing one to each team. The Colts won the game, 20–17, and with a 10–3–1 record were deadlocked with the Pack- ers, setting up a showdown the day after Christmas in Green Bay.

"We put the plays on wristbands for Matte [a novelty then]," Shula said. "I've got one of them still. He's got one. I think the Hall of Fame has one, too. Our whole objective was just to make a first down. If we made a first down, we were keeping the ball away from them. Then maybe we could make another first down." Matte said, "Unitas had a big hand in redesigning the offense for me. 'Tom, I don't think you're going to be a pocket passer,' he said. 'Let's get you to the outside.' I'd roll right or roll left. The back would go one way, I'd go the other. John was having a ball. 'Tom, how about if you did this? Can you do that? What about this other thing?' He was just loving it. And we beat the Rams."

Matte, Unitas, Jimmy Welch, Bobby Boyd, and a couple of other players attended a postgame party in Los Angeles, "a typical L.A. party," Matte called it, "at an apartment complex. Full of young starlets. Wall-to-wall good-looking women. John and I were having a couple of beers, like we always did, chatting up the girls, when Welch—he was a defensive back—came out of one of the bedrooms, whispering, 'They're snorting cocaine in there.' I turned to John and he was already gone. With a cast on one leg, he hopped down three flights of steps faster than you could believe. By the time I got to the street, he had already flagged down a taxi. God, we were laughing. 'Three flights in under ten seconds in a leg cast,' I told him. 'Are you shitting me? That's the record that will never be broken!'"

From the day Matte signed his original contract ($10,000 salary plus $4,000 bonus money, which he gave to his parents for a down payment on their first house), he was the "noodge" on the team, the overgrown kid. Nobody else had the nerve to twist grass in Shula's ear or sneak up behind Unitas and goose him. ("You crazy, man!" John exclaimed, over and over.) Nothing about pro football threw a chill into Matte, though even Tom shut up in John's huddle. "Everything would get quiet," he said, "and John would start asking his questions. Was I open for this? Was Raymond ready for that? What could he do for us? How could he help anyone? Did the line need a screen play to slow up the rush? Danny Sullivan was a guard for us. After a blitz and a sack, Sully's head was down like this, and John said, 'Sully, do you want to play quarterback today?' 'No, John.' 'Then you better goddamn block your guy.' 'Yes, John.'

'And no more of those *lookout* blocks from you, Matte.' Whenever I'd miss my man, I'd yell, 'Look out, John!' And now I was the quarterback, and it was my huddle. It was like a dream."

"Trying to mimic Unitas," Shula said, "Matte asked Berry, 'What have you got, Raymond?' Whenever John asked him that, Raymond would give him the formation, the play, the whole deal. But when Matte asked it, Raymond said, 'Run a Flow Thirty-eight,' which was an end run around the right side, as far away from Raymond as possible."

But the play-off in Green Bay couldn't have started better for Baltimore. Not a half minute into the game, linebacker Don Shinnick picked up a Packer fumble and ran twenty-five yards for a touchdown. Caught in the backwash of flying bodies, Bart Starr had to leave the game with throbbing ribs, in favor of Zeke Bratkowski. The Colts led at halftime, 10–0. "Every time I came off the field," Matte said, "I ran straight to John. 'Quarterback draw,' he'd say. 'They can't stop you.' Or: 'Let's have a little counteraction here.' I think that day is when I won John's respect as a football player. I hope so."

"With two minutes to go, we're ahead in the ball game, ten–seven," Shula said, "and it's going to be the greatest upset in the history of the National Football League. That's when Chandler attempted that field goal." With 1:58 remaining, Don Chandler, the Giant punter from the '58 sudden-death game, kicked a twenty-seven-yard field goal that was called good and led to another overtime. Chandler's kick was either just wide or just inside, depending on the camera angle of several photographs later put into evidence, but also on the prejudices of the people viewing them. Chandler kicked an undeniably good one to win the game in the extra period, 13–10. The next Sunday, again at home, the Packers beat Cleveland for the last non–super world championship, the first of three titles in a row.

"That's why the uprights were raised ten feet," Shula said, "the so-called Baltimore extensions. The ref who made the call,

Jim Tunney, was standing in the middle of the goalposts. After that, they put a man at each upright, looking up. I see Jim a lot. He's a good friend of mine. We talk about it all the time. I mentioned it again just recently, and he said, 'Christ, can't you let that go? It's been fifty years!'"

The Colts' season wasn't over. *After* the title game, runners-up Dallas and Baltimore played a consolation bowl January 9 in Miami. "Get ready for a long day," Shula warned the defense, "I'm going to let Matte throw the football." During pregame warm-ups, Shula and Cowboy executive Tex Schramm stood together on the field watching Tom make a spectacle of himself. With nobody rushing him and nobody covering his receivers, he still could barely complete a pass. "When one of his throws went end-over-end," Shula said, "Tex started hitting me, elbowing me, just grinning from ear to ear. He couldn't wait for the game to begin. But when it did, Matte hit everything—Tom was a hell of a competitor—and we kicked the shit out of them [35–3]."

In his postmortem, Dallas's cerebral coach, Tom Landry, told the reporters, "They knew exactly what to do against our Flex Defense." When Landry's analysis got back to Shula and Unitas, they finally found something they could agree upon completely, and laugh about all the way home. As Shula said, "Tom Matte didn't have the faintest fucking idea what the Flex Defense was."

TWELVE

1968

"I've always felt that if I had started the second half . . ."

Jets 16, Colts 7

The number one draft choice of 1956, taken right after bonus pick Gary Glick, eight spaces before Lenny Moore, twenty-nine places before Sam Huff, 106 spots before Bart Starr, was quarterback Earl Morrall of Michigan State. The day after Unitas appeared in his first Blue-White game, back in '56, when John was introduced to the city of Baltimore with the *Sun* headline UNITAS STARS FOR BOTH TEAMS, a small item on the same page reported that Morrall had been elected cocaptain of the College All-Stars. He was a two-time Rose Bowl champion, cheering from the bench in the first victory but leading the Spartans from ten points behind in the next. With six seconds left in that second game at Pasadena, Morrall held for a field goal that beat UCLA, 17–14, and the San Francisco 49ers made him their top pick.

Earl was also the third baseman on a Michigan State baseball team that nearly won a couple of College World Series. "I broke Harvey Kuenn's Big Ten record," he said, referring to a Wisconsin shortstop who became a star for the Detroit Tigers. "Harvey had four errors in one game. I had five."

This is a typically self-deprecating remark from Morrall, who ended up a journeyman quarterback in the National Football League (emphasis on the journey) but had more than a few shining moments along the way. He played for San Francisco, Detroit, Pittsburgh, the New York Giants, Baltimore, and Miami. Relieving injured starter Bob Griese, Earl quarterbacked the Dolphins to eleven of their seventeen victories in the undefeated season of 1972. With the Colts in 1968, Morrall was named the NFL's Most Valuable Player. "Perhaps it is hindsight, perhaps it is sophistry," wrote the bard of Baltimore, Ogden Nash, "but the Colts owe a lot to Giant front-offistry."

⬤

After the '67 season, Raymond Berry retired. John's latest backup quarterback and roommate was a tough, smart kid from Gettysburg College, Jim Ward, who was glad to be understudying Johnny U and grateful not to have missed Berry. In the second-stringer's traditional quarters at Westminster, the middle room in a three-man suite between Unitas and Berry, Ward had eavesdropped into the night as Hector and Paris plotted their wars. "In sixty-seven," Ward said, "John threw a touchdown pass to somebody, and Shula came over to me on the sideline and told me, 'Make sure you sit down with John and find out how he read that defense.' So, when he got to the bench, I said, 'John, what was your read out there?' He looked at me and said, 'Goddamn if I know, Jimmy. The guy was open.'" As Raymond said, Unitas wasn't overly analytical.

"Shula was definitely the boss," Ward said. "When John would return to the bench from the field, I'd be standing right there. Boy, I could feel the electricity between them."

Coming off his second MVP season in four years, Unitas brought a weary arm into 1968, his thirteenth pro campaign. He was thirty-five years old. In the second exhibition game, against the Chicago Bears in Birmingham, Alabama, Ward injured a leg and Shula called Morrall in New York. Earl wasn't keen to make another move to another subordinate position, but Don told him in a whisper, "You may play more than you think." A deal was transacted (Baltimore gave up a substitute tight end named Butch Wilson) and Morrall arrived just before the second-to-last exhibition. In the final tune-up game, a 16–10 victory over Dallas in the Cotton Bowl, Unitas threw a long touchdown pass to John Mackey but, a little while later, returned to the bench with his right arm hanging by his side. "What do you got?" center Bill Curry asked. "I don't know," John said. "I think I've torn something."

"The two tendons that hold the upper and lower bones together at the elbow were torn off at the bone," Unitas said years later. They would "just lay in there" for thirty years, while he compensated as best he could. (Gradually all of the strength would be drained out of his middle finger and thumb, rendering him, in his fifties and sixties, a left-hander.) For the entire 1968 season, John attempted only thirty-two passes and completed eleven, for 139 yards, two touchdowns, and four interceptions.

With Morrall at the controls, the Colts opened the year against Earl's original team, San Francisco, in Baltimore. "The first pass I threw was a touchdown," he said, "for San Francisco." (Shades of John's Colt debut.) "But we got the ball back and—bing, bing, bing—we moved down the field to about the 49er twenty-one or twenty-two. The next play was supposed to be a pass to Tom Matte, but a linebacker jumped right on him. Just as I started to throw it somewhere else, I saw the weak-side safety breaking across the field. I stopped, turned to the outside, and lofted it to the wide receiver, Ray Perkins. Touchdown. Seven–seven. I'm feeling a lot better. When I came to the bench, Shula jumped in my face and shouted, 'Goddamn it, what the hell are you doing out there! You're lucky that ball didn't go the other way! You've got to read the defense! That pass should have gone to the flanker! We had one-on-one coverage! Read the fucking defense! The defense will tell you where to go!' "

"Shula used to piss me off, too," said Jerry Hill, the fullback. "I remember a couple of times he said, 'You're blocking like an old lady, Hill!' Something like that. I'd wake up at night sweating and wanting to smash him in the head, you know? But, looking back now, I don't think I would have played as long as I did if Shula hadn't pushed me. I think that's just the way he motivated, the way he coached."

The Colts beat the 49ers, kicking off the Earl Morrall victory tour over all of his old teams: San Francisco (27–10), Pittsburgh (41–7), Detroit (27–10), and New York (26–0). During the fourteen-game regular season, Baltimore lost only once, to Cleveland on the sixth Sunday at home, when John tried to play. He threw eleven passes and completed just one. In Memorial Stadium, he actually heard a rumble of boos. "It's a sin," John Steadman said on his radio show, "for a Baltimorean to boo Unitas." Waltzing through the next eight games, the Colts handled Minnesota in the first play-off (24–14), dismantled the Browns at Cleveland in the NFL Championship Game (34–0), and prepared to do the same against Joe Namath, Weeb Ewbank, Johnny Sample, and the AFL Champion New York Jets.

Unitas and Morrall might have been jealous rivals, but they weren't. They quickly became chums. "The two of them fit hand in glove," Fred Miller said. "We called them Hump and Rump. John had those sloping shoulders and Earl had that big butt." Unitas could not understand Morrall's devotion to chocolate, but in every other way John liked Earl. "I would come to the sidelines and he would tell me things," Morrall said. "In later years, when he got the starting job back, he would come to the sidelines and I would tell him things. We were pros, and pals." In retirement, they would cruise together with their families to ports as distant as Australia and New Zealand. John: "So this is the Great Barrier Reef." Earl: "It's the greatest barrier reef I've ever seen." John: "Let's go get a beer."

"Early in December," Ward said, "we played a game in Green Bay on a Saturday. It was our most crucial game of the regular season, and we won it by a touchdown and a few points—I can't remember the score [16–3]. What I do remember is how cold it was. It was as cold as Christmas, and we stayed in a rickety old hotel, where the wind seemed to be blowing right through the glass. John and I went up to the room, and pretty soon, there was a knock at the door. John opened it and here came Fuzzy Thurston [former boy-Colt, current man-Packer] walking in with a case of beer. He put it up on the desk chair and for two hours I was privileged to sit there in silence and listen to all of the fifties stories." John's arm was starting to come back by then, and he had been restless not to be playing. But for the moment, he was laughing again. "As they told their Weeb stories," Ward said, "I could see how much John loved it all."

◆

"Unitas had this great belief in his own ability," said Shula. "Sooner or later, John was absolutely sure, things were going to fall into place for him. And they did. In college and in the pros, they did. I'll bet he even had it in high school. But he was hurt now. He had that elbow. Earl had come in and become the player of the year, the MVP. We were pretty good with Earl. We beat the Browns, thirty-four to nothing. *Thirty-four to nothing!* But John was practicing again, so I had to make a decision. I had to deal with what I saw. The Unitas I saw wasn't the same one who won those championships. I saw a guy with a bad elbow trying to play injured. I saw a guy on the downside of his career. And I decided to go with Earl in the Super Bowl."

As the Jets' players were picking up their room keys in the lobby of a Fort Lauderdale hotel, Namath brushed off a Dayton, Ohio, newspaperman named Si Burick. When Namath reached his room, the phone was ringing. It was Frank Ramos, the team's public relations director, who had witnessed Namath's snub of Burick. "Joe," Ramos said, "that's one of the best guys in the business." Namath called Si, apologized, and offered to meet him at the pool. This led to an iconic photograph, reprised every Super Bowl Week, of Namath in his swimming trunks, stretched out on a deck chair, surrounded by reporters. Si is the one seated in the foreground under the tent of a folded newspaper shielding his bald head from the sun. It looks like a free-for-all interview session, but for the first half hour, every time anyone other than Burick posed a question, Namath responded, "Excuse me, I'm speaking to this gentleman here."

Burick wanted to write a column about Namath and Unitas, two western Pennsylvania quarterbacks ten years apart. "Oh man," Namath told him. "That crew-cut hair. Those high-top shoes. On Sixth Street in Beaver Falls, I wasn't Joe Namath. I was Joey U. My number was nineteen, too. [Joe Montana's boyhood number was 19, too.] For our away games in high school," Namath told Burick, "we didn't have a nineteen jersey, so I wore twenty-nine. It wasn't even a quarterback's number, but it was the closest I could get to him. I heard Johnny say once that every play he called had to be thought out completely, and it had to have a crystal clear purpose. I still tell myself that today."

Three nights later, at Jimmy Fazio's bar in Fort Lauderdale, Namath and left-footed Colt placekicker Lou Michaels bumped into each other, and the two of them got into a demented argument over which one was the better Catholic. They almost came to blows, which wouldn't have been lucky for Joe. When Michaels finally threw up his hands and said, "Unitas never talked like you," Namath replied, "Unitas is over the hill."

It was the first Super Bowl that called itself a Super Bowl, and maybe the first one that had the right. The cover of the official program was a Merv Corning painting of Colt defensive back Lenny Lyles and Jet wide receiver Don Maynard going up together for a ball. "I didn't even know that," Lyles said, "until many years later, when someone sent it to me."

"Tom Matte had a fifty-eight-yard run in the first half," Sample said. "That was a long way for Matte to go, as slow as he was. When he looked up and saw it was me who tripped over him at the end, he said, 'You dirty so-and-so.' I said, 'I don't have to be dirty against guys as slow as you.' We had a big discussion about that. 'You guys can't beat us,' I told him. 'You have no speed at all.' Every second I was out there, I was thinking of nineteen fifty-nine and sixty. Every second of the two weeks leading up to that game, I thought of nothing else. I wanted revenge in the worst way. I hit Matte out of bounds. Of course I did. When I ran by the Colts bench one time, I got slugged with six or seven helmets, too. I knew it was going to be a good day for us when they took the kickoff and drove to our twenty; when we fumbled at our own twelve and they recovered; when Matte had that long run all of the way to the red zone; and when they ran the Flea-Flicker almost to perfection—and ended up getting no points at all. Not one point out of that whole mess! We were ahead, seven–nothing, at the half."

The Flea-Flicker, the last pass of the half, was the signature play of the game. That was Paul Brown's favorite trick. He used to call it "the triple pass." Ewbank was sure it was coming (Weeb's knowledge of the Colts was probably the decisive factor in the outcome) and he tried to prep the Jets for it all week. But they couldn't stop the triple pass even in practice. "I hand off to Matte, he starts to go right but throws the ball back across the field to me, and I pass it deep to Orr," Morrall said. "Jimmy was jumping up and down, all by himself. ['I did everything,' Orr said, 'except send up a flare.'] I still don't know why I didn't see him. He was the primary receiver. I threw underneath to Hill instead, threw behind him. It was intercepted."

The clock had struck midnight and Earl had turned into a pumpkin. "I think Orr may have been camouflaged," said Hill. "The blue of his jersey blended in with the blue uniforms of the Colts marching band [marshaling in the end zone for the halftime show].'" "A lot of crazy things happened," Morrall said. "From their six-yard line I threw what should have been a safe pass to Tom Mitchell but hit him on a shoulder pad and the ball bounced straight up in the air for an interception in the end zone. I threw it a little behind Willie Richardson and Sample caught that ball about a foot off the ground at the goal line. We did everything *but* score. It was just crazy." Unitas said, "Right before halftime, on the field, Shula told me, 'I want you to be ready to go in the next half.'" John took that as a promise that he would start the third quarter. When he didn't, he counted it forever as a lie. "I've always felt," Unitas said years later, "that if I had started the second half, things would have ended up differently."

Shula said, "Everything that happened in the first half—the tipped balls, the crazy bounces, the missed field goals, Jimmy Orr jumping up and down—not all of it was Earl's fault. He'd had a great year. I decided to give him one more series." Circumstantially, with New York monopolizing the football, getting Morrall four more plays exhausted the third quarter. "When I made the decision to go with John," Shula said, "he took us eighty yards right down the field to score [not immediately; Unitas's first time-consuming drive foundered at the Jets' twenty-five when still another tipped ball was intercepted in the end zone]. But it was too little, too late. I have to live with that."

At the 6:11 mark, by Namath's calculations, the Jet players started to perspire a little. But they needn't have. "That was the longest six minutes and eleven seconds of my life," Joe said. Being such a good Catholic, Michaels followed the touchdown with a textbook onside kick that was recovered by Baltimore in Jet territory, and Unitas pushed the offense inside the New York twenty. On the sideline Namath looked at flanker George Sauer and whispered, "Johnny U." Sauer replied, "Come on, clock." But on fourth-and-five, Unitas's last-ditch pass to Orr was late, lifeless, and easily swatted away. "John couldn't throw the ball ten yards," said Hill, who scored the Colts' only touchdown. "But I'll tell you what, he tried." "I used to call him Zip," Matte said. "But he had no zip that day." Sixteen–seven was the final. The AFL had triumphed.

"When Weeb Ewbank died [November 17, 1998]," Ted Marchibroda told the sportswriter, "I was coaching the Ravens in Baltimore. I mentioned Weeb to my players after practice. They had no idea who he was. Not one of them had ever even heard his name. I told them, 'This guy coached the winning team in the two most important pro football games ever played.'"

●

With 85 percent of the old zip (by his own estimate), John retrieved the starting position in 1969, Shula's last season in Baltimore before moving on to Miami. As the NFL and AFL completed their merger, the Steelers, Browns, and Colts pocketed $3 million apiece for deigning to join the old American Football League teams in a new American Conference. At the close of the 1970 season, with Coach Don McCafferty at the helm, the Colts returned to Miami for Super Bowl V as the ironic representative of the outlaw league they had let into the game. The deepest question asked in the pregame press sessions was: why had Unitas let his hair grow out to a combable length? "I lost my regular barber," he said, leaving out the fact that the barber had gone to jail for operating an illegal lottery.

The Baltimore players called their new boss Easy Rider. In 1959, the year McCafferty arrived from Penn State to help coach the offense for Ewbank, he asked Unitas, "John, do you want any help on Sunday?" "Mac," the quarterback replied, "if you're *positive* they're going to blitz, let me know. Otherwise, sit back, relax, and enjoy the game." John and the Easy Rider got along splendidly.

Baltimore beat the Dallas Cowboys for Unitas's third world championship, 16–13. This time, in a blaze of symmetry and equity, it was Unitas who started the game and Morrall who came in for him. After John threw a twice-tipped pass to John Mackey for a seventy-five-yard touchdown, the Cowboys did a xylophone number on

Unitas's ribs and left him cuddling an ice pack the entire second half. Morrall wasn't stupendous, but he brought the team back. He was redeemed. The hard-hitting but homely game came down to a 13–13 tie and a thirty-two-yard field goal try with five seconds to go. Kneeling to hold the ball for rookie Jim O'Brien's kick, Morrall looked up at the clock and recalled that there had been six seconds remaining fifteen years earlier when he held for the winning field goal in the Rose Bowl. O'Brien was just eight years old then. Was he nervous now, at twenty-three? "Well," Morrall said, "he tried to toss up a few blades of grass to test the wind. 'Jimmy,' I told him, 'it's an artificial grass field. Just hit it solid, son. Everything's going to be all right. It'll go straight through.'" And it did.

"The best team I ever played on," Mackey said, "lost the Super Bowl. The worst team I ever played on won it." Mackey, a large tight end from Syracuse, had a way of saying things quickly and well. "Playing with Johnny Unitas," he said most famously, "was like being in the huddle with God."

Shula went on to win a couple of Super Bowls in Miami and a total of 347 NFL games, more than anyone else (even Halas or Brown) ever had before or probably ever will again. In 1972, he talked owner Joe Robbie into spending $90,000 on an insurance policy named Morrall. "Ninety thousand dollars for a backup quarterback?" Robbie squealed, but he forked it over. The Dolphins likely wouldn't have won in '72, and certainly wouldn't have gone undefeated, without Earl. This time, though, the instant Griese was ready to come back, Shula reinstated him.

In an epilogue to Super Bowl V, O'Brien was out of football within two years of his winning kick, four seasons before Morrall retired a full twenty-one-year man. "What do you do after you've won the Super Bowl?" O'Brien asked the sportswriter. "I was single, and I was immature. I did some dumb things." He got into a barroom fight, and a bottle in the face cost him some of the vision in one eye. "That's my badge of stupidity," he said. It took O'Brien quite a few years, but, with the help of a good wife, he said, "I finally figured it out. The thing about Americans is, we have no heroes of substance, only athletes and movie stars. The inventors, the cancer-cure finders, are in the real game. It could have been better for me if I had never made that kick. I'd have been more serious. But practicing every day as a kid, I always dreamed of the last-second field goal to win the biggest game in the world, and there it was."

●

"If you threw the ball at that wall," Unitas said, "that wall would have just as good a chance of catching it as John Mackey."

"Then why," the sportswriter asked, a little annoyed, "do I have this memory of him carrying whole teams down the field on his back?"

"Oh, he caught some," Unitas said, including touchdown passes from John of 51, 52, 54, 56, 57, 58, 61, 75, 79, 83, and 89 yards, the last being the longest TD pass Unitas ever threw as a pro. "No, Mackey was a hell of an athlete," Unitas said. "Johnny was a smart guy, too, and he was a good guy. But he had 'board hands.' He had hands like a toilet seat." Quoting Unitas at Hall of Fame caucuses, Baltimore delegate John Steadman managed to keep Mackey out of Canton for fifteen years before he was finally elected in the final year of his eligibility. He was the second fulltime tight end to go in. The first one, Mike Ditka, kept asking, *Where's Mackey?* When it came to tight ends, both Unitas and Steadman may have had a hard time letting go of Jim Mutscheller.

"Johnny Unitas was my quarterback," Mackey said, "and he was the best. Isn't that right, Sylvia?" "Yes, honey," said Mackey's wife of four decades, his former sweetheart at Syracuse. The next time Unitas's name came up at the table, Mackey said, "Johnny Unitas? He was my quarterback. I'm just pissed at the NFL. They let him die. I told them I'd kick their ass."

Mackey was wearing a brown leather overcoat and a brown leather cowboy hat that puzzled the other diners at the Mount

Washington Tavern in Baltimore. It was a sweltering August day. But every day, winter or summer, he wore that same coat and hat. He thought he always wore the same Hall of Fame golf shirt underneath, but Sylvia had ten copies of that shirt. "I take the dirty one out of the closet every day," she confided in an aside, "and hang the clean one up in the same place."

Mackey was a brilliant and eloquent young man, who in the labor skirmishes of the early seventies served as the president of the NFL Players Association. He and Fred Miller met in Illinois at the College All-Star Game of 1963, the twelfth-to-the-last edition, and became permanent friends. This was no small thing. One of the famed "Chinese Bandits" at Louisiana State University, Miller had played with no blacks in college, and against only one black his entire time at LSU. When Miller and Mackey shared an airport cab to catch a flight to Baltimore after the All-Star Game (a 20–17 stunner over Lombardi's Packers, the last time the collegians would beat the pros), it was the first time Fred ever rode in a car with a black man. "I love John Mackey," Miller said. "When I see him, I just have to hug him. Sylvia, too. Charlene and I just love her to death."

"I ran over nine Detroit Lions," Mackey said. "Do you remember that, Sylvia?" "I sure do, honey."

In December of 2001, he was diagnosed with frontal lobe dementia. How did it happen? "Who knows?" Sylvia said. "It could be from head trauma, of course. John led with his helmet a lot. And he didn't go down easy, as you know. I have to say, the diagnosis was almost a relief to me. To finally have an answer. It had been coming on for so long, for years."

Participating in a Hall of Fame golf tournament in 1994, Mackey lent the wife of one of the players $5,000. He seemed to confuse her with someone from Syracuse who had once showed him kindness. "The reason he thought he owed her the money," Sylvia said, "didn't fit. A feeling of dread shot through me. After that it was just a series of things, like mail piling up, little things."

Going from table to table to tell everyone in the restaurant that Johnny Unitas had been his quarterback, Mackey made a few of the customers uneasy. But Sylvia wasn't embarrassed. "It's not him doing it," she said. "It's the disease. We went to a party of some of my oldest girlfriends and I heard one of them say, 'Oops.' John had taken off a whole corner of the cake with his hands. Inappropriate personal behavior, like repeating stories over and over, is one of the symptoms. If John sits here and eats the flowers, I'll be frustrated and sad. But I'm not going to worry about the people at the next table. So they don't get it. I don't know them. What do they mean to me? I don't care. I love him."

The daughter of two educators who met in graduate school at Howard University, Sylvia had been confronting the illness head-on for about three years. "I've read everything I can on frontal temple dementia," she said. "I've studied his medications. I'm trying to take the ball and run with it." Sylvia should be in the Hall of Fame, too. After thirty years in Los Angeles, she moved the family back to Baltimore in 2002, hoping John would find the city familiar. He didn't. But in an almost unbearably touching development, it found him familiar. "He's not at the wandering stage yet," she said, "but we went to a football game at the stadium, and as we were getting ready to leave, he got lost in the crowd. Our daughter Laura was frantic. I said, 'Don't worry, Laura. We'll call home and he'll answer.' We did, and he did. Some old Colt fan had brought him home. He's gone missing a couple of times, but some old Colt fan always brings him home."

Their other grown daughter, Lisa, "doesn't deal with him at all," Sylvia said. "It's embarrassing to her. She's not over that stage yet. But Laura is staying with us now, helping out tremendously. And I'm back flying for United. John does card shows, autograph signings. We have things to do. Every year, the Orioles invite all of the old Colts to a ball game. That's coming up soon. We've got our tickets and we're all excited. John will enjoy that. Then he'll walk through the crowd at the stadium and sign autographs, which he loves to do."

Occasionally he'll tell someone to "go deep," as though they were in a huddle. Frequently he'll repeat a sexual joke that has to do with tight ends and wide receivers. Over and over he'll say, "Johnny Unitas was my quarterback."

Along the far wall of the restaurant, he was pacing. "He'll pace for hours at home," Sylvia said, "saying, 'When are we going?' Then the moment we arrive somewhere, like here, he'll say, 'When are we leaving?' I'll say, 'We *are* where we're going, John.' 'Oh.' 'And we'll leave when we leave.' 'Good.' Sometimes I have to talk to him like a mother. 'Shave if you're coming with me,' I'll say. 'I'm not shaving,' he'll answer. 'That's fine, you don't have to shave. Stay home.' 'No, I'll shave.' We go through this routine with showering, too, and changing clothes. Every day is exactly the same. I don't know if I'm being realistic or not, but if it stays just like this for ten years, I'll take it."

Returning to the table in his leather coat and hat, John looked somewhat softer than his old self, but still pretty fit. The sportswriter played a pickup lacrosse game against Mackey once. Like Jim Brown before him, John was a tremendous midfielder at Syracuse. From the perspective of the crease, you should have seen young John Mackey bearing down on the goal. "Do you remember lacrosse, honey?" Sylvia asked. "I remember everything," he said, "that I need to remember. Johnny Unitas was my quarterback." "Physically," she said, "he could take off running right now. You know, they honored the old Colts at halftime of a Ravens game, when they put their names and numbers up in the ring of honor at the new stadium. All of the former stars were on the field, sitting in chairs. Each of them was presented a football commemorating the date. When John got his football ["*number eighty-eight, at tight end, John Mackey . . .*"], he jumped out of the chair, ran fifty yards into the end zone, and held the ball up to the people. They went crazy. At that same moment, one of his greatest touchdown runs was showing on the giant screen."

The next player introduced, "*number twenty-four, Lenny Moore,*" duplicated Mackey's run exactly, fending off the same imagined tacklers, stiff-arming the same perceived threats, in a perfect display of grace.

THIRTEEN

1971

"The one cigarette started coming down the line."

Reefer Madness in San Diego

G ino Marchetti had given way to Lou Michaels, who had given way to Roy Hilton, who had given way to Bubba Smith, who had given way to Billy Newsome. And Unitas was still there. Bill Pellington had given way to Jack Burkett, who had given way to Dennis Gaubatz, who had given way to Mike Curtis. And Unitas was still there. Alan "the Horse" Ameche had given way to Joe Perry, who had given way to Jerry Hill, who had given way to Tony Lorick, who had given way to Norm Bulaich, who had given way to Don Nottingham. And Unitas was still there. L. G. "Long Gone" Dupre had given way to Alex Hawkins, who had given way to J. W. Lockett, who had given way to Terry Cole, who had given way to Tom Nowatzke.

And Unitas was still there.

"John and I were having a beer," Marchetti said. "'How are things going out there?' I asked him. 'Not so good,' he said. 'I don't have the receivers I used to have. I don't have the blocking. The backs.' Never once did he say, 'I can't throw it like I used to.' That's us. We always think we can do it. Years after you've retired, you're watching a game on television, and you don't even realize you're coming closer and closer to the edge of your chair, until you almost fall out of it onto the rug into a three-point stance. You don't want to admit what you can't do anymore. You don't want to give up what you love so much."

Unitas was thirty-eight years old in 1971, his sixteenth season in the NFL. On April 7, playing paddleball with Tom Matte at the Towson YMCA (John was probably right to shun paddleball back on William Street), Unitas exploded an Achilles tendon. But, rehabbing fanatically with therapist Bill Neill, he made it back into uniform for opening day of the regular season, a 22–0 whitewash of the Jets. John and Earl shared the position for a while. On guile mostly, they led the Colts to seven victories in their first nine games. By the tenth game, Unitas was a full-timer again. "One of my best memories of him," Morrall said, "was after a game when he threw five interceptions. There were so many writers around John that I was almost squeezed out of my own locker. I leaned in between arms and legs, straining to hear him. 'I threw five interceptions today,' he said, 'but we won. I'll be glad to throw five interceptions any day, if we win.' I wanted to cheer."

They dropped the tenth game, 17–14, in Miami. "We were reeling a little from that loss," said Ernie Accorsi, the assistant general manager (the Hershey kid who witnessed *you*-knee-*tass*'s first pro pass). "We had to win the next game at Oakland to stay in the play-off picture." Even at home, adhering to the Paul Brown playbook, most NFL teams spent Saturday nights in hotels. The Colts stayed at the Edgewater Hyatt, the Raiders at the nearby Hilton, and both corps of Catholics came together Sunday morning at Mass. "I'll never forget it," Accorsi said. "There had to be thirty Catholics on each side of the aisle. John Sandusky [one of the Colt assistant coaches, no kin to Alex] was sitting beside me. As Unitas went up to the altar to receive communion, Sandusky nudged me and whispered, 'Look at the way the Raiders are staring at him. They're in awe of him.' That was the last great day of John's career."

Unitas had been "dinking" the ball all season, to use Ernie's word. "But it was as if God said, 'I'm going to give you one last day to throw the ball the way you used to.' I swear, he threw lasers. When John walked off the field that afternoon, the score was thirty-one to nothing. We ended up winning thirty-seven to fourteen. It's the only time I can remember John Unitas ever approaching being giddy. On the plane ride back, he was so happy. We beat Buffalo next, then Miami at home, fourteen–three, after he put together two nine-minute drives. But John was back to swinging the ball out to Matte. He was back to dinking it. We knocked off the Browns then in the play-offs [20–3 in Cleveland] and actually had a chance to return to the Super Bowl and defend the title." But they were stopped in Miami, 21–0, the Colts' first blank in ninety-six games. John wasn't awful (twenty of thirty-six, for 224 yards), but he wasn't his old self either.

"At least," Accorsi said, "he had that one last day as his old self."

●

The following summer, the Colts changed owners. In a shrewd whirligig to avoid capital gains taxes, Carroll Rosenbloom arranged for a whiskey-faced Skokie, Illinois, air-conditioning impresario, Robert Irsay, to buy the Los Angeles Rams and swap them straight up for the Colts, lock, stock, and horseshoe helmets. Joe Thomas, a former player–personnel director in Minnesota and Miami (you could smell his hair tonic just watching him on television), brokered the deal for Irsay. His finder's fee was the general manager's job in Baltimore. "I don't know which one of them, Thomas or Irsay, was the bigger liar," Unitas said. "Both of them were world class."

"I was just a little kid from American International College, Division Two, that got a shot," said Bruce Laird, who would make the 1972 team and the Pro Bowl as a kick returner and go on to be an eight-year starter at safety. "My first memorable moment in the NFL," he said, "was, after the last exhibition game in nineteen seventy-two, watching a bunch of grown men cry when Carroll Rosenbloom came walking through the clubhouse saying good-bye to his old players. It was like saying good-bye to an era. That astonished me."

Irsay advertised himself as an ex–football player on the scrub team at the University of Illinois, but nobody in Champaign had ever heard of him, and he certainly never played for the Illini. He spoke of the four years he served as a marine officer in World War II, from 1941 to 1945, going so far as to bemoan the "touch of malaria" he contracted in the jungles of New Guinea. In fact Irsay was a stateside enlisted man for precisely 101 days in the middle of the war. According to the National Personnel Records Center in Saint Louis, he entered the service on October 23, 1942, and was separated on April 3, 1943. The instant this four-flusher signed on the dotted line, the Baltimore Colts were essentially doomed.

Unitas's new "backup quarterback" in 1972, John's seventeenth and final season in Baltimore, was Marty Domres of Columbia University, a well-dressed young man who had written one book and read several others. Domres was the author of *Bump and Run: Days and Nights of a Rookie Quarterback,* a roman à clef he wrote when he had nothing else to do in San Diego, sitting around behind Charger quarterback John Hadl. Almost nobody except Mrs. Hadl ever read it. She seemed to recognize her husband inside the pages and between the sheets. It didn't do much for their marriage, or for team morale generally.

The morning after an especially discouraging 34–33 loss in Oakland, San Diego head coach Sid Gillman went to see owner Gene Klein in Los Angeles. With four victories and six defeats, Sid's team was on schedule for its usual third-place finish behind Kansas City and Oakland or Oakland and Kansas City. Still, he had no idea this would be his last morning on the payroll. Besides the Chargers, Klein owned Bantam Books, Domres's publisher. "Since we're going nowhere anyway," Gene told Sid, "would you mind

starting Marty now so we can try to move some of these books?"
Gillman, the only head coach the team had ever known, went off
like a Roman candle and was fired. At a press conference later in
San Diego, he said, "I've got a message for the young people of
America. If anyone ever tells you that you have a lifetime contract,
make sure you get it in writing."

He was replaced by Harland Svare, the Giant linebacker from
the sudden-death game, who couldn't cover either Raymond Berry
or Alan Ameche and blamed Carl Karilivacz. Svare traded Domres
to Baltimore for a number one draft choice that turned out to be
Nebraska running back Johnny Rogers. In the next twist of the
kaleidoscope, Domres would bag himself a second legend and
Unitas would wind up in San Diego.

•

Beating only hapless Buffalo, the Colts lost six of their first seven
games in 1972. On the Monday following the fourth loss (21–0 to
Dallas in Memorial Stadium), Don McCafferty was fired, and in an
eight-second phone call from Thomas, Unitas was benched. John
Sandusky became the interim coach. He was known mostly, and
unfairly, as Don Shula's old pencil man, the clipboard carrier who
had sat next to Shula every morning at six-thirty Mass. Actually
Sandusky was a gifted teacher and a stand-up guy. Probably knowing it would end his hopes of ever being a real head coach, he accepted the impossible job in order to preserve the salaries of the
other assistants. Of course, he was honest with Unitas. "They told
me never to play you again," he said. By "they" he meant Thomas
and Irsay, but mostly Thomas. "They said you're never going to
play another down in a Colt uniform." "It's their team," Unitas answered typically, "but I'm going to tell you what, John. Don't ever
ask me to run the clock out for you."

Everybody's homecoming opponent, the Bills, came to Baltimore on December 3. Unitas of the offense, Fred Miller of the

defense, and Ray May of the special teams went out to midfield for the coin toss. "This is Captain Unitas, this is Captain Miller, this is Captain May." But Miller and May were wearing their helmets. John was wearing a jacket over his shoulder pads. It was the third-to-the-last Sunday of the season but the year's final game at Memorial Stadium, and everyone knew this was Unitas's valedictory in Baltimore. What happened at the end of the game is still a little hard to believe.

Sometime in the forties, probably when Irsay was on furlough, E. B. White wrote a football fable that foretold giant television screens in the end zones and all manner of aircraft, including little dirigibles, floating over the ballparks:

> High in the blue sky above the bowl, skywriters were at work writing the scores of major and minor sporting contests, weaving an interminable record of victory and defeat, and using the high-visibility pink news-smoke perfected by Pepsi-Cola engineers. Cheering, of course, lost its stimulating effect on the players, because cheers were no longer associated necessarily with the immediate scene. A football star, hearing the stands break into a roar before the ball was snapped, would realize that their minds were not on him, and would become dispirited and grumpy. Two or three of the big coaches worried so about this that they considered equipping all players with tiny ear sets, so that they, too, could keep abreast of other sporting events while playing, but the idea was abandoned as impractical, and the coaches put it aside in tickler files, to bring up again later.

Cheering lost its stimulating effect on the Colts and Bills players, who felt entirely disconnected from the day—because the more Domres and the Colts abused Buffalo, the louder the full house of 55,390 people chanted, "We want Unitas!"

Rolling out to the left side with just a few minutes to go, Domres scored on a quarterback keeper and was nicked on the hip. He came off the field walking like Walter Brennan. When the Baltimore offense was called back out for one more series, Sandusky didn't know what to do. That is, he didn't know what Unitas would do. The coach pointed to his own hip and John put on his helmet. A sound went through the stadium that played scales on people's spines. The pass Unitas lobbed to Oklahoma wide receiver Eddie Hinton wasn't a particularly wonderful pass—it was more of a pretty good dink—but Hinton's backbone was reverberating, too. He'd had a buzzard year, with only ten receptions and no scores. But, catching the ball in a traffic jam, Eddie somehow morphed into Gale Sayers, weaving another forty yards, for a sixty-three-yard touchdown. John ambled off the field, waving good-bye. "Just at that moment a peppy little plane flew over the stadium," said Bill Tanton of the *Evening Sun,* "pulling a banner that read, 'Unitas We Stand.'" It would fly again twenty-nine years later at John's funeral.

The final road games were 24–10 and 16–0 losses in Kansas City and Miami. When Unitas was finished as a Colt, Ernie Accorsi approached his Orange Bowl locker and said, "John, the Hall of Fame wants absolutely everything, even the tape off your ankles."

"Oh, Christ," Unitas said. "Well, they can't have the shoes."

Accorsi was slightly taken aback. "Don't tell me you're sentimental about the shoes," he said.

"They're great for cutting the grass," John replied.

"They particularly want the jersey." Hearing that, Unitas pulled the white 19 over his head and handed it to Ernie.

"Here," he said. "I *don't* want you to give it to them."

"What?"

"I'll get them another one. One that I wore. They won't know the difference. I want *you* to have this one."

And he does.

"The first day I met Unitas," Accorsi told the sportswriter,

"I was a young PR guy, totally intimidated by him. I asked John if he would do something or other, and he said no. As I was leaving the clubhouse, he called out to me, 'Get back here!' When I did, he said, 'You're never going to accomplish anything if you take the first no for an answer.' You see, he taught every one of us how to do our jobs. In nineteen eighty-two, in October, my wife and I separated. Thanksgiving was going to be my first holiday alone, but I got a call from John. 'Where are you having Thanksgiving dinner?' he asked. 'At Hillendale,' I said. 'No, you're not. You're coming to my house.' 'My mom's with me.' 'She's coming to my house, too.' Same at Christmas. Johnny U."

●

"Are you *sure* you want me to sign this?"

That's all Jerry Magee of the *San Diego Union* had to hear. At the Chargers' contract-signing ceremony, when Unitas looked up from the paperwork and put that question to Gene Klein, Magee knew John couldn't play anymore. It was a two-year deal at $250,000 per, exactly twice Unitas's highest salary in Baltimore. Klein had paid the Colts $150,000 for the rights to the man already named Quarterback of the Century, who was informed of his sale over the telephone, not by any executive of the team with which he was synonymous, but by Larry Harris of the *Evening Sun*.

To say San Diego was a culture shock to Unitas is the understatement of any century. "After practice," John told Steve Sabol of NFL Films, "I see a bunch of guys go into this one room. Well, you know, usually guys will go have a beer or something like that. So I figure I'll knock on the door and see what's going on. Well, when I knock on the door, gee, it gets deathly silent inside. Finally, after I knock a couple of more times, one of the players opens it up. I says, 'Do you guys have a beer in here or anything?' 'Yeah, yeah, come on in.' There are about fifteen guys inside. So I sit down, figuring

I'll shoot the breeze for a while. All of the windows are open. We're talking football when I see one guy light up a cigarette. I have no problem with that. Players smoke all the time. But then the cigarette starts coming down the line. I says, 'You've only got *one* cigarette?' All of a sudden this big lightbulb lights up over my head. 'Excuse me,' I says. 'I'm in the wrong room.'"

Sabol told the sportswriter, "We were doing a piece on the Chargers in nineteen seventy-three. My old roommate, Tim Rossovich, was playing for them. He and I lived together for about three years when Tim was with Philadelphia. Dave Costa was in San Diego then, too. So was Deacon Jones. After practice ended, Rossovich said, 'Come on up.' So I went up to the room and the first thing I saw was this big bong pipe. You know, on this team, you could walk into their meal and get high just breathing. Unitas passed through, saying, 'Are you guys smoking those funny cigarettes?' He was such an anachronism on that team. Here's everybody else walking around in tie-dye shirts, love beads, and Afros. And there's Unitas. It was like he was from the age of Magellan."

Recreational drugs aside, the Chargers' locker room was a pharmaceutical swamp. A medical reviewer from the State Board of Pharmacy would later call it "Drugsville, U.S.A." Houston Ridge, an injured defensive lineman, had filed a lawsuit against the Chargers alleging that the team physician and the trainer gave him steroids, amphetamines, and barbiturates "not for the purpose of treatment and care but for the purpose of stimulating his mind and body so that he would perform more violently as a professional football player." The action was brought in 1970, but excerpts from depositions were just finding their way into the newspapers as Unitas arrived. They were juicy. Coach Gillman admitted saying to Ridge, "Get rid of those crutches, Ridge. Throw them down and walk. You can't make the team on crutches. You can't play on crutches." But Sid characterized his remarks as "colloquialisms of our profession." He also testified, "I'm not a medical man," noting that team physician Dr. E. Paul Woodward was the one in charge of prescriptions. "Woodward," Gillman said, "and a possible Dr. Jay Malkoff." Malkoff was Sid Gillman's son-in-law.

Dianabol, Desbutal, Seconal, Librium, Noludar, and an avalanche of other medications were purchased by the team in lots that ran to ten thousand pills a year. *Ten thousand pills a year.* Quoting Gillman as saying, "Take your Dianabol so you can become big and strong," safety Kenny Graham described the sensation of popping two amphetamines before every game, and one at halftime, as "an incredible exhilaration. I was very talkative. I was hyperactive. And I know some instances where I received injuries and I didn't—you know, I didn't pay them any mind."

The examiner asked Graham what made him stop taking bennies.

"Well, the way I was conducting my personal life."

Meaning?

"Well, for instance, the hostility."

Wasn't Graham afraid he might lose his position on the team?

"No. Afraid I might lose my wife."

Woodward, who paid a portion of the settlement Ridge ultimately received, acknowledged under oath that speed was freely dispensed before games to any Charger who wanted it. According to Dr. Woodward, the trainer would hand out "two [pills] prior to the game, and he would give an additional one at halftime, if a player seemed to feel he needed it." In his deposition, Charger executive counsel and former Hall of Fame tackle Ron Mix spoke of an unnamed player "who carried logic to the extreme and felt that if one benny would be good for him, maybe ten would be better. I don't know the exact numbers, but the result was he was in some form of discomfort after the game."

Cereal bowls full of anabolic steroids, "little pink pills," were put out on the tables at training camp right next to the salt and pepper shakers. "We were encouraged to take the pills," receiver extraordinaire Lance Alworth told Magee, "but nobody ever said,

'If you don't take the pills you're off the team,' or anything like that. They only said, 'We think they'll make you a better football player.'" Alworth, who moved over to Dallas in 1971, acknowledged to Magee that he took the pink pills. A few players testified that they pretended to take them while actually tossing them out a dining room window onto the lawn below, "the greenest strip of grass on the property." Alworth said, "Some of us were worried we were taking estrogen, which is a female hormone. We used to kid each other about that a lot."

In April of 1974, when Unitas was beginning his last three months with the Chargers, Rossovich, Costa, Jones, Walt Sweeney, Coy Bacon, Bob Thomas, Jerry Levias, Rick Redman, and Harland Svare were disciplined by NFL commissioner Pete Rozelle with a blend of fines and suspensions and other probationary penalties "for violations of league drug policies." Svare was cited for a stupendous lack of vigilance.

"It's a sewer out here, Doc," Unitas told Dr. Edmond McDonnell back in Baltimore. "Times are changing," McDonnell said. "You drank beer. They smoke marijuana." "No," John said. "They are not the same things. Beer is legal. Marijuana is *il*legal." McDonnell told the sportswriter, "Unitas was a sterling, hardheaded character for whom right and wrong were always strong in his mind. Everything was either black or white. There never were any gray areas with John."

•

San Diego held one positive, as far as Unitas was concerned: a twenty-two-year-old rookie quarterback named Dan Fouts. He was a third-round draft choice from the University of Oregon, and John was impressed by his talent, and by him. At first Svare and offensive coordinator Bob Schnelker (the Giant tight end in the sudden-death game) were pleased to see Unitas take an interest in Fouts. ("I think he felt sorry for me," Dan said. "I wasn't very good.") But eventually Svare and Schnelker summoned John to the office and, if you can believe it, told him to leave the young quarterback alone. "I can believe it," Raymond Berry said. "That's one of the sad realities we run into in the real world, insecure people who care less about accomplishing things than guarding their own turf. John was totally secure in himself. He wouldn't understand people like that."

Back at the lockers, Unitas informed Fouts, "They've ordered me to stop working with you, Danny." Fouts's response was concise: "Fuck them. Let's just keep doing what we've been doing." For Fouts, it wasn't a hard call. "Here Bob Schnelker is telling me, 'You've got to read this linebacker to that linebacker, and throw this ball to that guy,' and I look over and I see Unitas is rolling his eyes. So we get out of the meeting and John goes, 'Come here,' and he starts explaining to me exactly how to read defenses. If I walked out onto a football field today, eighteen years after I quit, I'd still be reading defenses the way he taught me. Schnelker, of course, caught wind of it. He went up and down, shouting, 'I'm the god-damn coach here! Don't you listen to that guy! You do things my way or you'll never play!' There was only one problem with his argument. This was *Johnny Unitas.* If you're going to paint the ceiling of the Sistine Chapel—if you're going to paint the roof of your garage—who are you going to listen to? Michelangelo? Or Sherwin-Williams? Come on." One month into the season, Schnelker quit.

In build and bearing, Unitas and Fouts weren't much alike. They didn't throw the same kind of ball, either. But something about the way Fouts dropped back to pass was reminiscent of Unitas, and it stayed that way throughout Dan's fifteen-year career. "I knew John's rhythm," he said. "People talk about timing, routes, and all that stuff. Well, he invented all that. He's the guy. *Bounce, throw, completion. Bounce, throw, completion.* I'm looking at him and going, Well, that's the way to do it. The backpedal. A lot of coaches wouldn't let you do the backpedal. They thought it took too long. But not when *he* did it. I found that, backpedaling like John, I could see the whole field. I could put pressure on the whole field.

Of course, coaches think, every time you backpedal, you're throwing left. Well, you're going to throw a majority of the time to the left because you're trying to see out there. But all you have to do is throw a couple of times to the right and that key goes away in a hurry."

Besides Unitas's rhythm, Fouts got to know John's laugh. "One day, when a player screwed up in practice, Unitas gave me this incredible look and said, 'Too much rope.' I thought, *Rope?* 'How can you expect them to know the plays,' he said, 'when they're up there in their rooms all night smoking that rope?' John had a few sayings that cut right to the quick. I can't even tell you."

Tex Maule wrote in *Sports Illustrated,* "It is a little like watching a Neanderthal man walking down Fifth Avenue. He wears the high-top, black leather shoes he has sported since he came into the league . . . now cracked and fissured with age. 'Jim Thorpe left me his shoes,' Unitas says, smiling. 'They keep my ankles together.'" To Maule, John looked a little homesick. What did he miss most about Baltimore? "You know something?" Unitas told Tex. "We haven't even had a drizzle since we came to camp. I miss thundershowers. I like to sit on the porch and watch the rain come down. No way I could ever live out here. I'll put in the time I can, but when it's over I'm going back to where it rains in the afternoon and gets cold in the winter." He was forty.

In the mind's eye, nobody pictures Babe Ruth as a Boston Brave, or Joe Namath as a Los Angeles Ram, or Bob Cousy and Walt Frazier as Cincinnati Royals and Cleveland Cavaliers. But the sight of Unitas in Charger livery isn't an easy image to shake. It's like Willie Mays stumbling in the outfield as a New York Met. John's first full exhibition game in powder blue and lightning bolts was only a statistical success. He completed eighteen of thirty-one passes, for 286 yards and two touchdowns. But San Diego lost to the Rams, 30–17. The Chargers had won just four games the previous year, and would win only two this season, but in a minute and eight seconds at the end of the first half, Unitas drove the team eighty-seven yards for a touchdown, exactly as he used to. He passed on every down. In the two-minute drill that closed the game, he was in the process of doing the same thing when Dave Williams caught a ball on the Los Angeles fourteen and fumbled. Both touchdown passes John threw—a twenty-eight-yard rocket to Williams and a forty-one-yard rainbow to Bob Thomas—were from the "greatest hits" collection. But while the arm appeared to be okay, the legs were another story.

In the previous exhibition game, Unitas had been blindsided by a 49er rush. "One of their big defensive linemen hit me a shot," he said. "I was down and my leg was twisted a little and the guy fell on it and I could hear a pop. I walked off the field but the knee was sore; and a few days later, trying to favor it, my back went out and I had a muscle spasm. I couldn't straighten up. The doctor put it back in place and it doesn't bother me now, but the knee is arthritic and Doc McDonnell back in Baltimore says it will deteriorate a little every year. So I don't know how much longer I can play, and neither does anyone else. I'll take it week by week." Meanwhile, the New Age team bought him a waterbed. "Every time I roll over," he said, "it sloshes and wakes me up."

In a season that was essentially ended in one game, the Chargers opened at Washington and were obliterated, 38–0. After beating the Bills and losing to the Bengals, they went to Pittsburgh for what would be the final start of John's NFL career—and, incredibly, his first and only pro appearance in his hometown. Stepping out of the Pittsburgh Hilton for a quick bus ride across a bridge to Three Rivers Stadium, Unitas was greeted by a band of screeching high school students holding aloft a cardboard sign that read, "Saint Justin's Loves Johnny U." He shook hands with the boys, hugged the girls, and smiled for all their cameras. "That was nice," John told *San Diego Union* columnist Jack Murphy on the bus. "I probably graduated with the fathers of most of those kids."

When Unitas walked off the field that day (in the flipside of the Oakland game of '71), the Steelers led, 31–0, and Fouts came in for good. The final score was 38–21. "Do you feel sorry for

Unitas?" someone asked Terry Bradshaw after the game. "No, he doesn't want that," said the Pittsburgh quarterback. But Terry did allow, "He looked awfully funny in that San Diego uniform. I admire him for trying. He must have a tremendous love for the game. I sure wish I could have seen him when he threw great, though. I don't suppose I'll ever play against him again."

"That was rough," Fouts said. "I prefer the memory of seeing him go over forty thousand yards in San Diego. The first quarterback ever to touch forty thousand. That was a thrill for me, even though it should have happened in Baltimore. He got that record on one of the few days that we won, too, which was great. You know, what Svare was trying to do was copy George Allen's Redskins formula with 'over-the-hill' guys. The problem was, most of our 'over-the-hill' guys were the wrong guys."

"I was doing the radio for the Atlanta Falcons," said Jimmy Orr, "and we went out there the fifth or sixth week of the season to play the Chargers. Before the game, I watched John warm up, but I don't believe he played. He threw the ball pretty good. It looked like he'd gotten it back a little. You know, I played in a Blue-Gray game when Sammy Baugh was the coach. At practice one day, he was trying to show one of the quarterbacks how to throw the halfback out-and-up. The older a quarterback gets, you know, the lower his arm drops down. Well, Sammy took the ball and he threw it from way down here and hit the guy with a perfect spiral about twenty-five yards down the field on the dead run. That's what I thought of, watching John. Slingin' Sammy Baugh. After the game, John came over to the hotel and we sat around and talked for a couple of hours. He said, 'Nobody here cares about winning. They're more interested in going to the beach.'"

John made only two appearances after that, separating his shoulder in the eighth game, his last. Sometime earlier, in the San Diego clubhouse, Magee and the sportswriter were Bob-and-Raying Unitas at his locker. Gary Garrison, the Chargers' best receiver, had just gone on the disabled list. "Ain't that a kick in the head?" John said. "Gary's a good boy, too." Standing there wearing only a jockstrap, Unitas looked like the oldest man in the world.

"I wish John could have been around in my tenth or twelfth year," Fouts said, "so we could have talked football together, especially with the Don Coryell offense. He would have gone bullshit with Air Coryell. I mean, he would have done things—when you think of the numbers he put up in a two-back, two-receiver, one-tight-end offense, for his whole career [40,239 yards, 290 touchdown passes, 62.9 postseason passing percentage, 1,177 yards in championship games, 22 NFL records in all, including 47 consecutive games with a scoring pass] and then you see what the guys are doing today. Imagine him at the top of his game today."

In 1993, Fouts was inducted into the Pro Football Hall of Fame. "I mentioned him in my speech," he said. "I looked into the camera and said something to the effect, 'Johnny U, I know you're out there watching. Don't adjust your set. I'm actually here.'" After a laugh and a sigh, Fouts said, "He was real. There was nothing phony about John Unitas. In this day and age in sports—in anything—in life—knowing exactly what you're getting is almost impossible. That's what he was. He was almost impossible."

Near the end in San Diego, Unitas roomed with an assistant trainer named Jimmy Hammond, whom most of the players called Hambone. Affectionately, John called him Dummy. "I asked John if Dave Costa could throw in with us, too," Hammond said, "and he told me, 'Sure, Dummy, as long as he doesn't smoke any of those funny cigarettes.'" On July 24, 1974, Hammond and Unitas were walking off their dinners at the Miramar Naval Air Station near training camp when first one, then two, and finally scores of aviators surrounded John. "They pulled him down to a hangar," Hammond said, "put him in a fighter jet, and took turns taking pictures. 'We have to get back, John,' I whispered to him. 'You're going to miss curfew.' 'Don't worry about it,' he said. 'I'm retiring tomorrow.'"

They didn't get home until one-thirty in the morning. To mark the occasion—to show that he had a little outlaw in him, too, and to bid a fitting farewell to the San Diego Chargers—Johnny Unitas took a leak off the balcony. Later that day, at a hastily called press conference, John said, "Coach Prothro [Tommy Prothro, the Chargers' new head coach] doesn't believe in players coaching and coaches playing, so I can't think of any way that I can help the team this year. It's too much to ask a player to get around on a pair of ninety-eight-year-old legs." Without fanfare, he flew home to the land of thundershowers.

"A couple of years later," Hammond said, "we went to Baltimore to play the Colts. I had a standing invitation from John to come to his restaurant, the Golden Arm. I called, but he wasn't there. I left a message that the equipment guys and I were on our way. When we arrived, there was a long line outside. 'Do you have a reservation for Jim Hammond?' I asked the hostess. She scanned her list. 'No.' 'Are you sure?' I said. 'Would you mind checking again?' I was in shock. 'Wait a minute,' she said. 'Are you Dummy?'"

"At NFL Films," Sabol said, "it's always been my job to glorify the game. I'm such a romantic anyway. I've always looked at football in dramaturgical terms. It wasn't the score; it was the struggle. And what kind of music could we use? But when I met Unitas, I realized he was the antithesis of all that. Football to him was no different than a plumber putting in a pipe. He was an honest workman doing an honest job. Everything was a shrug of the shoulders. He was so unromantic that he was romantic, in the end."

FOURTEEN

1978

"I'm never going to sleep with that woman again."

Colts 28, Giants 14

I n the summer of 1978, *The CBS Sports Spectacular* observed the twentieth anniversary of the sudden-death game by presenting a six-man, two-hand-touch rematch in New York's Central Park, pitting Frank Gifford, Kyle Rote, Pat Summerall, Alex Webster, Rosey Brown, Dick Modzelewski, Ray Wietecha, and Charlie Conerly against Gino Marchetti, Raymond Berry, Jim Parker, Alan Ameche, Artie Donovan, Steve Myhra, Lenny Moore, and Johnny Unitas. "They asked me to play, too," Sam Huff said, "but I don't play no fucking two-hand touch." The field was seventy yards long. To get a first down, a team had to cross midfield. In the absence of goalposts, extra points were automatic. Looking quite official in a striped shirt, with a whistle lashed to his neck, Sonny Jurgensen was the solitary, all-powerful referee.

The players dressed in jerseys and shorts, most of them. John wore sweatpants. On the back of his 35 shirt, Ameche's name was misspelled, with a *K* for an *H*. Using clumps of adhesive tape, Myhra customized an 86 jersey into his old 65. Both teams looked more than a little raggedy, but nothing important had changed. Unitas hit Sputnik in the flat for the first touchdown, Berry downfield for the next, and Raymond even deeper for a third. "Twenty years have gone by," Jurgensen said to the Giants, "and you all still can't cover Berry." The Colts led at halftime, 21–0.

Hiding Rote among the standing-room-only crowd framing the perimeter—no seating in Central Park—New York finally scored in the third quarter on a sneak pass to Kyle from Gifford. "That was a totally illegal play," Jurgensen said, then, "Touchdown! Twenty-one to seven." Conerly's elbow was aching, so Gifford did most of the Giants' quarterbacking. But at one point, when Charlie reentered the game, Jurgensen showed his knowledge of history by announcing, "Conerly in for Heinrich." Don Heinrich.

Huddling up, John looked right at Ameche and called, "Four twenty-eight." This time Alan heard the "four," took the pitch right, and in the absence of Jim Mutscheller, flipped a pass to Berry. But Raymond was touched down on the one-yard line, and the ball went over. Scrambling away from Marchetti's and Myhra's rush, Gifford was at least ten yards beyond the scrimmage line when he skidded to a stop and threw to Webster for a touchdown. "Twenty-one to fourteen," Sonny said—"New York has cheated on both scores." Reaching all the way back to the Kingston Trio, Gifford said, "It takes a crooked mind to recognize a crooked play." As time was running out on the Giants, Frank fired a pass over the middle that was intercepted by Unitas. Modzelewski got a hand on John, but nobody could double-touch him as he cut over to the left sideline and loped to the end zone. The final score was 28–14.

"I got there just in time to see John intercept Conerly's pass [Gifford's pass, actually] and score the winning touchdown," said Johnny Sample. "It was around the Fourth of July [July 7] because Wimbledon had just ended. I was in town for a tennis thing, staying at the Warwick. When I heard about it, I walked over to Central Park from Fifty-fourth Street. After the game, the guys were eating sandwiches and waiting their turns to be interviewed by Summerall. I'm standing by myself off to the side when, all of a sudden, *boom,* the ball comes to me. I caught it just by reflex. I wasn't even looking.

Unitas jogged over. I said, 'Why are you throwing to me, John?' He handed me a sandwich and said, 'Because you're back on the team, Johnny.' I'm glad he didn't throw me another one, though, because I couldn't have caught it. My eyes were full of tears."

⬥

"Here's a story about Unitas," Cameron Snyder said, "that hasn't been written. He picked me up at camp—don't ask me what year—towards the end of his career. In all of the years I'd known John, he'd never said one personal thing to me, or even in front of me. But driving along, without taking his eyes off the road, he said, 'Cameron, I'm never going to sleep with that woman again.' 'Who, Dorothy?' 'Yeah, I've slept with her for the last time.' 'What happened?' 'Well,' he said, 'my mother's husband'—Howard Gibbs— 'got cancer. She called me and told me he had cancer.' And when John hung up the phone, Dorothy asked, 'What was *that* all about?' He said, 'Mr. So-and-So has cancer.' And Dorothy said, 'So what?' Right away, that did it. *So what?* He took the whole family on a trip they had been planning to Hawaii, and while they were over there, the old man died. John got on a plane to San Francisco and connected to Pittsburgh. But Dorothy stayed in Hawaii. She refused to go to the funeral. That was the end of their marriage, as far as John was concerned. You know John. Commit the absolute mortal sin and you're excommunicated."

"I think I met Dorothy only once," said Norma Bender, the wife of Unitas's Louisville teammate Bob. "But I know she was the complete opposite of John. She was as loud as he was quiet. That last year at school, he went home for Thanksgiving and got married. We were out together on a double date just two days before. You know, John dated all of the girls in our wedding party. To tell you the truth, I don't think he was too thrilled about getting married."

But John and Dorothy had five children together, and he must have loved her. Marriages don't end in one phrase, and they can't be described in a few words. Jerry Hill, the old fullback, was trying to think of a single word to describe Dorothy. When "earthy" was suggested, he said, "She was earthy, all right. John could be earthy, too. He could be anything. He could fit into absolutely any situation, kings or commoners. John was equally at ease with the guy who owned the building or the guy who swept up the floors. Dorothy was a tough gal. She was a good gal, but tough, not overly refined." She expressly reminded the wives of the other Colt quarterbacks that their husbands were just substitutes. Jabbing her finger, Dorothy gave all of them the "Don't get any ideas" speech. "I stood up to her," Jane Morrall said. "I think she respected me for that. We didn't have any trouble." But the Colts had to move Dorothy from the wives' section at Memorial Stadium because she wouldn't stop screaming epithets at the husbands who missed the block or dropped the ball. If Gary Cuozzo's name was murmured in the crowd, Dorothy might jump up and shout, "Go ahead and put Cuozza in at quarterback, if you want to lose the game!" Never mind that Mrs. Cuozzo was sitting right there.

"She could make the other wives cry," Tom Matte said. "She made my wife cry. Dorothy could outcurse a sailor. She did a little play on words about the Golden Arm. 'The Golden Penis,' she said. She was embarrassing." "Remember that time John broke his ribs and we had to reinflate his lung?" said Dr. Edmond McDonnell. "George Shaw came to visit John in the hospital, and in front of all of us, Dorothy lit into him, screaming, 'You're just after John's job!'" "Dorothy was different," Marchetti said. "A bunch of us would be having dinner, and suddenly she'd announce to the room, 'If it wasn't for my husband, the Colts wouldn't beat anybody.' John looked like he wanted to crawl under the table. I mean, it might even have been true, but that was the last thing he'd ever say." Hill said, "John and I used to hang out at training camp. We'd sometimes go to this little bar outside Westminster, listen to a Western band, drink a Rolling Rock beer. Then, during the season, my wife and I and John and Dorothy often went out together after games. I remember a night when Dorothy got mad, thinking she was being excluded from the conversation, and started walking home from the restaurant. My wife got along with her. A lot of people didn't. We accepted her the way she was. She loved John. After the divorce [in 1972], she and my wife continued to call each other." "Whenever John ran into Dorothy after that," Fred Miller said, "he'd give her a little kiss. It wasn't ugly." "I suppose not," Hill said, "but from her side, I think she stayed pretty sour about the whole thing."

◆

"When he first told me that he loved me, I said, 'I don't love you.' He looked at me with that cocky little grin of his and said, 'But you will.'"

Sandra Lemon was a stewardess (was that still a word in 1970?) for National Airlines. Her base was Miami, but she met John in Baltimore at Stewart's department store, across York Road from the Golden Arm. She was doing some side work in the marketing of several products, including the Johnny Unitas Football Game. "The first time I saw him," Sandy said, "he was walking down the staircase from the parking lot with John Mackey. John [Unitas] had just started letting his hair grow out. He was wearing a dark suit, and I thought, Oh, my God, he looks so old. I walked up to him and said, 'Hi, Mr. Unitas, I'm Sandy Lemon.'" He was thirty-seven; she was twenty-six. "He said, 'Hi, little girl, I know who you are.' He later told me that at that instant, he already knew we were going to be together. 'You're crazy,' I said."

"If you want to go someplace to eat and feel safe," Unitas told her, "I own a restaurant just across the street." Almost the first person she spotted in the Golden Arm was Matte. "He was so good-looking," she said. "Years later, I told Tommy, 'I can still remember what you had on: an all-white cable-knit turtleneck sweater.'" Joining in with John, Tom, Rocky Thornton, and the rest of Unitas's gang, Sandy had a good time. After she left, Rocky asked John, "Can you get me her number?" "No," Unitas said, "you can't have it." "Why not?" "Because I'm going to marry that little girl."

John courted her on the telephone. "I've never talked so much on the phone in my life," he told her, laughing. "John had this crazy, crazy laugh," she said, "which Joey and Chad started, too. The three of them would get to laughing over some stupid thing or other, and of course they would all end up crying." Joey, Chad, and daughter Paige, the eighth child of Johnny Unitas, are the products of John's and Sandy's thirty-year marriage, her only marriage. It wasn't idyllic ("We had our moments," she said), but it was awfully close. Before John, without going into details, Sandy had limited experience with kind men and gentle fathers. Joey, Chad, and Paige are experts on both.

"Dad was strict but fair," Paige said. "'You're going to drink, I know you're going to drink,' he'd say. 'Don't drive. You're going to screw up, and that's your own fault. But call home. And don't lie to me.' That was his biggest thing. If Dad told you to do something, you jumped up and did it. He could get this look in his eyes that made you say, *Oh, no,* especially when we were going over the American Express bills and his reading glasses dropped down to the end of his nose. But he was a very gentle man, really. When my friends came over, they'd give him a hug and he'd hug them. 'Do you need anything?' he'd ask them. 'Can I do anything?' [*Just as though he were back in the huddle. Should we run a draw play? What do you got? How can I help*?] He was very involved in all three of our lives and we loved him very much."

Almost fifty when Paige was born, John may have had a grandfather's perspective with his second wave of children, but he still had a father's sense of duty. "When I'd screw up, he'd be my father," Chad said. "The rest of the time, he was my best friend." "One time, when Joey was in high school," Paige said, "he called Dad to tell him he was at a party and that there was some drinking but the parents were there. Hanging up the phone, Dad said,

'Okay, he's lying.' He got in the car, went to the party, picked Joey up, threw him over his shoulder, and walked out."

Joey's full name is Francis Joseph Unitas. He was named for the coal man from the Toner Institute and Seraphic Home for Boys. As a freshman quarterback of fourteen, Joey was practicing quick pitches at home, bringing the ball down to his knees, swinging it like a pendulum, when his father said, "That isn't the way to do it," and tried to show him. Not being overly coachable, Joey kept reverting to his own method. "Look, I'm telling you," John said, "here's the right way to do it." Finally, Joey blurted out, "What do *you* know about it?" John threw up his hands and said, "Okay."

But Joey is also the one who sent a letter to his mother on a particularly sad Christmas, quoting a saying that used to hang in the Unitas bathroom: "The greatest gift you gave us was your love for each other."

In 1976, Unitas appeared in a Disney movie called *Gus,* about a mule that kicked field goals. Sitting alongside *Hogan's Heroes* star Bob Crane, John played a football announcer. It pretty much cured him of appearing in movies. But when the Julia Roberts– Richard Gere film *Runaway Bride* was being shot in Maryland more than twenty years later, Unitas was sprung on director and avid sports fan Garry Marshall for his birthday. "And Dad ended up in the movie," Joey said, "sitting on a street bench in a purple letter jacket with a big white *H* on it [for Hale, the fictional town]. He had a couple of lines in the script, too, but they were cut out of the film. 'Did you see that?' Richard Gere asks him when a woman walking by and slugs Gere. 'Yeah,' Dad says, 'but I've been hit harder than that.' 'By her?' 'No, by my wife.'"

Later, John was offered a cameo in Oliver Stone's *Any Given Sunday.* "My dad could care less about doing movies," Joey said, "because they take forever and all you do is sit around. But I whispered, *'Dad, Dad, tell them the only way you'll do it is if I get to be in the movie with you.'* When I told him acting was my dream job in life, he said, 'Okay, I'll tell them.'" They went to Dallas and sat around on the Stone set together. "He was bored out of his mind," Joey said, "but he did it for me." Not long after that, Joey declared for Hollywood. "Most fathers would probably tell their sons to forget it," he said, "and then ask for a refund on that college education they paid for. My dad had a different response. He told me, 'If that's what you want to do, then do it. Follow your heart and work hard. If you do those things, you can accomplish anything. Just remember that your mother and I will always be here to help and support you in anything you want to do.'" Joey won small parts in *The Princess Diaries, Max Keeble's Big Move, Bandits,* and *Raising Helen.* The responsibilities of marriage and a family have since required him to take a steadier job, in advertising and marketing. But he still has his Screen Actors Guild card and his dream. Joey's little boy, born in 2005, is named Colten John Unitas. "I'm sure, one day," Joey said, "his buddies will call him Colt."

If a movie were made of Johnny Unitas's life, Chad wouldn't require any makeup to play the lead. He is the spitting image of the young Johnny U. "He always told me I'd grow out of that," said Chad, sporting even the brushcut hair. "I got it cut this way," he explained, "because I lost a bet. Dad looked at me and said, 'What in the hell did you do? You look like a goofball.' 'What are you talking about?' I said. 'You had a flattop for a number of years. People say I look like you. You must have looked like a goofball, too.' About a week later, he put his hand in my chest and said, 'Stop! You have to go back to the barber and get this fixed. Here, here, and here.' He got all excited about it. Oh, my God, I thought. 'He's reliving fifty-eight and fifty-nine again.'"

In the shaping of Chad's dream, his discussions with his father weren't much different from Joey's. "When I graduated from high school, Dad asked me, 'What are you going to do?' I said, 'I kind of want to play football and I kind of want to play golf. There are some colleges where I might be able to do both. What do you think?' He looked at me and asked, 'Do you want to walk with your own legs when you're sixty?' I said, 'Yes, sir.' He said, 'Then get your ass on the golf course.' Every time some charity invited him to play golf—he called it 'the disease tour'—he'd say, 'I'll be more than happy to play, but I'd appreciate it if you'd also make a spot for my son, Chad, who hopes to be a pro golfer.'" Chad turned pro in 2004 and, a year later, was working with the legendary teacher Bob Toski, testing the shark-filled waters of the hustler circuits, and aiming for the PGA Tour.

"People ask me," Chad said, "'What was it like growing up as Johnny Unitas's son?' I say, 'I don't know. What was it like growing up with your father?' All I can tell you is that he and my mother are the most loving, understanding people I've ever met, and Dad never got caught up in the glory. Whatever we were into, he was into. He always said that he got more enjoyment out of watching us play sports than playing sports himself. I don't know how much he enjoyed getting up at four in the morning to take us to hockey practice all those years, but he did it. Growing up, friends would ask me, 'Do you think he'd sign a football for my dad on Father's Day?' 'Yeah, sure, go ask him.' 'Oh, no, I can't ask him.' 'Dad, Kris wants to get a football signed for his father, but he's too much of a chicken to ask you.' 'Get your butt over here, boy. You don't have to ever be afraid to say anything to me. Whatever you need, we'll take care of it.'"

Paige was very much Daddy's little girl. "He was never embarrassed to talk to me about anything," she said. "We went to dinner a lot, just the two of us, and talked." Her memories may describe him the best. "'You gotta eat' was one of his favorite sayings. He'd get up and cook breakfast every morning, after going around and taking our orders the night before: pancakes, eggs, whatever. You gotta eat. He'd bring me lunch at school, usually from a deli nearby. Everyone would say, 'Your dad's here, Paige,' because they could hear him whistling in the hallway. He whistled all the time; not songs, just whistling, like a bird."

When Paige went off to a little college in Florida, she flew with her mother, Sandy, while John accompanied her car on the auto train from Virginia. But the school wasn't what she had expected. "I hated it, hated it, hated it," she said. The 9/11 attack and the anthrax scare in Florida made her wish she was home, and her parents were equally anxious to have her home. Simultaneously, Paige and John called each other. "Your mother's coming to get you," John told her. "I'm sorry, Dad," Paige said. "I know you've already paid." "That doesn't matter. I don't want you to be unhappy. Pack up the car. You can pick your mother up at the airport." "'Um, do you remember how my car got down here?' I told him. 'Um, do you think it could go back the same way?' And he goes, 'Paige, get your ass in the car and drive home.' 'Okay, Dad.'"

When she started dating Adam, her sweetheart still, "he never said anything about my last name, which I loved. Eventually, when it came time for them to meet, I told Adam, 'You *do* know who my dad is, right?' 'Yeah, I know who he is,' he said. 'And you're not freaked out?' 'No, I can't wait to meet him. But I'm dating you, Paige, not your dad.' Adam's friends were saying, 'Oh, my God, not only are you meeting her father, but her father is Johnny Unitas! Are you *so* scared?' No, he was a little nervous, but he was fine. They got along really well. Dad loved him. He called him Smiley. He never made it hard for Adam. My brothers were worse. But now Adam is part of the family." John had an uncle named Adam, an orphan who was killed by a train.

Paige and her father attended a function once at Towson University, where the stadium is named after John. She was ten months shy of twenty-one. "Everybody always took me for his granddaughter. He'd say, 'Here's my granddaughter.' And I'd say, with a smile, 'I'm *not* your granddaughter! I'm your daughter!' 'Do you want a beer?' he asked me. I said, 'Sure.' When the beers arrived, he went, 'Wait a minute, how old are you? Who said you could have that?' 'Um, you did.' 'Okay, here you go.'" For the thou-

sandth time, he cautioned her about drinking and driving. John
never mentioned the Louisville accident or the death of Battering
Bill Pence, but she could tell that it wasn't a casual warning. This
was August 2002.

◆

Unitas was no good as a TV analyst, though he had a few memorable lines. "Billy Kilmer throws an option pass," he said. "You
have the option of catching either end of the ball." John was worse
as a businessman, especially bad at picking advisers and partners.
The former ran to ex-high school basketball coaches, the latter to
old teammates. Bobby Boyd, a Colt cornerback for nine seasons in
the sixties, was co-owner of the Golden Arm until, late one night,
Bobby came out of the back room, dropped some paperwork in
front of John, and introduced him to his new partner. Without
telling Unitas, Boyd had sold out.

Bowling alleys were put up before liquor licenses had been
nailed down. A hotel in Orlando anticipated Disney World by too
many years. (In Florida, John avoided bankruptcy only by cashing
in his deferred salaries and paying creditors so much on the dollar.)
Later, in a computer circuit board fiasco in Baltimore, he couldn't
avoid Chapter 11—he would have lost their home. The story was
played on page one of the Sunday *Sun*. "But he kept making pay-
ments to creditors then, too," said a close friend, Richard Sammis,
"even though he didn't have to. I know that for a fact."

"When the electronics thing was going bad," Gino Marchetti
said, "John called and asked if I could make him a loan. Big money.
I didn't have that kind of money, but he didn't moan about it or
anything. He was himself." "He called me," Bob Bender said, "and
asked to borrow a half a million dollars. I didn't have it to lend
him. I was doing well, but all of my money was tied up in business.
And I wasn't willing to go in on a note with John, not with his

record. I have five kids. But the next year, I made a score, and I called him up and said, 'John, last year I couldn't help you. This year I can. Whatever you need, I got, or I can get.' He said, 'Bob, I'm fine, but I really appreciate it.' And I know he really wasn't."

John's Towson friend, the Hall of Fame golfer Carol Mann, said, "Professional athletes come from a kind of fantasy land. When you venture outside the gates of the magic castle, you leave behind all the structure, order, and predictability of sports, and you suddenly find yourself in a game with no identifiable rules. You try to play by your old rules. You conduct yourself with your old integrity. But you discover that not only aren't the other people playing by your rules, they aren't playing by any rules at all. Often you discover it too late."

"Sometimes," his sister Shirley said, "John would call me late at night, and we would talk for a long while. I'd ask, 'How's business?' and he'd say, 'The birds fly over and they shit on me, too'— excuse my language. But he wasn't depressed about it. John wasn't that way. During his football career, when people talked about him never getting too up and never getting too down, it wasn't an act. It was John. Somebody sent him a sculpture of a guy sitting on a park bench with birds flying over, and the caption said, 'Go ahead, you might as well, everyone else has.' He loved that. He laughed. Of course, John wished that everyone he'd had dealings with had been as honest and as professional as he was, and he certainly wished that all of his various enterprises had succeeded. But John knew what it was like for a man to be entirely happy with his work, and those things weren't his work. He knew what it was like for a man not to want to be anybody other than who he was. A setback in business might take something out of him for a while—as a matter of fact, it absolutely did—but he was never ashamed of himself and so he was never what I would call truly unhappy. 'I was talking to our brother,' he told me on the phone. 'You mean that silver-tongued devil?' I said. And we just started laughing. We laughed for fifteen minutes. I mean, it wasn't that funny. We were really laughing about everything, all the way back to the beginning. You know, John had a wonderful laugh."

•

"In nineteen ninety-three," said Bill Neill of the Colts training staff, "he had a second total knee replacement at Kernan. Thirty-six hours after the surgery, he was in his room having his supper and I just stuck my head in and said good night. His wife, Sandy, was there. At home thirty minutes later, I had just walked in the door when Sandy called to say, 'John's having a heart attack.' We rushed him down to University, where the chief surgeon cracked him immediately. He had terrible coronary artery disease. They did the bypass." "Heart disease ran in John's family," said Dr. Edmond McDonnell. "His brother, Leonard, had a procedure about ten years earlier."

Sandy said, "The nurses kept asking, 'On a scale of one to ten, Mr. Unitas, how bad is the pain?' 'Oh, maybe a three.' 'Don't listen to him!' I said. First of all, he'd just had his knee replaced the day before. John had a tremendous tolerance for pain [*try spitting on it; that seems to work*] and he just would never tell anybody how much he hurt." "Over the years," Neill said, "he had about twelve fairly major surgeries, just for football. He was an orthopedic textbook, for Christ's sake." Of course, his hands were broken down. A plastic middle finger had ultimately replaced the one he shot with the Colt 380. "Over the course of years," Neill said, "those muscles in his elbow that had ripped off the bone and hemorrhaged so badly had healed, but they reattached in not quite the right place, and a lot of fibrous tissue, scar tissue, was left behind. In an insidious, creeping way, it had curled around the nerves, making his right hand weaker and weaker and weaker." Dr. McDonnell said, "Whenever a Colt player went down during a game, I never came on the field until I knew he was really hurt. But anytime John stayed down for more than a second, I ran out there as fast as I could. He rarely admitted to injury. He just didn't believe in injury."

Visiting John in the hospital, Leonard Unitas looked at all of the tubes and machines and thought, *Oh, little brother. What's happened to you?* "I never left John alone in a hospital," Sandy said. "I always stayed with him, for a lot of reasons." About a week after the operation—"He lost a whole week," she said; "he was completely out of it for that long"—Sandy was standing outside the door to his room when somebody in the corridor said, "Code Blue," and the whole service rushed past her into John's room. "He was sitting up in bed," she said. "He had taken the heart monitor from around his neck, and was holding it in his hand. 'I can't get this damn TV set to work,' he said."

In a hushed voice, as though it were still a secret, Neill told the sportswriter that the cardiologists "privately gave him two years." With a look of triumph, Bill said, "We got him *nine.*"

"I'm the quarterback."

A Jack Daniel's Manhattan

"**I** played golf with him once in North Carolina," Joe Montana said. "Remember when Kathryn Crosby moved Bing's Clambake there for a few years? On the first tee I said, 'John, I just purchased a Johnny Unitas jersey, making yours the only football jersey I've ever actually paid for.' He said, 'Why did you do that? You should have called me. I'd have given you one.' Our paths had crossed a number of times before, but this was the only full day I ever spent with him. It was a great day."

Playing peewee and Pop Warner football like a lot of kids in western Pennsylvania (and not just western Pennsylvania), Montana wore number 19. "I don't remember how I picked it," he said. "Maybe my dad picked it for me. But that's why I took nineteen at the end in Kansas City." Joe was glad to have had 16 in San Francisco. "Nineteen would have been a lot of pressure," he said.

In every sport to which an honest timepiece or yardstick can be applied, today's players are demonstrably better than yesterday's. Johnny Weissmuller's gold medal times in the 1924 and 1928 Olympics would bring howling laughter to eight-year-old girls at a modern swim meet. Is it reasonable, then, when the sport is one that defies exact measurement, to insist that Joe DiMaggio is better than anyone playing baseball today, and that Johnny Unitas is the greatest quarterback of all time? Unitas was named the Player of the Decade for the 1960s. He was selected the Greatest Player in the First Fifty Years of Pro Football. He was picked for the NFL's fiftieth and seventy-fifth anniversary teams. But it is probably enough now just to say that Unitas may have been a quarterback in a sense that quarterbacks aren't anymore, and can't be. Would Montana agree with that?

"I don't know whether anyone today is the boss to quite the extent that he was," Joe said. "If you can do it, and you've proved that you can do it, the coaches are going to give you a lot of prerogatives. But they're not going to hand over the whole game to you. If you're asking me who else could have taken it upon himself to throw that ball to Jim Mutscheller in overtime, I don't think anybody else could have. We'd have probably kicked the field goal on second down, maybe on first."

Could Joe have played in the fifties? Could John have played in the nineties?

"Sure, I think I could have played in his time," he said. "I'm positive he could have played in mine. I've always believed that the game's the game. It's a little different, but it isn't *so* different. They had their struggles, we had ours. But it's still football. It's what it is while you're there, which is the only way you can look at it. No one would argue that the game isn't a little faster now, but it may have been a little tougher then."

"I played two years in the fifties," Jimmy Orr said. "I believe pro football was the toughest it ever was in the fifties. They didn't have any rules. I once saw a defensive guy kick a tight end in the face. No flag. They could bury your ass and not call a penalty. Roughing the quarterback? Forget about that."

"Johnny Unitas," Jim Brown said, "could play anytime."

"Talking to Johnny U," Montana said, "listening to his experiences, almost made me wish I *had* played in the fifties. How well did you know him?"

Not terribly well.

"You had to love him, though, didn't you?"

Peyton Manning said, "I wore black high-tops at Tennessee because of him. When I met John, I gave him a pair. My father's sports heroes were always Mickey Mantle and Johnny Unitas [Archie Manning was the first and, for a long time, only hero of the New Orleans Saints], so maybe that's why Johnny U always meant so much to me. I have a wall of pictures at home, me posing with quarterbacks: Starr, Staubach, younger guys, too—Marino, Aikman, Favre. But the one of Unitas holding up the black high-tops is my favorite."

Reminiscent of John, Manning is superfastidious about completing his fakes after the ball is gone. "Looking at highlight films, I could see what a technician Unitas was. He cared about the smallest details. So do I. It's the little things that make the big difference. The true timing in the passing game, that came from him, too, from the after-practice and off-season work he did with Raymond Berry. 'This is how we're going to do it. Here's what we want to happen.' They knew you couldn't just show up in September and expect to have timing. I'm a firm believer in that. So is Marvin Harrison [Peyton's Berry]. Marvin has great recall. A throw you might make in May in a situation versus a certain coverage is going to show up on third and five in November; and *boom,* because of all of that preparation, it'll be there."

How would Manning compare himself to Unitas?

"I make no comparison with myself to him," he said. "I hold John in such high regard, it's an honor just to wear the same uniform. The fact that my number is one below his, and the fact that I wear the same horseshoe helmet, inspires me. He was the ultimate field general. He called his own plays and was in complete control out there. Aggressive. Fearless. Utterly fearless. He was convinced that if you did things right and had worked on them, it didn't matter what the situation was. I asked him about the Mutscheller play. He said, 'If it's there and you execute it, it's the right call.' I do kind of have that same mentality. I call a lot of my own plays. I have a great deal of freedom. As my offensive coordinator, Tom Moore, says, 'No guts, no blue chips.' [That could have come straight from Unitas.] If you call a play you believe in, what does it matter if it's first and ten on the opening drive of the second half, or if it's fourth and five with thirty seconds to go? If this is the play you believe in, this is the play you call. You make it work. That's Unitas."

When Robert Irsay moved his franchise to Indianapolis on March 28, 1984, sneaking away in the dark of night, Unitas asked to have his statistics stricken from the Indy guide. "I never played there," he said simply.

"When I was drafted by the Colts [number one overall, 1998]," Manning said, "I thought, Wow. That's Johnny Unitas, Raymond Berry, Gino Marchetti, Lenny Moore. But it wasn't. When I got here—I should have known this—I found out that none of them embraced Indianapolis. Coming from the University of Tennessee, I was used to unbelievable tradition and history. The players of yesteryear—the [coach] General Neyland days—were around all the time. It was really neat. Now, we had this incredible Colt tradition, but none of the old players ever came to practice. It disappointed me. I wanted to feel connected to them."

"The Baltimore Ravens gave me a thousand-dollar camera," Jim Parker said, "which was damn nice of them. But the Colts gave me everything. I can't watch a game on television and root against the horseshoes." Craig Kelley, the Indianapolis public relations director, said, "Raymond Berry called me in two thousand and three. We had just won a game in Tampa, scoring three touchdowns in the last four minutes. We finally won in overtime, throwing all the way. 'I don't know whether Tony [head coach Tony Dungy] wants any advice,' Berry said, 'but I played in a game like that'—or maybe it was that he had coached in a game like that—'where we threw and threw and threw. Going from there right back to our regular practice routine, we ended up getting injuries and being unable to compete the following week.' Tony got on the phone with Raymond and they talked about it. 'Anything Raymond Berry wants to tell me,' he said, 'I want to hear.'"

"Yeah, Raymond has written me a couple of nice letters," Manning said. "Maybe they *are* part of us a little. I just wish they were around, telling us their stories. I guess most people would say that Eric Dickerson and Marshall Faulk are the best players who ever played for Indianapolis. I hope we're in the process now of making our own legacy, but I still look to Baltimore for our history. That's why it was always a big deal to me when we visited the Ravens, because Johnny U would be on the sideline. I always made a point of going over to him. He told me he liked the way I played the game. I consider that the ultimate compliment."

"Of the great quarterbacks today," Roger Staubach said, "Manning is the one who reminds me most of Johnny U. Peyton's bigger, of course. He finishes the fakes, like you say, but there's something else that's familiar, maybe just the way Peyton holds his shoulders. In terms of making the right decisions, Montana was a lot like John. Only about five or six times a game did Unitas do something different from what any other great quarterback would do. But those five or six plays made all the difference in the world. Knowing when to throw it to the tight end. Knowing when to drop it off. There's just something that makes you do the right things, and Montana had it. Johnny U was the best."

Staubach's plebe summer at the Naval Academy was in 1961, two years before he won the Heisman Trophy, three before he was commissioned. "For six months then," he said, "I was an ensign working in the athletic department. I saw a lot of Colts games that year. Unitas was hurt. It was the Tom Matte year. You know, the questionable kick by Green Bay? The big catches by Jimmy Orr down in that one corner of the end zone? It was a fun time in pro football. When I got to the Cowboys, John was nearing the end. But it still felt special just being on the same field with him."

On the telephone once, Dallas coach Tom Landry told the sportswriter that, at first, he had preferred Craig Morton to Staubach, but that the players always favored Roger. Landry was fascinated by the idea of shuttling in plays with alternating quarterbacks. He tested the system first with Don Meredith and Eddie LeBaron, then he tried it with Morton and Staubach. "Morton had a better arm than Roger's," Landry said, "and he was more predictable. ["Controllable" may be a better word.] When Roger played baseball, they couldn't keep him from trying to steal home. But it quickly became obvious to me that the players blocked harder for Roger, whether they realized it or not. They ran harder for him. They got behind him more. He had this thing that made him the quarterback. All of the great ones had it, starting with Johnny Unitas."

"Let me ask *you* one," Paul Brown fired back at the sportswriter. This was in the mid-seventies. They were arguing about Brown's long-established policy of sending in the plays, usually with "messenger guards" like Chuck Noll. "What's the first thing the quarterback does after he takes the snap?" As usual, Paul answered his own question. "He turns his back on the field. Because we know what's coming, all of the coaches, upstairs and down, can concentrate on the point of attack, see exactly what happens, and get ready for the next call."

"If you had had Unitas, would you have sent in the plays?"

"I almost did have Unitas."

"Yeah, yeah, would you have sent him the plays?"

"It's a superior system."

"If you had had Unitas, would you have sent in the plays?"

"I had Otto [Graham]."

"Would you have sent in the plays?"

Paul was too honest to answer.

"I quarterbacked sixteen years in the pros," Babe Parilli said, "and I called my own plays for fifteen of them. That one year I played for Brown, I felt like a robot, like most quarterbacks are today. Young pro quarterbacks now don't want to call their own plays. They didn't in college. Ask them if they'd like to call them now, and they'll say, 'No way! I got enough to think about.' But the best ones are good at checking off at the line, though the decisions they make there are still programmed by the coaches. [If you see this, this, this, or that, you may do this, this, this, or that.] To be honest with you, I was kind of programmed by Bear Bryant at Kentucky. We met every day after practice to play this little game of his, 'down and distance,' on a board. When the real game started, he never sent me a play, but I always knew exactly what he wanted. I remember once, we're playing Georgia Tech, and it comes down to a fourth and one. If we make a first down, we're going to win the game. He sends a fullback in, and I ask the kid, 'What did he say, Tom?' 'Nothing.' Okay. So, I call the play, the kid slips and falls, and we don't get the first down. We lose the game. Ten years later, at a Bear Bryant reunion, I said, 'Coach, why didn't you send me a play in the Georgia Tech game?'—when you don't lose many games, you tend to remember the ones you did. Bear looked at me and smiled. 'Babe,' he said, 'I did send you a play. I sent the one you called.' I knew exactly what he meant."

●

Unitas had many celebrity friends—actors, singers, athletes, and politicians—but his closest friends were nobodies. One of them, Richard Sammis, was actually called Mr. Nobody. He was a Baltimore auto dealer whose main competitor declared in a radio advertisement that "nobody will sell it to you for less." "I thought, 'You know what? I'll become Mr. Nobody, and I'll sell it to them for less.'" Mr. Nobody is the coinventor of the Unitas Golf Club Grip.

"As his right hand kept deteriorating," Sammis said, "John went from shooting in the low eighties to shooting a hundred and ten or a hundred and fifteen. Finally, he said, 'Tricky'—he called me Richard, then Rick, then Ricky, then Tricky—'I've got to find some way to hold on to the club or I'm just not going to play anymore.' He had no strength left in his thumb and index finger. If he pinched you as hard as he could, you wouldn't even feel it. So, we hopped in the golf cart—we were at Chestnut Ridge—and went over to my house to see what we could manufacture. I figured we needed something like a woman's girdle. But all I could find was an elastic knee brace. So, we returned to the course, and I said, 'Now put your one hand in here and your other hand in there.' I had him so tied up and we got to laughing so hard that we had to get off the course. But he went home saying, 'I'm going to figure this thing out.'"

Unitas came up with the idea of wearing two golf gloves, the right one fitted with a strip of Velcro for strapping his hand to the club. He practiced wrapping and unwrapping until he was as deft as a pickpocket. "I don't want to hold up the whole course," he told Mr. Nobody. And, before long, John was back shooting in the mid-eighties.

"I thought you were going to call Monte Blue?" Unitas asked the sportswriter after a round at Hillendale Country Club.

"Who's Monte Blue?"

"Oh, I'm sorry. Sleater."

This represented a new record for the Unitas memory. In the late fifties, at a golf tournament that included many of the Orioles and Colts, pitcher Lou Sleater won. But Lou was playing hooky from his off-season job that day and thought it might be a good idea to leave his name out of the paper. So he borrowed the name Monte Blue from an old movie cowboy. John never forgot anything.

The old memory record was set in the eighties when, in *Time* magazine, the sportswriter ripped Unitas, Brooks Robinson, Walt Frazier, and Phil Esposito for donning tuxedos and dancing around in a craps-game commercial, shilling for Bally's Park Place in Atlantic City. Shaking imaginary dice, they warbled, *Bally's, Bally's,* "like so many Sky Mastersons in a velveteen sewer." A full two years later, John turned to the sportswriter and inquired academically, "Who the fuck is Sky Masterson?"

Ernie Accorsi said, "I got a call from Pete Rozelle. Because of John's tout sheet [the Johnny Unitas All-Pro Football Report], Pete said we had to discontinue our relationship with him. Of course, Joe Thomas was gone, so I had brought John back just to be a part of the Colts, to give speeches for fifteen hundred a pop, maybe to help talk legislators into a new stadium. He was totally above board about picking point spreads [the guy who didn't know what they were in 1958]. He said, 'What's the league doing for me? This is honest work. I'm not hiding anything. I have to make a living.' But it made me sad. Of course, you know how mad he was with the league at the end about things like pension and disability."

"Maybe the stubbornness was part of the greatness," said Rozelle's successor, Paul Tagliabue. "It's like, 'Once I've reached my point of view, to hell with the rest of the world.' Unitas refused to attend anniversary celebrations. He just wouldn't give in. I think everything to him was like a football game."

"We had never retired his jersey," Accorsi said, "and I asked John if he'd put the uniform back on. I'll tell you, it was really tough to get him to do it. The Dolphins were in town and we were losing early, twenty-eight to seven. By halftime, it was twenty-eight to twenty-four, but when I went to the locker room just before the end of the first half, I still wasn't sure whether he was going to put the uniform on."

Coming out of the dugout on the run, carrying his helmet, Unitas almost collided with his last Baltimore coach, John Sandusky, who had joined Don Shula's Dolphins staff. Sandusky and Unitas embraced. Continuing on, Unitas nearly crashed into Shula next. Don put his left hand on the side of John's head, and John bumped Shula's butt with his helmet. Unitas went to a microphone at midfield, thanked the crowd, and took off his number 19. It was a sweet tableau for everyone but the Dolphins, who went on to lose the game, 45–28.

"How's your buddy, Farricker?" John asked. (Lord, what a memory he had.)

A few years earlier, Pete Farricker wondered if John might be willing to speak at a family fund-raiser. "Do you pay?" the sportswriter asked him. "Just expenses." "I doubt he'll do it. That's how he makes his living now. But I'll call him." "I can't do it," John said, "but give me his number." "You don't have to call him. I'll call him." "Give me his goddamn number!" "I can't do it," John told Farricker, "but I'll sign a football and send it to you, if that'll help. Maybe you can use it for a door prize." Farricker said the entire length of the ball was signed "Johnny Unitas." His hand was so bad then that, holding the pen like Bob Dole, he needed every inch of a football to write his name.

"John, Farricker's dead," the sportswriter answered.

"Aw, no."

"He died of Lou Gehrig's disease. He melted from the inside out. It's the worst way to die."

"No, it's not," Unitas said softly. "Alzheimer's is the worst way. My mother died of Alzheimer's. You can't think. You can't remember. To tell you the truth, I'm a little afraid of it."

They were in a restaurant-bar in Towson whose decor consisted mainly of a stuffed polar bear. The sportswriter ordered a beer and a sandwich. "Just give him half a sandwich," the quarterback said. "The sandwiches are big here. If you're still hungry, they can bring you the other half." Then, in the most unexpected call since Alan "the Horse" Ameche broke through the Giants' line on a trap play, the all-time beer drinker ordered "a Jack Daniel's Manhattan with no cherries." Not only that, he wanted it served in a brandy snifter.

"You're killing me."

"Oh, I'll have a drink with a meal. I'll have a glass of red wine with dinner. I'll even have a stinger now and then."

"Crème de menthe?"

Mr. Nobody said, "John and I drank a pitcher of stingers once. I haven't been able to look at a stinger since. We were arguing over a football play. He was trying to draw it for me on a wet napkin with a ballpoint pen. Well, that's impossible. Finally, he looked at me and said, 'You're the car guy. Take my word for it. I'm the football guy.'"

●

He died on an exercise machine at Kernan. Bill Neill heard the gasp and went to him. A little while later, the phone rang at Gino Marchetti's home in West Chester, Pennsylvania. "My wife answered," Gino said. "I heard her say, 'Oh no.' Because it was September eleven, my first thought was that those bastards had run another plane into a building. When she told me John was dead, I couldn't say anything. I just sat down." He'd have cried if he wasn't Gino Marchetti.

Jim Parker did cry. He drove out into the country, pulled over to the side of an empty road, and wept. "It was the first time," Jim said, "that I wasn't there to protect him."

Eighty-six-year-old Cameron Snyder called the *Sun* office to check if the bulletin was true. At Unitas's induction into the Pro Football Hall of Fame, John had spotted Cameron in the Canton audience and, pausing in the middle of his prepared speech, said, "Then there was a newspaperman before my first football game in Baltimore, a little, funny, fat guy with a beard, sitting down here, by the name of Cameron Snyder, who came over to me and knew I was nervous and said, 'John, I just want you to remember this, that the game you are playing today is a kid's game played by men. Go out and do a job.' And I thank you for that, Cameron."

Peyton Manning asked the Colts if he could wear black high-tops in the game that week. The team checked with the league. The league said no. "Sometimes, with the NFL," Manning said, "if it's not their idea, they're against it. I wish I had never asked. I wish I had just done it. I think every quarterback in the league should have worn black high-tops that Sunday."

"When Sandy called," Raymond Berry said, "she asked me, 'Will you speak at his funeral on behalf of the team?' I said, 'Of course.' Putting the phone down, I realized I had never broached the subject of the spiritual with John. I never felt free to do that, and I never did. Of course I knew he was Catholic, and not only that, I knew that all of the Catholics on the team always followed him to church. Coming out of east Texas, I'd never been around Catholics. But I figured a lot of them just went through the motions and didn't have a clue as to what it was all about. Because, you see, I had been that kind of Protestant. There's a big difference, a huge difference, an eternal difference, between head knowledge and heart knowledge. I didn't know about John Unitas's heart, when you got right down to it, you know? I started praying right then. I said, 'God, you've got to give me some clarity on this. You're the only one who really knows Johnny U. You're going to have to let me know.' A day or two went by. We had a trip to Florida coming up with my son—he's a missionary in Peru. After that, I went to Baltimore. I was still praying. I can't really explain what happened, but I just began to have a real sense of peace about John. It's like the Lord let me know that John had a lifetime of faith in Jesus Christ, and though it was a different experience than I had, everything was okay."

Berry's eulogy at the Cathedral of Mary Our Queen in Baltimore:

> *For all of us who were fortunate to be a part of the Baltimore Colts—whether as team members or fans—by now we all realize it was a once-in-a-lifetime experience. And all of us know that the main reason was John Unitas, a*

once-in-a-lifetime quarterback. I think I can safely speak for all of us in saying, "Thank you, John. You elevated us to unreachable levels—both on the field and in the stands. You made the impossible possible. You filled our memory bank full. Those images of your performances are still there and will never fade. But you did more than perform on the field. Individual achievements and glory didn't have a place on your priority list. All of us knew you were focused on moving the ball into the end zone and winning the game. You didn't care who did what. Just do our jobs when called on, and we all win together. The Colts were a team, and your example and leadership set the tone.

Football is a physical game. Even in that respect, you set a tone and were a leader and an example. Personally I think toughness was your number one asset. Not just physical—the hits you took—but mental toughness. You just kept on coming at 'em. In a different body, you would have been an ideal middle linebacker. All of us are glad God gave you the body to be a quarterback. I guess it is appropriate at this time to thank the Lord, not only for your talent but for sending you to Baltimore to bless all of us. You were more than a teammate to me. You were a special friend. And I came to love you like a brother. Because of your lifelong faith in Christ, you now have experienced the truth of the scripture—to be absent with the body is to be present with the Lord. So, as we come here today to thank God for what you meant to each of us, and to celebrate your life, we don't question his timing. But we are going to miss you, Johnny U.

Janice Ann, the first of the eight children, the little girl who had moved with her parents back into Dorothy's bedroom (Dorothy had died four months earlier), said,

*I'd like to tell you about the man who studied his play-
books at night with dedication, who watched game films
in the basement with at least one child on his lap, who
would let the little girl on his lap hold and work the button
that put the film into reverse so he could watch a particular play over and over ... who would come home from
practice with Raymond Berry in tow and continue to play
catch in the yard, making sure they got their timing just
right. He became a father in nineteen-fifty-five, when I
was born. The last time he became a father again was in
nineteen-eighty-two. Those first and last times produced
girls. Sandwiched in between my sister Paige and I are six
of the strongest, brightest, most loving and sensitive boys
I know. Each of us has a little of that same independent,
hard-headed streak that Dad had, that both endeared us
to and exasperated our mothers. . . . He was a man who
was strong in his faith, who made success a requirement,
who made mistakes and suffered the consequences, but
who was lucky enough to come out on top.*

At one point in the requiem Mass, John Mackey went to the
men's room and couldn't find his way back to Sylvia. "Who's in the
box?" he said, wandering up to the altar. Roy Hilton, a left defensive end after Marchetti, went to Mackey, gently put his arm
around him, and brought him home.

Lenny Lyles said, "They filled a whole cathedral, and people
were lined up on the street and sidewalk outside. Baltimore *became* a cathedral. The whole town. Coming down the church steps,
I heard the engine, looked up at the sky, and there was that little
plane again. 'Unitas We Stand.' *[Who's going to the drive-in? Get
in the trunk, Lyles. You're going.]* I don't know why, but I thought
of the Green Hornet."

On the first Tuesday of every month, the old Colts who are still in town get together for an evening of "Schlitz and bullshit," as Artie Donovan said, usually at Fowler's Baltimore Tavern. But this was a special Tuesday, the end-of-the-summer crab feast, in Jerry D's backyard, Jerry Dotterweich being a Mount St. Joe's kid who made it big in the saloon business. All of the wives were along. Donovan was there on a cane. Jim Mutscheller and Alex Sandusky were retelling stories and laughing. Tom Matte was cracking crabs with one hand and eating corn on the cob with the other. The "young" guys like Sam Havrilak and Bruce Laird joked with Andy Nelson and Buzz Nutter as though they had been teammates. They *were* teammates. The franchise had been gone for twenty years, but the team was still there.

"When Dad passed away, I lost a father," said Chad Unitas, who came with Sandy and Paige, "but I gained about thirty-five uncles. Uncle Artie, Uncle Gino, Uncle Lenny, Uncle Buzz . . ."

Havrilak, a dentist from Bucknell University, had been number 17 with the Colts. Sort of a quarterback, but more of a utility receiver and running back, he dressed alongside Unitas for John's last four seasons in Baltimore. "I grew up in the Pittsburgh area," Sam said. "My father was a steelworker for thirty-seven years. So, John and I sort of spoke the same language. He loved telling off-color jokes, and I loved hearing them. But the only football advice he ever gave me didn't do me much good. 'Pass when they think you're gonna run,' he said, 'and run when they think you're gonna pass.'"

Unitas wasn't there, but he was everywhere.

". . . and the Bears started blitzing the hell out of us, knocking John's ass off, and he jumped up off the ground finally and said, 'I ain't taking this shit no more. Everybody cut your patterns down two yards,' and . . ."

". . . and we were down the eastern shore, playing a basketball game in Salisbury. Driving back, the car hit a patch of ice and made a complete spin. John just calmly waited for it to stop and never touched the brakes. I swear to God, he was whistling. He just put out his right arm so Roy Hilton wouldn't hit the windshield. 'Everybody okay?' he said. You can have the sudden-death game. The coolest I ever saw Johnny U was on the road to the Chesapeake Bay Bridge. Another time, we . . ."

". . . and John would just be standing there at his usual spot by the locker room door, and Fred Miller would ask him, 'Do you have anything to add, John?' And he always said the same thing. 'Talk's cheap. Let's go play' . . ."

". . . and we're all sitting around Oz and Jenny's Pit in Westminster, and Lou Michaels is a little drunk and making a lot of noise. 'Lou,' John says. 'Sit down and shut up.' By God, he did, too . . ."

". . . Christ, then I had to go all the way out to Pueblo, Colorado, to speak at Benny Trotta's nephew's son's wedding. I remember telling John, 'There sure seem to be a lot of Italians out in Pueblo. Is it a hub for the witness relocation program or something?' 'Naw,' he said, 'it's the mines' . . ."

". . . so John mentions that his regular barber, across the street from the liquor store, is in prison. We decided to go visit him, and son-of-a-bitch if he didn't give me a haircut right there in jail, which is probably why the FBI came around later to ask me, 'Do you know a Frankie Spagnola?' And I told them, 'Hell yeah, he's my favorite fucking barber' . . ."

"You see," Miller said, "John's still here. He always will be. John, Gino, and a fella named Leo Sanford were my first heroes. You don't know Sanford [the linebacker who went out early in the sudden-death game, replaced by Steve Myhra], but he worked for a company over in Shreveport, so I had met him back home. I remember the morning John Mackey and I pulled up to Colts camp in Westminster, coming from the College All-Star Game. Unitas was the first person we saw. He was heading out to early Mass. 'Hello, I'm John Unitas,' he said, and shook my hand. I just stood there and watched him as he walked away. It reminded me of something.

The first time I ever played organized football was in the sixth grade. We weren't a very big school and we didn't have a very good team. Our opening ball game was against Minden, one town over, which had a great program and whatnot. When I lined up on the field for that very first kickoff, a sensation went through me. I fell in love with the game of football. I had that same feeling watching John walking away."

In retirement, Unitas often drove out to Miller's place in the country. They sat in the living room with an old stove going, and petted the dogs and talked. John was a frustrated farmer. "I gave him a few chickens," Fred said, "and he had a little pen at home. He loved those chickens. He'd go out and get himself two or three eggs. Sandy got even with me by giving us a cat. Oh, and I once swapped him a hog for a chandelier!"

●

Just a small stone, a couple of vases, and a simple bench sit beside a lake in Dulaney Valley. Somebody also put a horseshoe there. Sandy decided to leave it. "I found out only two companies made the benches," she said. "One was in Pittsburgh, and I said, 'Well, that has to be the one.'" The phrases she chose included "Your smiling face no more we'll see, your whistle in the wind. . . ."

"He always sent a beautiful card on my birthday," said Shirley Green (Tootsie), whose birthday happens to be September 11. "I have a whole stack of them. You could always tell that he did it himself, that it wasn't Sandy. He'd write down some funny little message. This last one actually came three days before my birthday, three days before John died."

What was the final message?

"'Don't forget to take the time to smell the flowers. Watch out for the bees.' And then he signed it as he always did, 'Your loving brother, John.'"

John's older sister, Millie, recalled the last time the whole family was together, at Shirley's house, the Thanksgiving before John died. "It was a beautiful autumn day in Pittsburgh," she said, "and John was out in the yard tossing a football around with the kids and grandkids. Not just ours, all of the kids in the neighborhood. Everybody came out to see him. They all wanted to catch a pass from Johnny U. He was laughing and having the grandest time." Watching him through the kitchen window took Millie back to a fall day when John was a little boy, and came running into the house with a hole in his head. "It wasn't bleeding," she said. "It was just a tiny little hole. They had been throwing stones, playing war, I think. I cleaned it up and put some Mercurochrome on it.

"'Come on, come on, come on,' he said.

"'What's your hurry?'

"'The football game is about to start,' he said. 'I'm the quarterback.'"

I started to read the few books that have been written about Unitas but stopped at the point where every one of them said his father's name was Leon. I did reread my friend Bill Gildea's 1994 book, *When the Colts Belonged to Baltimore.* The heart of it is Bill's relationship with his father. The fun of it, for someone who once lived there, is returning to Haussner's restaurant, the Two O'Clock Club, the Lexington Market, and the 1950s themselves, with the easiest-going tour guide since Thornton Wilder's Stage Manager. Bill's familiarity with the town and the time extends even to the fact that the drugstore cowboys in their ducktail haircuts were called "drapes." They were. Read's drugstore. Turning back to Gildea was a way of drifting back into a Baltimore state of mind. Reading beautiful writing is always a good place to start.

The late John Steadman's 1988 book, *The Greatest Football Game Ever Played,* was the handiest of manuals, being a treasury of dates, places, statistics, and attendances. But I'm even more beholden to Steadman for the lucky fact that we were friends, and I was around him enough to hear many of his Unitas stories firsthand. I'm equally grateful to Steady's *best* friend, Lou Sleater

("Monte Blue"), who, like Gus Triandos catching knuckleballer Hoyt Wilhelm using Paul Richards's oversized catcher's mitt, scrambled to backstop my Steadman memories. Sleater was a good-hitting left-handed pitcher with the Orioles when Billy Loes was the looniest right-hander on the staff. For some reason of his own (all of his reasons were unique), Loes called Lou "the Count." To this day, Brooks Robinson won't know whom you're talking about unless you say "the Count." But I call Sleater the MVP.

I began the interviewing on the first Tuesday of August 2004, when Larry Harris and I crashed the regular monthly get-together of old Colts still living in Baltimore. I was the interloper, actually; Larry was an invited guest. Thirteen months later, in September of 2005, I delivered the manuscript. It was a wonderful year's work, for which I'm especially thankful to the players, who all seemed to want to meet at some old Colt haunt. "Let's have breakfast at the Bel-Loc Diner," Tom Matte said. Alex Sandusky suggested the Sunset Lounge in Glen Burnie. "If it's not there anymore," he told me, "I'll meet you where it used to be." Unlike Sweeney's bar on Greenmount Avenue and Thirty-third Street, it was still there. As the waitress took our orders, she asked Alex, "You used to play for the Colts, didn't you?" This was thirty-eight years after he retired.

Buzz Nutter was working at a warehouse in Waldorf. "All we Nutters ever did was work," he said. "That's all we still do. I can't wait to go to work tomorrow morning." Jim Mutscheller was in his usual suit and tie, still selling insurance. Jim's a bit smaller than he used to be ("We've all shrunk a little," said Ordell Braase), but he's still a giant. "May I ask you a favor?" Mutscheller said as we walked to the office elevators. He wanted me to leave out a detail—a true detail—about his marine career. He thought it put him in too glorious a light. Every conversation with every old player contained a similar note of decency. At his home in West Chester, Pennsylvania, Gino Marchetti wondered if I had called Braase yet. "You have to talk to Braase," he said. "I received way too much of the credit in Baltimore. Ordell was a hell of a defensive end."

Braase told me, "I have just one photograph framed over my office desk. It verifies that I got to the quarterback one time before Gino."

At his home in the Randallstown section of Baltimore, Lenny Moore and I sat and talked away an entire afternoon in front of two large paintings: one of Lenny and the other of Big Daddy Lipscomb. Hidden behind a door in the basement was a four-foot-tall silver trophy signifying that the players of both the Western and Eastern Conferences had voted Moore the NFL Player of the Year in 1964. "Nineteen sixty-four," I said, "was Jim Brown's championship season." "Amen," Lenny said. It was Moore who told me, "Go see Parker, and if he's not himself, go back the next day, and the next. Eventually, he'll be Jim." Thanks, Lenny. And thank you, Jim.

Four of the men I interviewed died during the year: Parker, Carl Taseff, Chuck Thompson, and Johnny Sample. In that little room at the rest home in Columbia, Maryland, Moore was with Jim when he died. Sonny Hill found Sample for me. I'm going to send Sonny the tape, so he can hear Johnny's voice again. When I told Chad Unitas about the mortality rate, he said, "I have to go now." Like Steadman, Weeb Ewbank was a posthumous source. In the early seventies, when I was the sports columnist at the *Cincinnati Enquirer,* I visited Weeb twice in Oxford, Ohio. Around that same time, I saw Secretariat in the home stretch and Muhammad Ali in the Congo, but few images have stayed with me like the sight of Weeb riding on the back of Smokey Alston's motorcycle in Darrtown. For a practical joke aimed at one of Alston's hunting cronies, the former Dodger manager and I boosted Ewbank up into a forked tree, where he wired a stuffed pheasant to an upper branch. Both Alston and Ewbank called me later to report that the caper had gone off like clockwork and the taxidermy had been blasted to smithereens. I can see why John loved Weeb.

Still another posthumous source was Fred Schubach, the Colts' equipment manager, talent scout, and all-around good football man. A hundred years ago, Fred would call me up to say the floor had been reinstalled at the Civic Center and the brethren were gathering again for a game of murder ball, basketball with no rules. Those games usually included the old commissioner's sons, Upton and Bert Bell Jr., assistant coach Chuck Noll, broadcaster John Sterling, and a few other guys with blackened eyes and blistered lips. Before and after those bloody sessions, I gleaned a lot of Colt lore that helped here.

Raymond Berry got up in his living room in Colorado (he has since moved to Tennessee to be near grandchildren) and ran pass patterns for me. His cuts are still precise. Redskins coach Joe Gibbs once told me that anyone who has ever been alone in a room with Raymond Berry walked out of that room a better person. Raymond introduced me to Unitas in 1967, in the Colt clubhouse at Memorial Stadium after a Bears game. I was fresh out of Mount Saint Mary's. "John, this is a friend of mine, Tom Callahan," he said. (We had known each other exactly five minutes.) "He wants to ask you a few questions." "Hey, Tommy," John said, and I was Tommy to Unitas from then on. While I was with Berry in Colorado, the telephone rang, and for a few minutes, he took off on an animated conversation with somebody named Frank. "He's a friend from Los Angeles," Raymond said after hanging up, "a real character. I met him the weekend President Kennedy was assassinated, on the airplane flying out to our game in L.A. He called the hotel to see if we were still going to play [to Pete Rozelle's everlasting regret, the Colts and the rest of the NFL did play that Sunday; Baltimore lost to the Rams, 17–16], and for some reason the operator put him straight through. I have a lot of interesting people in my life. My kids like to say, 'Dad, do you find them by mail, or phone, or what?' The truth is, many of us used to think it was a privilege to be something in the lives of people. Through the years, I met more than a few Colts fans who became my friends."

Once, when I was a guest on Dick Schaap's TV panel show, *The Sports Reporters,* the topic was a new proposal to include instant replay in the officiating of NFL games. "There have been a lot of changes through the years," I said, "every one of which I've opposed. But if Don Shula is for it [and he was], I guess I'm for it. If Ted Williams says it's a ball, I guess it's a ball." Unitas happened to see that show, and when I was talking with him on the phone several days later, he chided me about it. "I know how you feel about Shula," I said, "but you must know that you're the only one." I expected him to reply with an epithet, but surprisingly, John said, "He did a hell of a job with the Dolphins in seventy-two. He left absolutely nothing to chance." I still say their main problem was that they were the same guy. Shula and I talked so long at his Florida home on Indian Creek Island that, by the end of our conversation, his voice was a squeak. Don has always been an easy guy for a writer to be around, because he doesn't measure his words and he tells the truth.

Other stops on the carousel: Earl and Jane Morrall in Orlando, Florida, just before they embarked on a cruise to Norway ("Earl," Shula told me, "is one of the finest human beings I've ever met"); Alex and Charlie Hawkins in Denmark, South Carolina ("I moved here when Atlanta got too congested," Hawkins said. "I think I may have overcorrected"); Fred and Charlene Miller, and Artie and Dottie Donovan, in their respective kitchens in Baltimore. Dr. Edmond McDonnell, the old Colt physician, was just leaving Donovan's place as I arrived. "Every Friday, Arthur Donovan and I have a session," he said. "My wife calls him my psychiatrist. We lie to each other and tell stories. We just enjoy each other."

As you can see, more than a few wives kibitzed. I'm particularly indebted to Sylvia and John, the cochampion Mackeys. To a man (and woman), it seemed everyone I talked to had a little story about Unitas that was their own. "I think he was that way," said Jim Ward, the backup quarterback from Gettysburg. "If I saw him this afternoon, the first thing he would say is—he wouldn't say hello or anything—he'd look at me and say, 'Jimmy, how's Turtle?' That's my wife. That was her nickname in college. Somewhere along the line, in training camp, on team trips, or rooming with

John, I had shared with him the fact that Pam used to be called Turtle. And over the years, whenever I ran into him, the first thing out of his mouth was always, 'How's Turtle?' " Along with the football plays Unitas put in the back of his head for later, he appeared to have stashed away in his memory bank some tender little reference point for everyone he knew.

Whatever door I knocked on, I was invited in and offered a beer. I found Jimmy Orr at a golf course on Saint Simons Island, Georgia. Unitas was often described as a "Mississippi riverboat gambler," but Orr actually became one. He dealt blackjack on showboats and at casinos like Caesars Palace in Las Vegas and Atlantic City. "That's the only game you have a real chance at, I think," he said. In an early sixties photograph several Colts are pictured playing cards in the rear of a plane. All of them are wearing white shirts and neckties, including Unitas. What kind of cardplayer was he? "Average," Jimmy said. "But there was a lot of cheating going on in those games. Cheating was legal." "John was a *horrible* poker player"—Hawkins begged to differ.

Naturally, I went to Pittsburgh. Thank you, Joe Chilleo, for taking me back to 345 William Street before it was paved. Steeler president Dan Rooney let the work pile up on his desk as he filled me in on the boroughs and the valleys, North Catholic, Central Catholic, and Saint Justin's. Later, one by one, Tim, Art Jr., John, and Pat Rooney chipped in valuable details. It turns out, John and Pat are Mount Saint Mary's guys, too. I knew their father. Every sportswriter in the country was Art Rooney's friend. In Three River days, his office was just off the back and down the corridor from the Steeler locker room. On Saturday mornings, when the deadline was far away, he'd rescue you from the clutches of Mean Joe Greene, Dwight White, and Fats Holmes, trundle you down to his office, and fill you up with coffee and Billy Conn stories. On the road, Art sat in the press boxes, not the owners' suites, usually next to Ed Kiely. Thanks, Ed. Jack Butler, the Steeler defensive back who dubbed John "Clem," put me on the practice field in

Olean. So did Ted Marchibroda. I appreciate it. Like Baltimore, Pittsburgh is one of those eternal places where, if you go looking for something from fifty years ago, you might actually find it. John's sandlot coach and second-string quarterback, Chuck "Bear" Rogers, was both a wellspring and a delight.

Thank you, Bert Rechichar (I mean, Forty-four), Andy Nelson, Bill Neill, Jerry Hill, Dick Bielski, Dave Pivec, Adrian Mehrling, Sam Havrilak, Bruce Laird, Roy Hilton, Richard Sammis, Jerry Dotterweich, Carol Mann, Rick Smith, Dick Stockton, Lesley Visser, Jerry Caraccioli, Julian Pavia, Loran Smith, Scott Tolley, Jack Nicklaus, Doc Giffin, Arnold Palmer, Bill Duarte, Jeff Blumb, Dave Anderson, Chuck Antony, Greg Aiello, Paul Tagliabue, Craig Kelley (whose Indianapolis Colts Media Guide is a work of art; I rank it somewhere between *Wuthering Heights* and the Holy Bible), John Ziemann, Hugh McNally, Jim Kelly, Sonny Jurgensen, Sam Huff, Babe Parilli, cousin Joe Unitas, Steve Sabol (who opened up the NFL Films offices to me; Steve and his father, Ed, are the permanent poet laureates of professional football), Dan Fouts, Jimmy Hammond, John Cunningham, Eric Fernandes, Joe Montana, Roger Staubach, Bart Starr, and Peyton Manning. Not too many days after Hurricane Katrina slammed New Orleans, I picked up the phone and it was Manning. "How can you have time to talk to me now," I said, "with everything that's going on at home?" "You've been on my list," he said, "and I'm sick of talking about the other. I'd rather talk about Johnny U." It took some doing, but Peyton's old friend at the University of Tennessee, assistant athletic director Bud Ford, found the 1953 film of Louisville's 59–6 loss in Knoxville. All of the Vols' touchdowns had been snipped out. Thanks to Bud, I was able to see Unitas play a game as a college quarterback. Kenny Klein at the University of Louisville was helpful in myriad other ways, but only a three-minute reel of Unitas's plays survives there.

I made two trips to Louisville, where Frank Gitschier led me by the hand to fountainheads like Clark Wood, Joe Trabue, Nancy Camp, Walter Fightmaster, Lee Corso, and Bob and Norma Bender.

Bob Bender and I started out to have breakfast together and ended up having lunch and dinner, too. After Gitschier's five-year run as an assistant football coach, just long enough to discover Johnny Unitas, he had an eventful twenty-three-year career as a special agent for the FBI, and on his telephone answering machine and license tag today, he goes by "G-Man." But Unitas never stopped calling him Coach. For much of Gitschier's time in law enforcement, his baili-wick was New York City (not Frank's favorite place in the world), and among the most malevolent criminals he encountered there was a bank robber named Tommy Callahan. "You do look a little like him," he said, suspiciously. As the force behind the Johnny Unitas Golden Arm Educational and Charitable Foundation, and the custo-dian of the Golden Arm Award (presented annually to the best senior college quarterback in the nation), Gitschier is the loving keeper of both John's flame and coach Frank Camp's memory. These days the G-Man is back in a red ball cap at Cardinal workouts, with a pretty good team to watch, too. Beside the helmetless statue of Unitas out-side the Louisville stadium, to go with the helmeted one outside the new stadium in Baltimore, a lineup of honored jersey numbers is tacked to the upper deck. All of them, including Lenny Lyles's 26, are red—except one. Number 16, the only retired number, is gold. But the best monument to the kid who failed the entrance exam has to be Unitas Hall ("U Hall, for Johnny U," said a smiling coed studying at a table outside), the tallest building on campus.

Louisville's largest minority-owned retail development is the Lyles Mall across the street from the Lyles Plaza shopping center on the west end of town. Lenny came back and built things. Lyles's name is also on a boys' football league. He is known as a commu-nity leader who never drops the ball. Showing me his scrapbooks and other mementos, Lenny said, "I wonder why I've kept all of this stuff. Maybe because you were coming."

John's siblings, Leonard, Millie, and Shirley, and Shirley's husband, Ralph Green (John's old Saint Justin's teammate), were not just necessary sources; they were indispensable collaborators.

Probably violating some sacred code of journalism, I sent Shirley the first chapter to make sure I had all of the dogs' names right. "I found a mistake," she said. "Father Connie visited us at Christmastime from Tiltonsville, Ohio, not Chiltonville, Ohio." "What else?" I asked. "That's it," she said. God bless you, Toots. Meeting Leonard at a McDonald's in Jacksonville, I immediately flipped on my tape recorder, and he said gruffly, "Did you ask my permission to do that?" As I broke into a stammer, he burst into laughter. He was John's brother, all right. I consider Leonard to be the hero of both John's life and this book.

Special thanks are obviously due Sandy, Paige, Joe, and Chad Unitas, who let me inside their family. "It was amazing to watch Richard Gere's face," Paige said at John's funeral, "as he realized that the stranger approaching him was Johnny Unitas. Dad was so laid-back, as always. While Richard Gere may have been in seventh heaven standing next to my dad, I was in seventh heaven standing next to Richard Gere." Through Gitschier, I tried to contact John Unitas Jr., but the word came back, "*I'm* writing the book." Fair enough.

Morgue workers Sandra R. Levy and Sharon Reeves at the *Baltimore Sun* and *San Diego Union-Tribune* helped tremendously. My daughter, Rebecca, was the chief researcher; my son, Tom, the main sounding board. Thanks to Angie Callahan for raising such beautiful people while I was at the play-offs. Cited throughout is the professional work of old friends like Red Smith, Jack Murphy, and Si Burick, along with the contributions of many other hardworking newspaper reporters, living and dead. But I owe the most to the Baltimore writers, starting with Bill Tanton, who brought me into the business, Cameron Snyder, and Larry Harris.

By way of a footnote, the records of the Elias Sports Bureau say Unitas threw two passes—an incompletion and an interception—against Detroit at Baltimore on October 6, 1956, two weeks and a day before John relieved George Shaw in Chicago. To believe that this isn't a statistician's mistake is to believe that Unitas and everyone else forgot his NFL debut. Everyone else, possible. Unitas, no. "Either way," Berry said, "the first pass he ever threw that was caught by anybody was caught by J. C. Caroline."

Though he started out as a newspaperman and once covered a Masters for the *Evening Sun,* Ernie Accorsi rightly belongs with the football people. However, like many sportswriters, I've never stopped thinking of Ernie as one of us. As you might imagine, Unitas isn't high on the icon list in the offices of the New York Giants. The most prominent photograph on the general manager's wall at the Meadowlands shows Pat Summerall kicking the snowy field goal that led to the sudden-death game. But if you push aside a few books on Accorsi's bookshelf, you'll uncover a picture of John. "Though he never played for a New York team," Ernie said, "on the day he died, he was the back page of both New York tabloids."

The players call Harris "Deep," only partly because, in the writers' pickup games, he always thought he was open downfield. Like Jerry Magee in San Diego, Deep's a thinking man's football writer. His wife, Kathleen A. Klein (she of the magical crab cake recipe), and their lovely daughter, Sarah Klein-Harris, made me feel at home again in Baltimore.

Thanks to my agent, David Black, and to Doug Pepper, Rachel Kahan, and Rick Horgan at Crown. Pepper bought the book, Kahan squired it along, Horgan rolled up his sleeves. Thanks to my usual troop of unpaid advisers: Mike O'Malley, John Hewig, Dave Kindred, John Huggan, and MaryAnne and Christian Golon.

Thanks, two-minute drill. Thanks, three-step drop. *Bounce, throw, completion. Bounce, throw, completion.* Thanks, caterpillar, for becoming a butterfly and staying a caterpillar. Thank you, John.

Turn the page for an exclusive excerpt from Tom Callahan's *THE GM: The Inside Story of a Dream Job and the Nightmares That Go with It*, a journey into the inner sanctum of the League's most senior general manager, the Giants' Ernie Accorsi, in his final season with the New York Giants.

First Game of the Last Season: The Manning Bowl

For the first time in sixteen years, the New York Giants were perfect in preseason, beating the Ravens, Chiefs, Jets, and Patriots.

By contrast, the New Orleans Saints and their rookie head coach, Giants castoff Sean Payton, were one-and-three. Obviously, these were two teams going in opposite directions in the National Football Conference. "I have no idea where we're going," Giants head coach Tom Coughlin said. "I'm not the great philosopher."

New York opened the regular season on a Sunday night at home in a game against Indianapolis that was inevitably dubbed "The Manning Bowl." For the first time in NFL history, brothers were starting as quarterbacks against each other in a real game. Hours before the kickoff, on different patches of the field, Peyton and Eli Manning were loosening up with their respective teammates, tossing the ball around lightheartedly. Everybody wore comically baggy shorts that went way past today's basketball bloomers, almost all of the way back to the boxer Archie Moore. Archie Manning, once a very good quarterback for very bad New Orleans teams, looked down from high above, the press level. He was the picture of crossed signals and mixed emotions. "This feeling of dread may be a Saints hangover thing," he said, "but I know how, if it gets going bad, how really bad it can get—for the quarter-back." Archie and his wife, Olivia, had accepted invitations to watch their sons from the Reebok box upstairs. "Peyton says I like to get to the games in time to see the cheerleaders stretch," Archie said, "but the truth is, I just like watching warm-ups. I'm completely nuts."

This night, more than ever. "Inside of me, I'm not sure what I'm supposed to be hoping for," he said. "Usually you can relax a little bit during the parts of the game when your boy is off the field, but what am I going to do tonight? Olivia and I didn't mean to raise quarterbacks, I swear to God. Like all parents, we just wanted them to be well rounded, go to school, grow up to be good people, do the right things. Believe me, I never tortured them on practice fields. Heck, I didn't mold them or anything. I just watched them have a dream that I understood, that I remembered having myself. I watched them work their rear ends off to attain it. Olivia was always a good sport and only pretended to get mad about spending her whole life cleaning up after football players. 'And another thing,' she'd shout. 'I'm sick and tired of washing jock straps!' Both Olivia and I mostly stood off to the side and smiled, or moved a little further away and cried."

Earlier that Sunday, Archie had told each of his sons the same thing, what he always told them before games: "I love you. Play hard. Have fun."

The New York GM, Ernie Accorsi, also stood off to the side, in one of the end zone tunnels at Giants Stadium, the one nearest both the home and the visitors' locker room, the position he had long since staked out as his game-day headquarters and bunker. Ernie was too nervous to watch from the press box and too appalled by the modern press box in any case. Those gentlemen sportswriters of sentimental memory, most of them decked out in suits, neckties, and fine felt fedoras, have all died off. They have been replaced by a convention of class clowns, some of them dressed like sharecroppers. After every play, three or five or ten or twenty of them yell out strained witticisms, the first things that pop into their heads—absolutely everything that pops into their heads—as though they were auditioning for sports talk radio, which perhaps they are. Though "press box wags" have existed since the Roman Coliseum, they used to have a drier style.

At an early Super Bowl, when streaking was in fashion, a naked woman who ran on the field was trundled off by four policemen. "And they took her away," someone in the press box said with a sigh, "two abreast."

"Ron Sellers was this big, tall receiver from Florida State," Ernie said, "who was constantly on injured reserve. He typified the futility of the early-seventies Patriots, who couldn't get anything right. He was always hurt. So now he's coming back again, this big bastard with all that talent. Jim Plunkett drops back to pass, and here comes Sellers over the middle. He leaps into the air—the ball is this far from his hands, left safety Jerry Logan is this far from his shoulders, right safety Rick Volk is this far from his legs—and, a split second before the crash, Will McDonough of the *Boston Globe* yells out, 'Eight to twelve weeks!' You had to laugh."

One of the Giants exercising in shorts was twenty-three-year-old Mathias Kiwanuka, New York's first pick in the most recent college draft, a 6-5, 262-pound defensive end from Boston College. His grandfather, Benedicto Kiwanuka, became Uganda's first elected prime minister in 1961 and was assassinated by Idi Amin eleven years later. With three and a half preseason sacks, Kiwanuka had made a more-than-promising start. In the final exhibition game against New England, he shrugged off 320-pound tackle Wesley Britt to bring about a tip and force an interception.

In the draft room, Accorsi had been the last one to come aboard for Kiwanuka, which was unusual. "I was thinking of maneuvering to get University of Miami corner Kelly Jennings, who ended up going to Seattle. But Jerry [player personnel director Jerry Reese] and Tom both wanted another pass-rusher, and I liked Kiwanuka, too. I decided to let them have their way. A GM shouldn't always be heavy-handed. The front office is a team, too. This was good for the team. And, obviously, it wasn't a franchise-changing decision. If it had been a franchise-changing decision, I'd have ignored everybody and insisted on having my own way. If it's a quarterback, absolutely, I'm making the call."

Just then, the franchise-changing decision, Eli Manning, passed Accorsi in the tunnel on his way back to the locker room to get suited up for the game. "Hi, boss," Eli said.

Ernie first saw Eli in person at an Auburn game Manning's junior year at Mississippi, November 2, 2002. The word then was that Eli might come out of school early. He did not. But the scouting report Accorsi typed out in bold capital letters didn't change the next year and, to Ernie's way of thinking (although almost no one else's), it hadn't changed in the years since:

WEARS LEFT KNEE BRACE . . . DURING PREGAME WARM-UP, DIDN'T LOOK LIKE HE HAD A ROCKET ARM . . . AS GAME PROGRESSED, I SAW EXCELLENT ARM STRENGTH UNDER PRESSURE AND THE ABILITY TO GET VELOCITY ON THE BALL ON MOST THROWS. GOOD DEEP BALL RANGE. GOOD TOUCH. GOOD VISION AND POISE.

SEES THE FIELD . . . IN A SHOTGUN ON MOST PLAYS AND HIS ONLY RUNNING OPTION IS A DRAW . . . HIS OFFENSIVE LINE IS POOR. RED-SHIRT FRESHMAN LEFT TACKLE. ELI DOESN'T TRUST HIS PROTECTION. CAN'T. NO WAY CAN HE TAKE ANY FORM OF DEEP DROP AND LOOK DOWNFIELD. WITH NO RUN-NING GAME (10 YARDS RUSHING THE FIRST HALF) AND NO REAL TOP RECEIVERS, HE'S STUCK WITH THREE-STEP DROPS AND WAITING TIL THE LAST SECOND TO SEE IF A RECEIVER CAN GET FREE. NO TIGHT END EITHER. NO FLARING BACK. SO HE'S TAKING SOME BIG HITS. TAKING THEM WELL. CARRIED AN OVERMATCHED TEAM ENTIRELY ON HIS SHOULDERS. I IMAGINE, EXCEPT FOR VANDERBILT, HIS TEAM IS OVER-MATCHED IN EVERY SEC [SOUTHEAST CONFERENCE] GAME . . .

HE'S BIG, NEVER GETS RATTLED. RALLIED HIS TEAM FROM A 14-3 HALFTIME DEFICIT BASICALLY ALL BY HIMSELF. LED THEM ON TWO SUCCESSIVE THIRD-QUARTER DRIVES TO GO AHEAD, 17-16. THE FIRST TOUCHDOWN, ON A 40-YARD STREAK DOWN THE LEFT SIDELINE, HE DROPPED THE BALL OVER THE RECEIVER'S RIGHT SHOULDER. CALLED THE NEXT TOUCHDOWN PASS HIMSELF, CHECKING OFF TO A 12-YARD SLANT . . . MAKES A LOT OF DECISIONS ON PLAY CALLS AT THE LINE OF SCRIMMAGE, BUT THEY ASK TOO MUCH OF HIM. THEY DON'T LET HIM JUST PLAY. THIS IS A GUY YOU SHOULD JUST LET PLAY . . . WHEN HE'S INACCURATE, HE'S USUALLY HIGH, BUT RARELY OFF TARGET TO EITHER SIDE . . . PLAYS SMART AND WITH COMPLETE CONFIDENCE. DOESN'T SCOLD HIS TEAMMATES [DID ACCORSI WISH HE DID?], BUT LETS THEM KNOW WHEN THEY LINE UP WRONG OR RUN THE WRONG PATTERN [AT LEAST] . . . THREW THREE INTERCEPTIONS. TWO WERE HIS FAULT. TRYING TO FORCE SOMETHING BOTH TIMES. HE COULD HAVE RUN ON ONE OF THEM, A FOURTH DOWN PLAY. HE HAS A LOT TO LEARN.

SUMMARY: I THINK HE'S THE COMPLETE PACKAGE. HE'S NOT GOING TO BE A FAST RUNNER, BUT A LITTLE LIKE JOE MONTANA, HE HAS ENOUGH ATHLETIC ABILITY TO GET OUT OF TROUBLE. REMEMBER HOW ARCHIE RAN? IN THAT DEPARTMENT, ELI DOESN'T HAVE THE BEST GENES, ALTHOUGH I NEVER TIMED MOM OLIVIA IN THE 40. BUT HE HAS A FEEL FOR THE POCKET. FEELS THE RUSH. THROWS THE BALL, TAKES THE HIT, GETS RIGHT BACK UP . . . HAS COURAGE AND POISE. IN MY OPINION, MOST OF ALL, HE HAS THAT QUALITY YOU CAN'T DEFINE. CALL IT MAGIC. AS [OLD BALTIMORE COLTS DEFENSIVE BACK] BOBBY BOYD TOLD ME ONCE ABOUT UNITAS, "TWO THINGS SET HIM APART: HIS LEFT TESTICLE AND HIS RIGHT TESTICLE." . . . PEYTON HAD MUCH BETTER TALENT AROUND HIM AT TENNESSEE. BUT I HONESTLY GIVE THIS GUY A CHANCE TO BE BETTER THAN HIS BROTHER. ELI

DOESN'T GET MUCH HELP FROM THE COACHING STAFF. IF HE
COMES OUT EARLY, WE SHOULD MOVE UP TO TAKE HIM.
THESE GUYS ARE RARE, YOU KNOW.

ERNIE ACCORSI

"I remember everything about that day," Eli said. "It was a
heartbreaker. I threw an interception on the last play to lose the
game, actually. It was fourth down. I tried to scramble—maybe I
could have run it in. I probably could have run it in. The receiver
was crossing, but he turned away just as I threw it. The ball went
flying right by him. That one hurt for a long while. Still does."

Following Eli up the tunnel, Jim Finn, almost the rarest animal in the League—a fullback from the University of Pennsylvania—offered his own scouting report on the Mannings, and on the
night. "Peyton always shows his excitement and always shows his
disappointment," Finn said. "He walks off the field with his head
shaking one way or the other. Eli doesn't show anything. A touchdown and an interception look the same. That's who Eli is. He
keeps it inside."

"Yeah," quarterback coach Kevin Gilbride said, "but I think
there's something in there that would like to show his big brother
a thing or two."

"Any little brother has to be tough," offensive left tackle Luke
Petitgout said, "but Eli is Peyton Manning's little brother. He has to
be tougher."

At school—Tennessee and Ole Miss—Peyton was the antiso-
cial one, the football geek tethered to a film projector. Eli was the
one who liked the night, music, and beer. Who wouldn't have
guessed the opposite? Peyton, at thirty, the omnipresent pitchman
from Madison Avenue, was the oil-painted portrait of a com-
mander in chief who, up close, appeared taller even than 6-5. Eli,
at twenty-five, with permanently tousled hair, stood only an inch
shorter but somehow it seemed a foot. No NFL quarterback was in

more extreme need of black stubble on his chin, a jagged scar across one cheek, or at least a misspelled tattoo.

"I've been playing nine years," Peyton said. "Eli's beginning his second season as a starter. Let him breathe, will you?"

He said this after the game. Before it, the Colts' quarterback reappeared in Ernie's tunnel ahead of any of his Indianapolis teammates, helmet on but with the chinstrap unsnapped, standing completely still. Not ten feet separated them, but Peyton didn't seem to see Accorsi or anyone else. "Look at him," Ernie said, not bothering to whisper because Peyton couldn't hear him either. "He isn't moving a muscle. He isn't bouncing from one foot to the other the way they do. He's come to a stop. He's calm. *Now* does he remind you of Unitas? The best ones all have this same moment of serenity just before the storm. There he is. Tiger Woods on the first tee."

Adam Vinatieri, the most dependable place-kicker in the NFL, opened the scoring with a couple of field goals that Peyton stretched to a 13-0 lead in the second quarter with a short touchdown pass to tight end Dallas Clark. Near the end of the first half, beginning at his own 14-yard line, Eli finally replied.

GIANTS

1-10-G14	(out of the shotgun) Eli passes to Tiki Barber for 17
	Two-Minute Warning
1-10-G31	(shotgun) Barber runs for 11
1-10-G42	(shotgun, no huddle) Eli passes incomplete
2-10-G42	(shotgun) Barber runs for 11
1-10-C47	(shotgun) Eli passes to Amani Toomer for 6
2-4-C41	(shotgun, no huddle) Eli passes to Barber for 7
1-10-34	(shotgun) Eli passes to Plaxico Burress for 34 yards and the touchdown; Jay Feeley kicks the extra point

INDIANAPOLIS 13, NEW YORK 7

But twenty-eight seconds remained for rebuttal, enough time after a nice kickoff return for Peyton to push the Colts back inside Vinatieri's range.

COLTS

1-10-C38	Peyton passes to Marvin Harrison for 16
1-10-G46	(shotgun) Peyton passes to Harrison for 5
	Timeout (:15)
2-5-G41	(shotgun) Peyton passes to Harrison for 9
	Timeout (:10)
1-10-G32	Dominic Rhodes runs for 1
	Timeout (:05)
2-9-G31	Vinatieri kicks a 48-yard field goal

INDIANAPOLIS 16, NEW YORK 7

Up in the Reebok box, Archie Manning said, "They aren't football players out there. They're my little boys."

Receiving the third-quarter kickoff, New York spent nearly eight minutes moving 69 yards on eleven plays to close within 16-14 on Eli's 15-yard touchdown pass to tight end Jeremy Shockey. "Shockey reminds me of Ted Kwalick," Ernie said, recalling a Penn State tight end from the 1960s. "Looking at Kwalick once, Joe Paterno said, 'What God had in mind here was a football player.'"

Two points were still the difference, 23-21, with about five minutes to go in the game, when everything was resolved on a four-play Giants possession. "The reason I've always preferred baseball," Ernie muttered in his tunnel, "is that their umpires can't just blow a whistle and take away a three-run home run."

GIANTS

1-10-G10	Eli passes to Toomer for 6
2-4-G16	Barber runs for 2
3-2-G18	Eli passes to Tim Carter for 17

But Carter is called for interfering with defensive back Nick Harper, a venial sin all but invisible in the replay.

3-11-G9   Eli's pass to Toomer is intercepted by Harper

Vinatieri made another field goal, and the final score was 26-21, Colts. "Good game," Eli told Peyton at the center of the field. "I love you," Peyton said. "I'm proud of the way you competed."

To the media in the Giants locker room, Eli said forthrightly, "I think I was throwing to the right guy on the interception, but it was definitely the wrong kind of pass. You can't float that one. It has to be a line drive." Some days later, alone in a small classroom just off the clubhouse, Eli said, "Peyton is one of the best quarterbacks in the NFL, if not *the* best. In my opinion he is the best. He's the benchmark not just for me, but especially for me. He always has been.

"I'm five years younger than Peyton, seven years younger than our older brother, Cooper. When they were growing up, my dad was still playing. Cooper and Peyton hung around the locker rooms, got to know all of the players. They went along to Hawaii when Dad made the Pro Bowl. They were around it. They saw it. I just heard about it. On family car trips, Cooper and Peyton were always playing this numbers game. They would pick out a uniform number at random—eighty-four. Then, back and forth, they'd name all of the players in the NFL who wore eighty-four—sometimes college players, too. Sometimes high school players! They knew everybody. They knew everything. I was more than a little bit behind."

After Peyton elected Tennessee over Archie's alma mater, Ole Miss, "our whole family was harassed," Eli said, "especially my dad. There were death threats and everything. People expected him to force Peyton to go to Ole Miss, because he had starred there. But they didn't know Dad. 'I'm not doing that,' he said. 'It's not my job. He's a grown man. It's his decision.' Those fathers you near about who force their kids to play sports, who hang over them at school and try to be their coaches, my dad was never that. Never. He had lived his own athletic life. He'd already had his high school days, his college days, his pro days. He didn't have to live it through us. He said, 'You know what? I went my way, you go yours. If you love football, heck, go ahead. I did. But if you don't love it, don't worry about it. It's not that important.'" It's just sports.

In 2004, when overall number one draft choice Eli maneuvered his way out of San Diego and into New York, Chargers fans considered Archie the puppet master. "The heat he took in San Diego wasn't deserved," Eli said. "It was my call, it was always my call. I did what I thought was right for me. He actually got involved only to take the pressure off me, because I asked him to. I wanted him to kind of speak for me at one point, but I told him what to say. 'No problem,' he said. 'I'll draw the fire.' He did it to protect me, as always. It's like, it was entirely my decision to go to Ole Miss. I could have gone to Texas.

"There were other places where I might have had a shot at a national championship. But I had to do what I thought was best. And, whatever I decided, Dad was going to back me. I can't tell you what it's meant to me to have his support, and Peyton's."

When Eli signed with Ole Miss, Peyton presented him with a thick notebook he had been filling out all season on airplanes to and from Colts games. "Full of protections, plays, and reads," Eli said, "pages and pages and pages. He sat down with me and tried to teach me all of these things. I didn't ask him to do it. At the time I hardly knew what was going on. Everything in that book was new to me, and it all came into play. Now Peyton and I talk every week, a couple of times. Right after the game, I might call him just for a minute. Often he'll be on the team bus. Then, on Monday or Tuesday, we'll talk a little longer. We'll actually talk football. If we didn't see each other's games, we'll go over them some, you know, a series here and there. I may have seen a highlight of a pass to Marvin [Harrison]. 'Hey, what was that? Take me through that, will you?' You can't have conversations like these with everyone. Not even with your closest friends. 'Yeah, yeah, they were playing a cover two, so we ran, you know, the end thing, and got a great look until they shifted the strong safety, and we had to slide the protection, and . . .' Only another quarterback really understands. I'll tell you, it's lucky to have somebody to talk to who knows exactly what you're saying, exactly what you're feeling, exactly what you're going through, without having to spell everything out."

Statistically, their final passing marks were 25 of 41 for Peyton, 20 of 34 for Eli, 276 and 247 yards. Peyton threw one touchdown pass, Eli two. They both had a solitary interception, though Peyton bounced a few incompletions off Giants defenders' chests. A two-time NFL Most Valuable Player, the only man ever to throw forty-nine touchdown passes in a season, Peyton likely wasn't halfway through his career, but he was more than halfway to Dan Marino's all-time passing record of 61,361 yards. Of course, the Indianapolis quarterback was also married to Marino at the top of the list of statistically accomplished quarterbacks who never won a Super Bowl. In Peyton's case, he had yet even to play in the ultimate championship game.

Eli, meanwhile, was still pretty fresh out of the egg. The year before, his first as a full-time starter, he led the Giants to an 11-5 record and a division title before showing his age in a 23-0 playoff loss to Carolina at home. Bart Starr was in his fourth proseason before he got out from behind Lamar McHan and Joe Francis in Green Bay.

At Eli's stage, Jim Plunkett hadn't yet been run out of New England, let alone San Francisco, on his long way to Super Bowl titles with the Raiders. At that juncture, coaches Dan Reeves and Chuck Noll were losing patience with John Elway and Terry Bradshaw. Noll was about ready to take a harder look at Jefferson Street Joe Gilliam.

Obviously New York isn't the kind of town that wants to hear _y_ of that when its twenty-five-year-old quarterback throws an interception on what was supposed to be the winning drive. At the same time, wide receiver Plaxico Burress, known for a mastery of jump balls and an economy of language, made a quiet suggestion: "Shouldn't four hundred and thirty-three yards of total offense have been enough?"

Coach Coughlin was steely in the locker room. "We have to stop talking about being good," he said, "and get good." When Coughlin was hired two years earlier, Accorsi presumed Tom was going to run his own offense. "I'm not saying you're going to call every play," Ernie told him, "but it's going to be you, right? That's what we're buying, right?" Instead, hard-working, well-traveled offensive coordinator John Hufnagel was at the wheel. "He's a former Canadian League quarterback," Ernie said, "and he thinks like a Canadian League quarterback. Only three downs in Canadian football, you know." At the close of the 2005 season, Accorsi tried to talk Tom into calling Hufnagel a cab and taking over the play-calling himself. But Coughlin resisted. "Okay," I told him, "have it your way. You won the division. But, I warn you, it's at your peril."

Accorsi expected Tom and Eli to be much closer by now. To Ernie's way of thinking, the coach and the quarterback have to be connected tighter than everyone else. "[Pittsburgh Steelers patriarch] Art Rooney told me that years ago," Ernie said, puffing on his cigar, Rooney-like. "He said, 'The most significant relationship in all of sports is the one between the head coach and the quarterback.' How one goes, so goes the other. Come the end of this season, we won't be saying Tom had a good year and Eli a bad one, or vice versa. They're going up or down together."

Sitting in his office, Coughlin said, "Eli's such a good person, such a good kid, so dedicated. When we went to Baltimore and Washington his rookie year, and we lost both of those games pretty big, he came up here and sat down in that chair right there. 'I played awful, Coach,' he said, 'but I'd like you to know something.

I want to be the quarterback of the New York Giants. I want to be as good a quarterback for this team as I can possibly be.'"

Now, at 0-and-1, a daunting Giants schedule looked even worse. Next up were the Eagles in Philadelphia, followed by the Seahawks in Seattle. From beneath the blackened cloud that follows most GMs everywhere, Ernie murmured, "We could be 0-and-3. Then we get the Redskins here, Atlanta on the road, and Dallas on the road. Somehow, someway, we've got to get to 3-and-3."

Running back Tiki Barber, defensive end Michael Strahan, and linebacker Antonio Pierce—the Giants' most corporate players, the leaders among the ones who walked around the clubhouse like stockholders instead of employees—had already declared for the Super Bowl. "I didn't like that," Accorsi said. "Tom's right about that. Say it to yourselves, but don't say it out loud."

The Monday after losing to Indianapolis, Ernie wrote what he knew was a pointless letter to Mike Pereira, the NFL's head of officials, invoking the name of Wellington Mara, the Giants owner and NFL pioneer who died in the middle of the 2005 season. It began, "Mike: Wellington Mara had a great saying. 'I say this more in sorrow than anger . . . '"